D1380588

ETHICAL ISSUES IN MENTAL ILLNESS

Ethical Issues in Mental Illness

CAROLINE DUNN

Ashgate

Aldershot • Burlington USA • Singapore • Sydney

Published by
Ashgate Publishing Limited
Gower House
Croft Road
Aldershot
Hants GU11 3HR
England

Ashgate Publishing Company
131 Main Street
Burlington, VT 05401-5600
USA

Ashgate website: http://www.ashgate.com

Reprinted 1999, 2000, 2001

British Library Cataloguing in Publication Data
Dunn, Caroline
    Ethical issues in mental illness. - (Avebury series in
    philosophy)
    1. Moral illness - moral and ethical aspects 2. Mental
    illness - Treatment - Moral and ethical aspects
    I. Title
    616.8'9'06

Library of Congress Catalog Card Number: 97-76954

ISBN 1 85972 608 9

Printed in Great Britain by Biddles Limited
Guildford and King's Lynn

Contents

Acknowledgements

First and foremost I would like to thank all those who shared their experiences of mental illness with me; their help enabled me to locate mental illness in the lives of people, instead of approaching it as a purely theoretical issue.

I cannot adequately express my thanks to Harry Lesser, of the Department of Philosophy at the University of Manchester, whose perceptive and constructive criticism was always accompanied by an enlivening degree of humour. Finally, and most importantly of all, I would like to thank my husband, without whose patience, kindness and love, this book would never have been written.

1 Introduction

People have always been fascinated by the human mind and its functions and dysfunctions. Over the centuries, philosophers and scientists have suggested a variety of explanatory models for the nature of the mind and its relationship to the body; the causes of mental dysfunction have been examined and treatments for it prescribed. Today we may marvel at the explanations offered in times past for mental illness and shudder at the barbarity of the treatments inflicted upon the mentally ill. We consider ourselves to be more enlightened, both in our explanations of, and treatments for, mental illness. In the contemporary world, with ever-increasing amounts of knowledge, specialisation has entered the arena, and mental illness is now the province of a variety of 'experts'; doctors, nurses, psychologists, psychotherapists and social workers all have their part to play in the care and treatment of the mentally ill. These experts, whose assumptions in the main often appear unchallenged and even unacknowledged within in their own fields of expertise, and in some cases, outside them, all have their corners to fight in the professional hierarchy and power stakes. All these different experts have their own models of mental illness; these may overlap and share significant characteristics, or they may diverge sharply from each other, often causing hostility and friction between their protagonists; and there may be little real understanding of these different models by professionals from the different fields whose jobs involve them in treating the mentally ill. All too often opinions polarise, the result of simplistic stances on both sides, and meaningful debate is stifled before it even begins. Thus the ethical issues involved in mental illness may be reduced to antagonistic posturing by the most vociferous members of the opposing sides in the debate; those who stand to lose most from this unseemly wrangle are the mentally ill.

Predominant amongst the experts are psychiatrists, for nowadays, the disorders of the mind are fundamentally considered to be the province of medicine. The discipline of psychiatry has sought, and some would argue, increasingly achieved, scientific exactness. Psychiatry seeks to organise the phenomena of mental illness into patterns of symptoms in order to classify different types of mental illness; applying the classification system to the experiences described by a mentally ill person then enables the 'expert' to diagnose what type of illness the patient is

1

suffering from, and this in its turn indicates the appropriate treatment. Not surprisingly, such a relatively simple approach to the complexity of mental illness, resulting as it frequently does in the application of a simplistic medical model to the definition and treatment of mental illness, has its limitations; when it is coupled with an appalling catalogue of abusive practice in the treatment of the mentally ill, it is hardly surprising that a vociferous anti-psychiatry movement has developed. The term 'anti-psychiatry' is not used to imply any homogeneity amongst theorists who may be included under this heading, for the theoretical stances of those opposed to psychiatry are many and varied. Notwithstanding the valuable work such theorists have done in exposing the limitations of a purely medical model of mental illness, and the abuse of much mental health practice, these theories purporting to offer explanations other than medical ones for the causes of mental illness, and alternative suggestions for its treatment, are often as dogmatic and simplistic as those of the medical profession.

Mental illness involves behaviour which is often a problem to society; it often results in behaviour that is perceived by others as irrational, and consequently it poses questions relating to autonomy which have considerable implications for the treatment of the mentally ill. I have considered the general issue of autonomy and mental illness in the Chapters 2 and 3; in Chapters 3 to 6 I have considered the specific issues raised by different forms of treatment for mental illness. I suggest that there are two fundamental models of autonomy that inform treatment of the mentally ill, each of which is essentially too impoverished to deal with the complexities of mental illness; each model may result in grave injustice, even though in the best cases of its application it may be intended to do good.

In Chapter 8 I have considered community care, the aim of which was to improve the care and treatment of the mentally ill, but in a great many cases, and for a variety of reasons, it has failed them. Finally, in the Conclusion, I consider what improvements are necessary to present care systems in order to try and provide humane treatment for the mentally ill.

I have based my arguments wherever possible on the stories of those affected by mental illness; in some cases I have used written material sent to me in response to advertisements I placed asking for people's experience of mental illness in users' magazines such as *Open Mind*. I have also used material already published which gave accounts of the experiences of the mentally ill and/or their loved ones, and newspaper reports, of which there have been a significant number in the past few years, as concern mounts about the implementation of the policy of community care for the mentally ill. There are dangers in such an approach; one only has one side of the story; certainly newspaper reports often seem to have a particular slant to them; and there is always the likelihood that such material will be biased towards those who have had unhappy experiences. Nevertheless, I chose this approach because it seemed to me that in all the vast 'expert' literature on the subject of mental illness, the voices of the mentally ill and their loved ones were conspicuous by their absence. I can therefore claim no scientific, 'objective' status for any of the evidence I have used to support arguments; it was not my intention to carry out a sociological survey, however, so I do not consider this to be a problem. If nothing else, one can accord the status of 'thought experiments' to the cases discussed, as a valid method of exploring the issues they raise. But wherever the mentally ill and their loved ones do try and make their voices heard, there is such an overwhelming catalogue of misery reported that I do not have the slightest doubt that there is very considerable cause for concern about their treatment. If I had to sum it up in one brief sentence, I would say that the overwhelming complaint made by the mentally ill and their families is that of not being listened to or not being taken seriously.

For despite the growth of user groups, special interest groups such as MIND and SANE, the various protests made by made by those who take an 'anti-psychiatry' stance, and the community care movement, it is still hard to avoid the conclusion that the mentally ill do not have a voice, or, if they do, it is one that is not taken very seriously. The mentally ill appear to be largely inaudible and invisible until and unless they are perceived to pose a danger or nuisance to society. Then there appears a spate of articles in the press asking what went wrong with the system, following another tragic case concerning a mentally ill patient who has killed someone whilst in the care of the community; or perhaps the increasing numbers of mentally distressed people occupying the gutters of our cities causes concern or offence to 'normal' society.

I have also relied quite heavily on the two volumes of the *Report of the National Enquiry into the Human Rights of People with Mental Illness* carried out under the auspices of the Australian Federal Human Rights Commissioner, Brian Burdekind, and published in 1993. This report received many oral and written submissions from people affected by mental illness, their loved ones, professional carers, community organisations, members of the public and Federal, State and Territory governments. It is an up-to-date, comprehensive report; an interesting, illuminating and thought-provoking document. Although it relates to another country, I am satisfied that the nature of society in Australia is sufficiently similar to that in the United Kingdom to make the issues raised in this report equally applicable here; in the absence of any comparable British document, it has proved extremely valuable, and the British government might be well advised to consider a comparable exercise in the UK.

The issues surrounding mental illness are great, and I am acutely aware that there are many gaps in this book; I have not, for example, had the space to consider specific groups, such as the elderly, children, women or ethnic minorities, all whom could be argued to raise specific issues within the overall ethical issues which mental illness raises. All the issues that have been considered would warrant an entire book being devoted to them, not merely a chapter. And over and above all these issues there is the fundamental question of whether or not mental illness can be considered to be a valid category.

3

In its starkest terms, the debate about the validity of the concept of mental illness may be reduced to those who accept the term at face value and those who deny the very existence of mental illness. This issue must be acknowledged because what is termed 'mental illness' expresses itself in deviant behaviour which frequently causes problems to society at large. Consequently, it has been argued, most notably by Szasz, that the concept of mental illness is merely a myth, a convenient way of controlling those whose behaviour and beliefs pose a threat to the established social order. Szasz considers that the term 'illness' relates only to physical conditions, and that physical illness can be approached in a value-free, scientific manner; whereas 'mental illness' relates to behaviour, and because 'human behaviour is fundamentally moral behaviour' (Szasz, 1972, p. 27) conditions considered to be mental illness are really moral issues.

This then begs such questions a what is meant by 'illness' and how is 'mental' to be defined? And it begs consideration of the issues raised by the mind-body debate, for classifying illnesses as either physical or mental immediately suggests that a dualist approach to the mind-body problem is being adopted; Szasz's approach to mental illness is certainly unrelentingly dualist.

These issues, fascinating and important though they be, must remain outside the scope of this book; I have chosen to accept mental illness as a valid concept, as I believe that there are convincing arguments to support this stance, and to consider the ethical issues raised when considering the care and treatment of the mentally ill, but these issues must be acknowledged for they are fundamental questions in the consideration of the ethical issues involved in mental illness.

All illness has an ethical dimension because illness alters one's moral status; as Sontag has pointed out, it suggests 'judgements of a deeper kind, both moral and psychological, about the ill.' (Sontag, 1990, p. 43) Illness may cause a paradoxical moral state, for the ill are likely to lose certain rights, but at the same time acquire others, and will be excused certain moral obligations while at the same time acquiring others. Such changes in moral status will at least partly depend upon the meaning that is ascribed to an individual's illness.

Meaning and morality are social enterprises into which an individual is inducted and becomes a participant; thus the experiences of the ill person are greatly influenced by the meaning that is attached to illness. In earlier ages the meaning of illness frequently had an overt moral element, often being associated with evil, sin and bewitchment; contemporary sociological analysis of illness has illustrated that this moral element, although different in form is no less present. (see, for example, Parsons, 1951, 1958, 1978). Such work shows that being classified as 'ill' is far from being merely a straightforward, scientific medical decision, but is also a culturally determined, social state, as indeed, are attitudes to illness and health.

The ethical implications of being defined as 'ill' will depend upon the time and place inhabited by a given patient - that is, a given society at a particular time in its history. For the inhabitants of Butler's Erewhon, illness was treated as a crime, crime treated as an illness. The inhabitants of Erewhon are taken to hospital and treated as if they were ill if they commit what would be regarded as a crime in the narrator's world: fraud, arson, robbery with violence are all met with sympathetic understanding. The 'cure' for such behaviour may be unpleasant, and the 'sufferer' is expected to pursue the relevant treatment regardless of its degree of unpleasantness, but nevertheless, she is regarded as unfortunate rather than morally deficient.

> The strange part of the story, however, is that though they ascribe moral defects to the effect of misfortune either in character or surroundings, they will not listen to the plea of misfortune in cases that in England meet with sympathy and commiseration only. Ill luck of any kind, or even ill treatment at the hands of others, is considered an offence against society, *inasmuch as it makes people uncomfortable to hear of it*. (Butler, 1987, p. 102, emphasis mine)

It is easy to dismiss this as the artistic licence of the author, but in certain forms, illness, sin and crime have had a perilously close relationship throughout most periods of Western civilisation. Butler's perceptive comment on the discomfort caused to the Erewhonians by hearing of the misfortunes of others is particularly relevant when considering the meanings attributed to illness, for sickness that is perceived as in some way carrying a potential threat to the non-sick can cause considerable discomfort, and with such discomfort the treatment of the sick person is affected. Such threat is not limited to a direct threat to the non-sick person's health; it can be the fear provoked by the realisation of one's own ultimate mortality, or the feeling of 'there, but for the grace of God, go I.' Cancer patients tell of being avoided by friends when the nature of their sickness is disclosed; parents of handicapped children tell of attitudes which express disgust towards their children, remarks such as, 'You should have let it die'; 'Why are you bringing it out in public?' 'Spastic' is used by some as a term of abuse. Our supposedly rational and scientific era is far from relinquishing guilt and shame as possible meanings attached to sickness. Sontag, examining the metaphors relating to AIDS, argues that:

> With AIDS, ... shame is linked to an imputation of guilt; ... Indeed, to get AIDS is precisely to be revealed, in the majority of cases so far, as a member of a ... community of pariahs. ... The unsafe behaviour that produces AIDS is judged to be more than just weakness. It is indulgence, delinquency - addictions to chemicals that are illegal and to sex regarded as deviant. (Sontag, 1990, p. 24)

Perhaps we are less removed from the citizens of Erewhon than we might like to think.

Certain forms of illness have meanings whose implications are even worse; such illnesses appear to remove the sufferer from the ranks of humanity altogether, and in the process remove rights which are normally taken for granted; morality often appears to become irrelevant if the sick person is not perceived as human. Kafka's *Metamorphosis* conveys this situation starkly. Gregor Samsa's metamorphosis into a giant insect is perceived as repulsive by his family; their initial reaction to his metamorphosis is one of shock and disbelief as they struggle to come terms with what Gregor's illness means to them; Gregor's metamorphosis represents to the Samsa family a form of moral judgement upon them, but for what they do not know. Although Gregor retains his human feelings, his family begin a slow process of dehumanising him; dirt is allowed to accumulate in his room and it is used as a repository for any unwanted items in the apartment. His metamorphosis creates a 'spoiled identity' for Gregor, and he is increasingly regarded as contaminated and potentially contaminating until eventually there is no pretence at regarding him as the person he was: Gregor suffers as Donne described, centuries earlier:

> As Sicknesse is the greatest misery, so the greatest misery of sicknes is solitude; when the infectiousnes of the disease deterrs them who should assist, from comming; Even the Phisician dares scarse come. Solitude is a torment, which is not threatened in hell it selfe. ... When I am dead, & my body might infect, they have a remedy, they may bury me; but when I am but sick, and might infect, they have no remedy, but their absence and my solitude ... it is an Outlawry, an Excommunication upon the patient, and separates him from all offices... (Donne, ed. Raspa, 1987, p. 25)

Mental illness may result in sufferers experiencing many of the injustices so graphically described in Kafka's fictional story because mental illness is associated with the loss of rationality, which is considered to be a prerequisite for being considered fully human. Just as Gregor's metamorphosis strips him of his humanity and denies him the moral considerations which we take to be a right, so too do the moral consequences resulting from the pejorative meanings ascribed to mental illness have great ethical implications for the mentally ill. It seems that for many people, the degree of humanity, and therefore human rights, that is attributed to anyone bears a direct relationship to her conforming to an acceptable (and by implication, non-threatening) model of a human being.

It is these issues which I propose to address in this book. I am very conscious that it is alarmingly easy to inhabit an ivory tower and offer tidy theoretical solutions to those whose profession it is to care for the mentally ill, secure in the knowledge that one will never be faced by the intractable problems that mental illness often poses in the 'real' world. I would therefore like to have included more views and experiences from professionals, in order to consider the issues mental illness poses for those in the difficult position of trying to provide care and treatment for the mentally ill, but response from the institutions that I approached was virtually zero, and constraints of time meant that it was not possible to approach a larger number of institutions knowing that this only *might* result in a better response.

Despite the omissions that are inevitable when one considers all the many ethical issues raised by mental illness, I hope that this attempt to address what I consider to be some of the fundamental ethical issues raised by mental illness will be a small step on the way to raising the most basic issue of all, the right of the mentally ill and their loved ones to have their voices heard and what they say taken seriously.

2 Mental illness and autonomy

At the outset it must be acknowledged that some of those values which should govern our treatment of the mentally ill - benevolence and humanity - do not require detailed discussion at the conceptual level, although how they should inform treatment does require consideration, and this will follow.

However, autonomy is a different case. Autonomy is a central feature of the conception of the nature of persons and a central philosophical constituent of ethical theories in post-Enlightenment Western culture, which normally involves the belief that people are autonomous beings with the ability to make their own decisions and determine their own lives. Autonomy consequently features prominently in ideas of liberty and equality; and it is a focal point for much of medical ethics, in which specific context it relates to issues of informed consent and paternalism. However, even a cursory examination of the way the notion of autonomy is used by various authors demonstrates that its definition varies considerably. As Gerald Dworkin (1988) has pointed out, autonomy is used in a variety of ways in moral and political philosophy:

> It is used sometimes as an equivalent of liberty, ... sometimes as equivalent to self-rule or sovereignty, sometimes as identical to freedom of the will. It is equated with dignity, integrity, individuality, independence, responsibility, and self-knowledge. It is identified with qualities of self assertion, with critical reflection, with freedom from obligation, with absence of external causation, with knowledge of one's own interests. ... It is related to actions, to beliefs, to reasons for acting, to rules, to the will of other persons, to thoughts, and to principles. About the only features held constant from one author to another are that autonomy is a feature of persons and that it is a desirable quality to have. (Gerald Dworkin, 1988, p. 6)

Dworkin considers that 'It is very unlikely that there is a core meaning which underlies all the various uses of the term.' (ibid., p. 6). However, he does manage to find a common feature, necessary to any definition of autonomy, if not sufficient, and either specific or presupposed. This is:

... the capacity to reflect upon one's motivational structure and to make changes in that structure. Thus, autonomy is not simply a reflective capacity but also includes some ability to alter one's preferences and to make them effective in action. Indeed, to make them effective partly because one has reflected upon them and adopted them as one's own. ... Autonomy is a second-order capacity to reflect critically upon one's first-order preferences and desires, and the ability either to identify with these or to change them in the light of higher-order preferences and values. By exercising such a capacity we define our nature, give meaning and coherence to our lives, and take responsibility for the kind of person we are. (ibid., p. 108)

Now, to be able to make and modify one's own decisions in accordance with one's chosen plan of action in this way, requires two things: not being constrained by others and not being constrained *by limitations in oneself.* Irrespective of the variations in their definition of autonomy, all who try to define it rightly agree that one cannot be considered to be autonomous if one is constrained by limitations in oneself, and all consider serious irrationality to count as *a limitation in oneself.*

Thus the notion of autonomy is inextricably tied to the concept of what it is to be human and rational, for without this, autonomy is irrelevant. Heelas and Lock have made the point that:

It is not possible to live as a human being without having an idea of what it is to be human. People have always considered their nature. (Heelas and Lock, 1981, p. 3)

Serious irrationality can affect four different groups of people: young children, considered irrational to some degree by virtue of their immaturity, constitute one group; such irrationality is considered normal, and will be outgrown. Restricting the autonomy of young children in the interests of their own safety, providing it is done in an appropriate manner, is generally not considered to pose any great moral problems (although what constitutes an appropriate manner can cause problems). The irrationality of young children is not considered pathological; it is an entirely normal aspect of their development.

The second group that can be affected by serious irrationality is the elderly, where degenerative changes in the brain can result in the ability to reason being impaired. In such cases it is often necessary to restrict autonomy in the interests of the sufferer's safety. The situation is not as clear cut as that relating to children, however. To some extent, irrationality as a result of old age is accepted as part of the normal ageing process. However, it is also seen as abnormal, in that not all elderly people experience it, and it is at least sometimes the result of pathological changes in the brain, for which researchers are seeking a cure. Nonetheless, despite the greater complexity of the situation relative to that of children, I think it is fair to say that it remains the case that at present some degree of irrationality in old age is common enough to be considered 'normal', and that restricting the autonomy of an irrational elderly person for her own safety is justified, with the same proviso as for children, that it be done in an appropriate manner.

The remaining two groups who may be affected by serious irrationality are the mentally handicapped and the temporarily and permanently mentally ill. Both these groups raise considerable ethical dilemmas when the question of whether irrationality can be considered a sufficient condition for restricting autonomy is considered, but I shall only be concerned in this book with consideration of the mentally ill.

Thus the scope of autonomy may be considered to be restricted to those who are mature, conscious and rational. There are problems of definition with these criteria; for example, one may have a very mature eleven-year old and a hopelessly immature twenty-year old; yet age is generally the criteria for determining maturity in relation to autonomy. One might have a patient slipping in and out of consciousness, and have to decide the degree to which any decisions made while she was conscious were compromised by her lapses into unconsciousness.

From this it may be seen that both the internal and external conditions for autonomy admit of degree. Maturity, rationality and consciousness are not 'all or nothing' states; and society, although it always and necessarily interferes both socially and legally with its members' autonomy to some extent, does so to different degrees at different times and places. Since the conditions for autonomy admit of degree, so does autonomy itself; the importance of this will emerge in later chapters.

The criterion of rationality poses particularly difficult problems in relation to autonomy, and it is this criterion which is particularly relevant when considering autonomy in relation to the treatment of the mentally ill, for irrationality may both excuse someone from the consequences of her actions, and at the same time it may impose serious restrictions on her autonomy.

> Rationality is the fundamental premise by virtue of which we understand ourselves as human beings; that is, as creatures capable of adjusting their actions as reasonably efficient means to intelligible ends. Being mentally ill means being incapacitated from acting rationally in this fundamental sense. (Moore, 1980, p. 60)

Thus rationality would also appear to be a necessary condition for both personhood and autonomy, and the consequences of this may be enormous for the mentally ill, for the relationship between irrationality and autonomy informs two extreme models of the treatment of the mentally ill, both of which may have disastrous consequences; I shall discuss these models of treatment in the next chapter.

Culver & Gert have pointed out that psychiatrists have not formulated explicit definitions of rationality and irrationality, and that irrationality is treated as more basic than rationality, so that rationality is defined in terms of the absence of irrationality. They distinguish two classes of rationality:

10

... that which it would be irrational not to do (or believe or desire) - [this class of rational actions (or beliefs or desires) we call rationally required].

... that which it would not be irrational not to do (or believe or desire) - [this class of rational actions (or beliefs or desires) we call rationally allowed]. (Culver & Gert, 1982, p. 21)

The notion of a rationally allowed act, belief or desire is weaker than a rationally required one; thus although an action or belief may considered rational, this does not imply that it must necessarily be advocated, because it may only be rationally allowed. Any act that is not irrational must fall into one of the two categories of rationality.

However, this does not help us to decide what actions, desires or beliefs are rational or irrational; it is generally agreed that to describe an action, belief or desire as irrational is equivalent to saying that it is undesirable, but it does not say why an action so defined is undesirable. In contemporary Western society, the constructed social world is based on order, reason and understanding; through understanding, the world is explained and controlled. Irrationality will almost inevitably be seen as undesirable in such a culture, and indeed, rationality is considered an intrinsic element of human nature; 'losing one's reason' is an expression used to denote madness, for example. It is more useful, however, when considering rationality and irrationality in the context of mental illness to regard these terms as normative judgements that people make about the actions of other people, and consequently such judgements are inevitably subjective to some degree. (The same applies to judgements made about beliefs and desires, but until these are transformed into actions of some sort, they cannot be judged, because there is no way for others to know of their existence. Thus I may believe that my milk is delivered by the milk goblin, who lives on the farm across the road, but unless I do and/or say something, for example, leaving his breakfast for him every day and telling my husband that this is the purpose of the food I leave on the back doorstep, no-one can judge this belief to be irrational, because only I will know of its existence.)

How then might a standard for rationality be decided? If the standard set is too restrictive, one can reach the situation where to disagree at all with a doctor is to be considered irrational (not as ridiculous at it might seem, given the power and authority of the medical profession, and the arrogance of some of its members). If, at the other extreme, the parameters are too wide, then we encounter a situation in which 'anything goes', which may have appalling consequences, and in fact runs counter to common-sense intuitions as to what are rational actions and what are irrational ones.

The difficulties encountered in deciding what is to count as an irrational action, behaviour or belief are easily demonstrated by considering two very different scenarios. I find it seriously irrational to leap off the side of a mountain with only a large kite strapped to one's shoulders; devotees of hang-gliding assure me that it is tremendously enjoyable. I find it equally irrational that Jehovah's Witnesses should refuse to accept life-saving blood transfusions; they are equally convinced that it would be worse to save one's life at the expense of losing one's soul. Neither hang-gliders nor Jehovah's Witnesses are considered to be mentally ill as a result of what many people would consider to be irrational behaviour or beliefs. How then do they differ from the mentally ill person who believes that the television is emitting harmful rays that will destroy her brain, and whose fear causes her to attempt to destroy every television that she comes across? Such behaviour is irrational enough to be considered to be mental illness and possibly irrational enough to justify the restriction of her autonomy. As Sims has pointed out, 'There is ... a dilemma, delusion may be very religious, religious belief may be very odd'. (Sims, 1992, p. 43)

Sims (1986) has argued that the differences between religious belief and mental illness (specifically, the symptoms of schizophrenia) can be identified. He argues that believers usually regard their religious experiences or teachings as metaphorical or spiritual, and that these experiences result in meaningful, goal-directed behaviour, unlike that of schizophrenic experiences or beliefs, which frequently result in bizarre behaviour which does not follow logically from the experiences. Schizophrenic behaviour is also often concrete, interpreting spiritual values in physical terms; he quotes a patient who interpreted the injunction 'if thy right hand offend thee, cut it off' by trying to sever his wrist from his arm. He suggests that religious beliefs are held concurrently with the possibility of religious doubts, as is the case with other abstract concepts, whereas schizophrenic beliefs are accepted without doubt. Religious beliefs, according to Sims, also differ from schizophrenic delusions in being based upon religious authority; and they result in no changes to the physical boundaries of the believer's self, which is not the case in schizophrenic delusions.

Sims argues in a 1992 paper that:

The key for making the distinction between belief and symptom lies in the use of phenomenology to explore subjective experience. ... In phenomenology it is important to distinguish between form and content. ... The phenomenological form categorises the subjective experience and reveals the psychiatric diagnosis;... The content is dictated by the cultural context. ... So the form reveals the nature of the illness whilst the content arises from the social and cultural background. Only the study of form can reveal whether a symptom is present or not, and this can be explored by finding out what is the meaning of the experience for the individual. (Sims, 1992, pp. 43-44)

12

The relationship between form and meaning in the differentiation between religious or ideological belief (no matter how odd) and mental illness rests upon the coherent structure of the former kind of belief, a structure that is understandable to other members of society in its form, even if they disagree with its content; the beliefs expressed by those suffering from severe mental illness lack this coherent, understandable structure.

We must consider, therefore, what are the necessary and sufficient conditions for a person's decisions based on their beliefs to be respected. These conditions are not hard and fast, applicable in all situations. To begin with, rationality and irrationality are not mutually exclusive absolutes. In practice, degrees of irrationality are acknowledged, as described by terms such as 'eccentric', 'silly', 'stupid', 'idiotic' and 'crazy', which allows for the situation in which an action is carried out or a desire expressed to be taken into account when considering its rational status.

There is also another distinction that may be made, between beliefs which may be considered to be seriously irrational, to the extent of constituting evidence of mental illness, and beliefs which may seem odd or irrational to many people but which do not constitute evidence of mental illness.

> However 'irrational', in the sense of 'unconventional' the Jehovah's Witness's belief may be, it may nevertheless be the Witness's *own* belief in a sense in which the schizophrenic's is not. By this I mean that the Witnesses come by their beliefs as part of the normal process of reflection on one's own life and experience which all of us engage in to a greater or lesser extent. ... Such beliefs may not be 'rational' in the sense of being justifiable by something like philosophical argument: but they are intelligible in the context of the believer's other experiences. This does not seem to be true in the case of the schizophrenic's beliefs. ... The beliefs of someone suffering from schizophrenia affect competency, not because they are out of line with standardly held beliefs in the community, but because they are not the outcome of the believer's normal development and reflection on his own experiences. Rather, they are the result of whatever it is which causes schizophrenia - whether it be a brain disorder or the lingering effect of childhood traumas or whatever. (Matthews, in Grubb, 1994, p. 110)

Thus many beliefs and actions which might appear to be irrational, such as any action that causes unhappiness to oneself, become intelligible in this context. However, actions such as self-mutilation, for example, that some mentally ill people engage in, which cause pain and distress and appear to serve no positive purpose, must be judged irrational on the basis that there is no way of rendering it intelligible, even in context, and therefore it can only be explained as being the result of illness. Such behaviour is must surely therefore constitute a *limitation in oneself*, which must necessarily diminish one's autonomy.

13

It would appear, therefore, that the answer to the question of whether irrationality is a justification for restricting an individual's autonomy can be 'yes' or 'no'.

For no member of a society can expect to enjoy unrestricted autonomy., there will inevitably be occasions where one person's autonomy is another person's loss of autonomy because individuals' interests frequently conflict and consequently, social systems must construct methods by which they can arbitrate on such conflicts of interests; these take the form of legal and moral systems.

> The common requirements of law and morality consist for the most part not of active services to be rendered but of forebearances, which are usually formulated in negative form as prohibitions. Of these the most important for social life are those that restrict the use of violence in killing or inflicting bodily harm. The basic character of such rules may be brought out in a question: If there were not these rules what point could there be for beings such as ourselves in having rules of any other kinds The force of this rhetorical question rests on the fact that men are both occasionally prone to, and normally vulnerable to, bodily attack. (Hart, 1961, p. 190)

Thus if the expression of irrationality poses a serious risk to the welfare of others, it might appear obvious that it justifies the restriction of the autonomy of anyone whose irrational behaviour poses such a threat. This is not the relatively simple situation it at first sight appears to be, however, for although unlimited individual autonomy is not allowed in situations where it threatens the rights of others, irrespective of whether or not irrationality is involved, irrationality complicates the issue. It does so because an individual's autonomy in such a situation may be restricted because of the *possibility* of their future behaviour threatening the welfare of others. This is not the case with legal penalties. If someone causes harm to others in the course of committing a crime, she will be punished for that crime by the law of the land, and after that she will theoretically be free to continue her life, having paid society's penalty for her crime. However, someone whose irrational behaviour threatens the welfare of others can find her autonomy restricted not as a specific punishment for a specific crime but instead as a deterrent measure designed to protect others from the possibility of future harm. I shall return to this issue in greater depth in Chapter 4.

A different situation arises where irrational beliefs, desires or actions do not threaten others but do pose a threat to the individual experiencing them. A depressed individual threatening to commit suicide exemplifies such a situation. The pain and misery of deep depression is immense, often made all the harder to bear because those around may have no understanding of the suffering involved, particularly if the depression has no apparent cause. If someone in this state commits suicide, she poses no threat to anyone else, so what justification can be made for restricting her autonomy in order to prevent her suicide?

14

Durkheim defined suicide as applying to 'all cases of death resulting directly from a positive or negative act of the victim himself, which he knows will produce this result.' (Durkheim, 1952, p. 44.) However, knowing that death will result from one's actions is not the same as desiring death to result from one's actions; it might be an undesired but unavoidable consequence. For example, a Jehovah's Witness who refuses a life-saving blood-transfusion may have no desire at all to die; however, her religion does not allow blood-transfusion and she believes that she cannot therefore accept this treatment. If she dies, it will be an undesired but unavoidable consequence of her religious beliefs. Thus Durkheim's definition of suicide does not fit contemporary usage of the term, which includes the desire to die as a necessary element of the definition. In the past, suicide was considered as a religious sin or as morally prohibited, which led to suicide and attempted suicide being made criminal offences. Suicide was only decriminalised in Britain as late as 1961; subsequently, it has become medicalised instead, for the value of life is so much taken for granted that the intention to commit suicide is nowadays considered as evidence of mental illness in the vast majority of cases.

Bloch and Chodoff have pointed out that we do not usually feel morally obliged to prevent sick people refusing essential medical treatment or committing heroic acts that are life threatening - acts which do not have death as their ostensible purpose, which they classify as passive suicide, but that we do appear to have a 'moral intuition' to prevent what they call active suicide, acts which are consciously intended to cause the person carrying them out to die. (Bloch & Chodoff, 1984, p. 196).

Suicide, however, must be the act of a seriously distressed person. It is simply inconceivable to imagine a perfectly happy person sitting down and deciding for no reason whatsoever that she will kill herself. The problem is, however, that those wishing to kill themselves often have perfectly rational reasons for doing so. In the case of a terminally ill person, who prefers suicide to a slow, painful death, most people would consider this a perfectly understandable, rational reason for suicide. But let us return to the case of the seriously depressed person who also wishes to commit suicide in order to obtain release from her suffering. Such a desire is likely to be considered evidence of mental illness and she would be considered irrational for feeling it. Yet this sufferer would probably argue that her pain is just as unbearable as that of the terminally ill person's, so why should she be denied the right to exercise her autonomy and choose to die?

There are those, prominent amongst whom is Szasz, (see, for example, 1971; 1972; 1983; 1989), who would argue that her autonomy should not be restricted because to do so would limit her freedom, and that if she chooses to die, that is her right. In this situation we are faced with Matthews' question of whether her desires can truly be said to be her 'own'; and there is a difference between these two cases. The terminally ill person has no hope of cure and can only expect to suffer pain in what is left of her life. In the case of depression, however, it is not accepted that nothing can be done for the sufferer, and that there is no hope of a cure. It is often argued that when such a depressed person recovers, after the appropriate treatment, she will be glad to have been prevented from killing herself, and thus that she will give her consent retrospectively to the restriction of her autonomy that led to her not being able to kill herself.

This is a very persuasive argument, particularly if one has seen depressed suicidal patients recover to enjoy their lives. However, Reznek (1991) has argued that the argument for retrospective consent cannot be justified, because the existence of brainwashing means that a person could have her political beliefs or sexual orientation altered by aversive conditioning and after such treatment be grateful for being 'helped' in this way. There is undoubtedly much food for thought here, but I think it can be argued that there is a fundamental difference between these two situations.

There is, first of all, the question of whether or not brainwashing could achieve the alteration of political or sexual orientation. It could be argued that this is irrelevant, as it is the principle that is of importance, but on the other hand, if such behaviour alteration is not actually achievable, the problem ceases to exist! I do not propose to begin a consideration of the efficacy or otherwise of brainwashing, and I shall therefore proceed as if it were effective, noting only that it is an issue that should be acknowledged; and there are serious doubts as to whether people's beliefs, as opposed to what they say, really can be altered in this way. The really important point is that what justifies the interference is not simply that the person retrospectively approves of it, but that they do so for valid, rational reasons.

Now, one can justify retrospective consent to being prevented from committing suicide, if one accepts the value judgement that life is valuable. In general, this is a judgement which underpins our whole moral system; if one removes it, it makes a mockery of laws that prohibit murder; medical care becomes unnecessary and a whole array of institutions whose aim is to improve the quality of life are rendered superfluous. Even religious systems which stress an afterlife of eternal bliss are generally strangely reluctant to encourage their followers to commit mass suicide in order to achieve this glorious state sooner. I would call such a value judgement a fundamental value judgement, in that very few people would disagree with it.

(Sexual and political orientation also involve value judgements, but are much more open to argument and disagreement. Therefore, providing that they do not involve others' suffering, they should be left to the individual to decide, and thus no-one has the right to try and alter another's sexual or political orientation by any form of coercion, such as brainwashing, even if it be the case that the subject would be 'grateful' afterwards.)

However, to give rational consent after the event one must also come to accept that one's own life is in fact valuable, though previously one thought it was not. The problem lies in the fact that the person suffering from depression cannot believe that she will ever feel free of pain. yet if her 'autonomy' is respected and she exercises her freedom to choose to die, her decision is irreversible, while if her 'autonomy' is restricted and she is prevented from dying, she may well recover, and in so doing regain her real autonomy and probably give her retrospective consent to it temporarily having been restricted. Given the irreversibility of suicide, it must be justifiable to restrict her autonomy in the short term in order to see if her depression, and consequent wish to die, can be treated, for it is arguable that in the worst case scenario, that of her depression never responding to any form of treatment, she still has the option of suicide. Once dead, however, she has no options at all - and no autonomy. Of course, this argument is only valid if it is accepted that the value of life is a fundamental value judgement, which I have argued that it is.

The above argument is valid when considering a mentally ill patient for whom there is no evidence to suggest that she mall never recover from her illness. However, is it equally valid when considering the case of a mentally ill person who has suffered for years with no improvement in her condition? Is this not a similar case to that of a physically ill person for whom there is no hope of cure and who is suffering appallingly? The problem, of course, is that the wish to die in the absence of any clearly defined and socially accepted cause is seen as evidence of mental illness, because it is seen as irrational. Yet in the case of a long-term mentally ill person for whom all treatment has failed, is it irrational to prefer to die than to continue suffering? Even if the wish to die is the result of, say, depression, if the depression has not been cured and there appears to be little hope that it ever will be, why should such a person be considered to be in a different category from someone suffering from an incurable physical disease?

Logically, I find it hard to argue that such a mentally ill person should be put into a different category from the patient suffering from a terminal illness. It can be argued that in the case of a terminally ill person the wish to die is a result of wanting to avoid pointless pain and suffering from an illness for which there is no hope at all of a cure, whereas the wish to die of a depressed patient is part of the illness itself, and so theoretically there is the prospect of cure. However, for someone who has suffered severe mental illness for many years it is arguable that the hope of a cure is more theoretical than actual, and therefore I cannot see any rational reason for her situation being considered to be in a different category from that of the terminally ill patient suffering front a physical disease. There is one aspect to this situation, however, that should not be ignored. I think it is quite possible, maybe even probable, that a person suffering from a terminal physical illness will have had a greater likelihood of having received all appropriate treatment for her illness than a mentally ill person. I am not suggesting that this is necessarily the result of a lack of concern for the mentally ill or some devious conspiracy to deprive them of treatment. Instead, I think it is more likely to be the result of any number of factors related to mental illness, or a combination of them. These include confusion about what is the appropriate method of treatment, lack of resources for some types of treatment and the vulnerability of the mentally ill which may lead them to be unaware of their rights or unable to assert their right to second opinions and different treatment. This is of particular importance, because if a patient is assigned, for example, to the care of an organically orientated psychiatrist she will be unlikely to obtain any other form of therapy, which might be more appropriate.

17

This point was underlined when I spoke to a psychiatrist who works as a psychotherapist in the NHS. She told me of a patient of hers who had been treated for severe depression for twenty years. During this time she had received a variety of drug treatments and ECT, and had spent many spells in hospital. Nothing had helped her significantly and she had reached the stage where she had given up all hope of ever being free of her depression and was suicidal. She had recently moved to a different area, and her new GP, noting that all previous treatment had failed, referred her instead to the NHS therapist. After many weeks, the patient revealed to her therapist a long history of child abuse, considered by the therapist to be the cause of her depression. When asked why she had never told anyone about this before, the patient said that there had never been the opportunity - because her illness had been treated organically, she had fallen into the treatment pattern of hospital, drugs and ECT. She was not an articulate, informed patient; instead, she was in awe of the medical 'experts', desperately ashamed of her past - and, quite simply, had never been given the right circumstances in which she could talk. This woman began to improve as a result of the appropriate therapy, and for the first time for longer than she could remember began to feel that there was hope that she might get better.

This example was not given to me as a argument that 'therapy cures' or is necessarily the right treatment in every case, nor from any anti-psychiatry perspective, but simply to highlight the difficulties involved in deciding whether a person suffering from mental illness is in the equivalent position to that of a person suffering from a terminal physical illness. There is also the fact that had there been no NHS therapy available, this patient would not have received the appropriate treatment because she could not possibly have afforded private treatment. None of these factors is exclusive to the treatment of the mentally ill, of course; it is perfectly possible to imagine these issues arising in the case of physical illness. I think these factors are likely to play a larger part in mental illness, however, and so although logically one can argue that an 'incurably' mentally ill person is no less rational in wishing to commit suicide to avoid further suffering than someone suffering from a terminal physical illness, I am aware of a greater degree of unease about such a conclusion in such a case.

All these issues involve the issue of paternalism, which is usually defined in terms of the denial of liberty justified by the argument that it is in the best interests of the person whose liberty is being denied. Buchanan, however, has argued for the enlargement of the definition:

> ... paternalism is interference with a person's freedom of action or freedom of information, or the deliberate dissemination of misinformation, where the alleged justification of interfering or misinforming is that it is for the good of the person who is interfered with or misinformed. (Buchanan, 1978, p. 372)

Dworkin, however, has argued that this definition implies that if a doctor does not misinform or fail to reveal information to a patient but tells the patient more

18

than he wants to know the doctor does not act in a paternalistic fashion. But when a doctor insists upon telling a patient what he does not want to know, for his own good, this is a clear case of paternalism. (Dworkin, 1988). He argues that autonomy, not liberty, is the idea against which paternalism should be measured, as it 'is a richer notion than liberty, which is conceived either as mere absence of interference or as the presence of alternatives.' (ibid., p. 107). Using autonomy as the idea against which paternalism is measured ultimately comes down to the question of whether 'the substitution of one person's judgement for another's', thus diminishing or even removing her autonomy, is justifiable.

However, as we have seen, it is arguable that a mentally ill person already has restricted autonomy by virtue of her illness affecting her ability to reason. The ability to reason is a fundamental constituent of adult human beings, thus any limitation of one's ability to reason must be construed as a constraint on oneself; to be autonomous means suffering no constraints on one's ability to be master of one's own destiny, whether those constraints be externally imposed or the result of limitations in oneself. Therefore, to be seriously irrational is, by definition, to suffer restricted autonomy to some degree, and consequently I would argue for the position of 'Justified Paternalism', which holds that paternalistic intervention can be justified, but only if

> ... the harms prevented from occurring or the benefit provided to the person outweighs the loss of independence or the sense of invasion suffered by the interference;

> ... the person's condition seriously limits his or her ability to choose autonomously;

> ... it is universally justified under relevantly similar circumstances always to treat persons in this way. (Beauchamp & Childress, 1983, p. 172)

The problem still remains, of course, that the assessment of the seriousness of someone's condition in limiting her ability to make autonomous choices is necessarily a subjective one: this, however, is a different issue from that of whether irrationality as such is sufficient grounds for restricting an individual's autonomy. Those who adopt an anti-paternalistic stance, however, would argue that this is an intrinsic weakness in the paternalistic view, on the grounds that the principles governing paternalism are simply too broad and too open to variations in subjective judgements, with the risk therefore of the restriction of autonomy in cases where it really cannot be justified.

This is a powerful objection and one that is particularly potent in the context of mental illness, where subjective judgements are impossible to avoid, because we are dealing with situations where, assuming that there is a right answer, no-one is in position to know what it is. In practical matters, therefore, we must rely on a 'best-guess'; and in the case of autonomy, it a 'best-guess' as to what course of action best promotes an irrational individual's autonomy. As a result, I think the approach of justified paternalism is one that can be defended. We do not inhabit a perfect world (arguably, in such a world mental illness would not exist), and there is no solution to these problematical issues that cannot be argued to have some drawbacks to it. Given this, I would argue that in some circumstances irrationality may justify the restriction of an individual's autonomy if it is sufficiently serious to pose a threat to others or if there is a serious threat posed to the life or welfare of the irrational person herself, and it is considered that treatment could alleviate or cure her condition and remove the irrationality that is the source of the threat.

The basic issue here is that of what best serves the promotion of autonomy. Those who regard any involuntary treatment and/or hospitalisation of the mentally ill as an unjustifiable restriction of their autonomy are making the simplistic assumption that leaving them to their own resources is equivalent to preserving their autonomy, which is patently not the case.

> I believe that we are witnessing a pendular swing in which the rights of the mentally ill to be treated and protected are being set aside in the rush to give them their freedom at whatever cost. But is freedom defined only by the absence of external constraints? Internal physiological or psychological processes can contribute to a throttling of the spirit that is as painful as any applied from outside. (Chodoff, 1976, p. 501)

If we accept Moore's argument that 'rationality is the fundamental premise by virtue of which we understand ourselves as human beings'., then it follows that irrationality may be a sufficient condition for restricting autonomy, providing that certain other criteria are met. (Irrationality, of course, is not a necessary condition for the restriction of autonomy). This means that irrationality may be used as a justification for paternalistic intervention in the treatment of the mentally ill in order to prevent or alleviate the harm that may result to them or to others as a consequence of their irrational state. I would argue that irrationality may justify paternalistic intervention even though it may be considered to be a restriction of the autonomy of the mentally ill because the behaviour which is the result of mental illness cannot be considered to be truly autonomous behaviour. Irrational behaviour is not the behaviour of people 'capable of adjusting their actions as reasonably efficient means to intelligible ends'. In the majority of cases, the irrationality which afflicts the mentally ill results in behaviour which is harmful to themselves; less often, such behaviour is harmful to others. In both cases, however, the behaviour must be considered to be outside the control of the sufferer and consequently, she cannot be held responsible for it. Therefore, if life and the quality of life is valued, and individual autonomy is seen as an important element of the quality of life, there must surely be a moral duty to try and restore autonomy to the mentally ill. This is not best achieved, under the spurious guise of not interfering with their autonomy, by putting the entire onus of sorting themselves out and taking responsibility for their lives onto those who, by virtue of circumstances over which they have little or no control, i.e. severe mental illness, are unable to do so, because irrationality severely limits autonomy. And paternalism need not be interpreted in a heavy-handed, authoritarian manner (even though it does involve substituting someone else's authority over that of an irrational person's). It can also be interpreted as caring enough for another to make difficult, and probably unpopular, decisions in the short-term in the hope that in the long-term genuine autonomy will be promoted. If it is accepted that the mentally ill have a right to protection and treatment, and surely any society which makes claims to be humane must accept this, then it must be accepted also that, by virtue of the nature of mental illness, this will sometimes involve difficult and painful decisions relating to their autonomy, which cannot be resolved by simplistic stances which grant the illusion of autonomy at the expense of hope and possibly even life itself. Therefore, in answer to the question of whether or not serious irrationality, inevitably subjectively defined, is justification for the restriction of autonomy, I would argue that the answer is a qualified 'yes'. The qualifications relate to the issues of the degree of irrationality; its consequences and the nature and degree of the restriction, which I shall consider in detail in the next chapter.

3 Autonomy and treatment models of mental illness

I have argued in the previous chapter that irrationality may be a sufficient justification for restricting a person's autonomy by virtue of the fact that irrationality itself restricts autonomy by virtue of imposing a *limitation in oneself* on the sufferer. However, although this may sound fairly obvious when stated simply, the consequences of this have been quite devastating for the treatment of the mentally ill.

In this chapter I propose to examine two models of the treatment of the mentally ill, both of which I shall argue are seriously flawed, and both of which are informed both by simplistic notions of the relationship between irrationality and autonomy and the nature of autonomy itself. The issue of irrationality lies at the heart of both these unsatisfactory models of treatment for mental illness; in what I have called the 'voiceless patient' model of treatment, the mentally ill are denied all autonomy by virtue of their illness being perceived as stripping them of one of the defining characteristics required to be considered as fully human, that of rationality. The other model, which I have termed the 'benign neglect' model of treatment, results either from a denial that irrationality may be a relevant factor in the behaviour of the mentally ill, so treating their sometimes bizarre behaviour as the product of a rational choice on the part of the ill person and consequently denying that any restriction of autonomy is justifiable; or from a belief that autonomy must be valued above all other rights, and irrespective of the condition of a mentally ill person, sets out to protect her autonomy at all costs.

I shall consider the consequences of each of these models in turn, and wherever possible, I propose to explore the ethical issues they raise by looking at people's stories of their experiences. I shall use examples taken from published accounts of mental illness and also accounts of personal experiences from ex-patients, carers and professionals in the mental health services which have been given to me directly, in response to requests that I made to organisations and institutions for information. The stories that follow do not make for pleasant reading, and I am aware that there are many people working with the mentally ill who have respect and compassion for their patients, and that good practice does exist. I am aware that people are more likely to complain than praise, and that some mentally ill people may have a distorted view of their treatment. Nevertheless, the issues raised

22

by the treatment of sufferers and their carers in the stories that follow raise immensely important ethical issues that must be addressed.

Using individuals' stories means that I shall be relying on anecdotal evidence and any account is likely to tell only one side of the story; I cannot therefore claim any scientific basis for the conclusions reached. That is not my objective, however. The stories I shall examine illustrate the ethical issues involved in the treatment of the mentally ill. It would not matter if every person who had experienced mental illness other than those whose stories I relate here had received exemplary treatment; the moral issues involved would still remain. Slavery has been abolished in the Western world, but that does not preclude us from discussing the ethical issues posed by it. Nor would such issues be irrelevant even in the unlikely event of it being proven that all slaves had been happy.

The 'voiceless patient' model of the treatment of the mentally ill may be seen as a consequence of the fact that all types of illness, including mental illness, have meanings attached to them which may alter the moral status of the sick and consequently affect their treatment, both in the medical sense and in the wider sense of the way society treats the sick - one only has to consider the case of AIDS to see how its association with 'judgements of a deeper kind, both moral and psychological' (Sontag, 1990, p. 43) has influenced attitudes to those unfortunate enough to contract this disease.

In the case of mental illness, one is confronted by the fact that to be mentally ill is to be different. Difference as such is not necessarily an undesirable state. It is perfectly possible to be positively different: witness the glory that attends the superb sports person or musician, whose difference from the majority of people is very visible. But the difference which is valued implies that one has more of a desirable characteristic, whereas the difference involved in mental illness implies either that one has less of a desirable characteristic or more of an undesirable one - and the characteristics involved are those which are considered to be indicative of our humanity; reason, rationality, self-awareness and self-control. Thus the difference implied by mental illness results from the perceived loss or diminution of the very characteristics that form the basis of the common identity that enables someone to claim a shared humanity with the rest of society's members.

The implied lack of certain desirable characteristics in the mentally ill is evident in the colloquial expressions used to describe sufferers.

> I realised that for some while back I had been hearing ... colourful euphemisms, all relying on someone being short of something. Whether they were descended from venerable concepts such as having a screw loose, or having lost your marbles, I don't know, but I can't be the only one to have picked up such descriptions as "he's two sandwiches short of a picnic", or "she's two cards short of a full house". (Kington, 1992, p. 28)

Mental illness puts sufferers from it into the category of a 'special race of people', set apart from 'normal' society.

> In and through its own creation, society creates the individual as such and the individuals in and through which alone it can actually exist ... individuals are made by the instituted society, at the same time as they make and remake it ... The institution, and the imaginary significations borne by it and animating it, create a world. This is the world of the particular society considered: it is established in and through the articulation it performs between a "natural" and "supranatural" - more generally, an "extra-social" - world and a "human" world. (Castoriadis, 1991, p. 145 and p. 146)

The difference between the "extra-social" world and the "human" world is exemplified by the difference between the ordered, social world, where reason and rational behaviour reign, and the heath of Shakespeare's *King Lear*, where anarchy reigns, 'where men have only their flesh in common, [and] some men treat the flesh of their brothers as so much meat'. (Ignatieff, 1990, p. 57). If rationality is seen as a defining characteristic of humanity, and mental illness is perceived as diminishing or removing entirely an individual's rationality, then mental illness may result in the dehumanising of sufferers. As a consequence, autonomy is diminished or denied because rationality is a prerequisite for autonomy, and this in turn further diminishes the perceived humanity of the mentally ill, as autonomy is considered to be a defining characteristic of persons. The mentally ill may therefore be, as it were, doubly dehumanised as a consequence of being perceived as irrational.

The following four stories illustrate the horrendous consequences which may result from what I have termed the 'voiceless patient' model of the treatment of the mentally ill. This model of treatment is a consequence of simplistic notions of autonomy as an absolute and rationality as a prerequisite for being included as an autonomous member of a common humanity.

> Then two nurses dragged her, one on each side, to an enormous room filled with baths. They dipped her into bath after bath of boiling water. Each bath was smaller than the last, with gold taps that came off in her hands when she tried to clutch them ... After the hot baths, they ducked her, spluttering and choking, into an ice-cold one. A nurse took a bucket of cold water and splashed it over her, drenching her hair and half blinding her. She screamed, and nurses, dozens of them crowded round the bath to laugh at her. ... She had human limbs, but she was not human; she was a horse or a stag being prepared for the hunt. ... She came out of [a] dream suddenly to find herself being tortured in her own person. A young man with a signet ring on his finger was bending over her, holding a funnel with a long tube attached. He forced the tube down her nose and began to pour some liquid into the funnel.

There was a searing pain at the back of her nose, she choked and struggled, but they held her down ruthlessly. At last the man drew out the tube and dropped it coiling in a basin. The nurses released her and all three went out and shut the door.

This horror came at intervals for days. She grew to dread the opening of the door, which was nearly always followed by the procession of nurses and the young man with the basin and the funnel. (White, 1982, pp. 431, 432, 433)

This horrendous description from Antonia White's novel *Beyond the Glass* is based on her own experiences whilst a patient at Bethlem Royal Hospital, where she spent a year after being certified insane. Her daughter in her memoirs states that the account of her madness in *Beyond the Glass* was the least fictional of all her mother's writing. She records that her mother was never able to forget the horrors of her stay in Bethlem:

The nightmares of last summer began again. They were always about the asylum, but now Antonia was an old woman being dragged protesting to 'the wire machine and the clippers'. (Chitty, 1985, p. 75)

The description of Antonia White's treatment reads more like an account of torture than of treatment of a mentally ill person. Even if one removed the distortions produced by the illness, and were to construct a purely clinical account of this force-feeding and public hot and cold bathing, it would still be horrible. But there are other forms of torture than the purely physical:

The two doctors insisted that I must go into a mental hospital. I pleaded with them. I argued that I was in no way a subject for a mental hospital - I would go anywhere else for recuperative treatment and a rest. ... I do not remember my actual admission. ... From then on it was a case of drugs, and still more drugs, drugs to break down one's resistance, drugs to loosen one's tongue, drugs to make one remember and then to make one forget. That, during that time, I became mentally unbalanced, I cannot deny. I believe that my unbalance was induced by drugs. ... [I was] locked up in this vast strange building; sometimes sleeping in a long dormitory, sometimes in a small side room off a long corridor, at others in a padded cell on the floor. Always the doors were locked. One could tell when nurses passed by the jingle of keys at their waists. Never had I felt so frightened, lost, lonely or desolate. (Johnson & Dodds, 1957, p. 70)

I was not allowed to write to my employers to notify them of my inability to continue my work, and I was not allowed to write to my best friend to tell her where to locate me. No reason was ever given for this breach of the rules; and no harm could possibly have resulted from my correspondence, since the ward sister read every letter written by patients, and failed to post those of which she, or the doctor disapproved.

These extracts are taken from *Plea for the Silent*, (Johnson & Dodds, 1957), a collection of cases from the post bags of two MPs in the 1950s. The stories they tell are horrifying chronicles of insensitive, callous treatment of those designated 'mentally ill'. These documents do not allow the excuse that the treatment these unfortunate people received was the product of a less enlightened age than the twentieth century. And if confirmation were needed that barbarity is alive and well and flourishing in the twentieth century, it is only necessary to read *Fifty Years in the System*, by Jimmy Laing and Dermot McQuarrie (1992).

In 1938, at the age of nine, Jimmy Laing was locked up in the Baldovan mental institution in Scotland; fifty years later, in 1987, he was conditionally released from Carstairs State Hospital. He had spent virtually all the intervening years incarcerated in mental hospitals. By his own admission he was a difficult child, although reading his brief account of his childhood it is not difficult to see why, for his family life could hardly have been described as happy.

The regime at Baldovan was regimented, implemented largely by untrained and unsympathetic - and in some cases brutal - staff. Punishment was severe and if it did not achieve compliance on the part of the inmates, paraldehyde would be used to sedate offenders.

There were some good, loving, caring nurses but they were in the minority. Where you have an authoritative regime where someone wants to rule with the whip, the good ones can only do so much. Even they can't change the system. (Laing & McQuarrie, 1992, p. 39)

After nine years at Baldovan, Jimmy Laing was transferred to Murthly, an asylum outside Perth.

The nursing staff at Murthly, like Baldovan, were not 'nurses' in the true sense of the word. While the majority wouldn't really bother you, there was a rotten minority. But it was a powerful minority. Even the good ones would never bear witness against the bad ones. (ibid., p. 47)

There is no indication that any of the patients were treated as individuals, and certainly no sign of understanding that their behaviour might be an acceptable adaptation to a life of unremitting boredom and aimlessness, for there was no form of therapy whatsoever at Murthly. Conformity appeared to be the only aim, at whatever the cost to individuals.

One of the most disturbing aspects of Jimmy Laing's years of confinement in various institutions is the fact that neither he nor any of the inmates anywhere had a voice. There was no right of appeal even against brutal malpractice, let alone the medical treatment, if it can be dignified with such a name, that those incarcerated in these institutions experienced. Even on the rare occasions when medical staff talked to him about his plight, there was an atmosphere of their knowing what answers they expected - indeed, demanded.

I didn't really respond to psychoanalysis; perhaps it was because of the questions, which were concerned with digging into your mind, or so they thought. For example, they would ask, 'Now, when you were crossing that bridge you did want to throw yourself off, didn't you?' If you wanted the interview over quickly then you'd make up a story of why you wanted to throw yourself off the bridge and what led up to it and they would be pleased. It was a game we were both playing. But again we're back to winners and losers. You thought you were winning but you weren't really. Psychiatrists are just as cunning and foxy as the people they're interviewing. There were other highly amusing questions which whatever answer you gave you'd be the loser. They'd ask you, 'Would you be comfortable talking to the Queen?' and 'If you were talking to the Queen could you take coffee with her without being embarrassed?' And the piece de resistance: 'Do you have any relations in the Royal Family?' If you replied that you could speak to the Queen, have coffee with her and not feel embarrassed then they put you down as having delusions of grandeur. If, on the other hand, you said that you'd be unable to talk to her and be very embarrassed to take coffee with her they put you down as having an inferiority complex. I think if you'd said you had relations in the Royal Family they'd have written you off right away! (ibid., p. 71)

The same appalling catalogue of inhumanity and abuse occurred again and again at all the institutions Jimmy Laing was incarcerated in; Baldovan, Murthly, Gartloch Hospital the Criminal Lunatic Department at Perth, Carstairs Hospital (the Scottish equivalent of Broadmoor) all had a proportion of decent staff unable to effect any significant change in attitudes to and treatment of the patients in their care, and everywhere the prevailing feeling is that the only definition of reality is that of the staff.

Jimmy Laing was eventually released from Murray Royal Hospital in November, 1986, 47 years and 2 months after being sent to Baldovan as a disruptive child. In all the years he was incarcerated the only crime with which he was charged was breach of the peace - his other 'crimes' were absconding from institutions so awful that it is beyond comprehension how anyone could not try to escape from them.

The following extract from a letter sent to me by an ex-patient is a contemporary example:

... far more harm than good was done to me by those who sought to treat me ... My first complaint ... is that they were grossly incompetent. Some of them were also unjustifiably violent. Without any explanation as to why they considered it justified, I was clapped in handcuffs, bundled into a police car and driven to a mental hospital. When I tried to escape, they locked me in a room. Having decided that escape was impossible, I lay down to sleep, only to be awoken by a psychiatrist and several nurses, who, between them, held me down on the bed and injected me with a drug which rendered me unconscious. Since I am over six feet tall, it is possible that these people were frightened of me. Yet I had done nothing, under the most severe provocation, which could indicate that I was likely to become violent. If I had ever used force to incarcerate someone, had prevented them from escaping by, again, forcibly detaining them and had finally resorted to drugging them into unconsciousness, it might have been justifiable to regard me as being sufficiently dangerous to warrant taking similar measures to prevent me from doing further harm to anyone. Even then it seems to me that there is some doubt about the ethics of meeting violence with violence. That these members of the psychiatric profession could find no other way of dealing with me is ... simply a measure of their incompetence.

This ex-patient prefers not to use the term 'patient' because he considers that 'it was entirely erroneous to regard what was wrong with me as a medical problem'; instead, he considers himself to have been a victim of the psychiatric system, a survivor rather than a patient.

These stories (and there are many, many more that could be used) illustrate the appalling mistreatment that may arise as a consequence of denying the mentally ill any autonomy. These people were treated as abnormal, lacking all autonomy and fundamentally sub-human, to be manipulated and kept quiet so that they cause no trouble to anyone. Consequently, they are denied a voice, because being seen as subhuman, by definition, denies them a voice. The relationship between them and their 'carers' is adversarial; 'them and us', with 'them' being categorised as other by virtue of their illness; for these patients their otherness has deprived them of their shared human identity and with the loss of a common humanity with their 'carers' they have lost their human rights in the sense of being treated as fully human beings, if not in the legal sense (although mentally ill patients may well lose some of their legal rights too, depending upon the circumstances of their admission to hospital). (See Bluglass, 1984, for the legal situation of hospitalised mentally ill patients.)

To treat anyone in the manner that these cases illustrate is indefensible and repugnant - even someone who is totally non-autonomous, such as a patient in a deep coma, should be treated with respect and humanity. It may be that these cases are the extreme, an horrendous but unrepresentative sample of cases demonstrating extreme cruelty. Nevertheless, even kindly treatment may be administered in the mistaken belief that mental illness necessarily renders the sufferer entirely totally non-autonomous as a consequence of irrationality. This is simply not the case. Mental illness may result in irrationality which restricts autonomy as a consequence of being a 'limitation in oneself'; in severe cases, the restriction of autonomy may be virtually absolute, as, for example, in cases of catatonia. But equally, in the majority of cases, although autonomy may be diminished it is not extinguished.

The 'voiceless patient' model of treatment denies the mentally ill any significant degree of autonomy and in so doing dehumanises them. At best, this is humiliating, at worst it may result in people being treated with extreme cruelty, as the examples I have included above illustrate. It inevitably means that the chances of helping the mentally ill are or non-existent. It is thus objectionable in three ways. Firstly, it is a violation of autonomy, since people with diminished autonomy may, as we have seen, have to be restrained, but are still entitled to have what remains of their autonomy respected and to be free from any *unnecessary* restraint. Secondly, it results in the infliction of physical and mental suffering, and thirdly, it reduces the likelihood of, or even prevents, any improvement.

Let us now consider the 'benign neglect' model. This model grew at least partly out of the well-intentioned aims of those who wished to redress the appalling situation that results from the 'voiceless patient' model. It was both fostered by the growth of community care and one of the rationales for it, and it illustrates one type of professional attitude to the mentally ill currently in vogue amongst some mental health practitioners. The following story illustrates the nowadays all too familiar consequences of this model of treatment for the mentally ill.

Anne Deveson's son, Jonathan, developed schizophrenia at the age of seventeen. Her book, *Tell Me I'm Here*, (Deveson, 1992), tells the story of her son's affliction with schizophrenia and her desperate attempts to obtain help and treatment for him She accepts the term 'schizophrenia': whether one does or does not accept it as a valid diagnostic category, there can be no doubt at all that her son became a severely disturbed, deranged young man.

> This is a story about a journey into madness. It was a journey where my son became a will-o'-the-wisp, leading us all into brambles and boglands. Now you see him, now you don't.

> Tell me, tell me, Anne, tell me I'm here. Open your right eye only when you're telling the truth.

> Jonathan had schizophrenia. He was seventeen when he first became ill. Its journey took him to lands of mythical happenings. The demons that plagued him were capricious, and he could not order their behaviour. Sometimes they brought him delight; more often they plunged him into horror.

My journey after him took me down a labyrinth of passageways, each labelled 'cure'. I never found one. Jonathan died of a drug overdose when he was twenty-four. ... We do not use the word 'mad' any more. We have banished it, together with words like 'lunatic' and 'asylum'; even the word 'insane' is rarely heard. These words evoke oppressions of the past; today the terminology has changed, become more technical and distancing, yet our oppressions remain. They are the oppressions of neglect. (Deveson, 1992, pp. 1 & 2)

Her descriptions of her son's torment make harrowing reading; the alternative reality he inhabited frequently reads like a description of a descent into hell. Equally harrowing is the response she received from many of the professionals with whom she made contact in her efforts to obtain help for Jonathan. Her account of her encounters with some of the professionals who were supposed to be trying to help Jonathan sometimes makes the reader wonder whether these professionals are also inhabiting an alternative reality of their own construction.

Jonathan was diagnosed as suffering from schizophrenia on one of the rare occasions when he voluntarily entered hospital, in Sydney, Australia. The drugs he was taking affected his weight, which increased, and caused a 'wooden appearance' (p. 36). These drugs 'took the edge off his madness but ... did not work as well as the doctors had hoped, and this was to be a recurring problem.' (p. 36).

The rest of this book is a heartbreaking chronicle of Jonathan's disintegration as a person; it is a catalogue of the torments and anguish suffered both by this unhappy young man, and his family and all who loved him. Whenever he stopped taking his medication his condition deteriorated; his behaviour was so bizarre and unacceptable that it put horrendous strains on his family, to the extent that the other children wanted to leave home when they were told that their elder brother was returning. He began attacking Georgia, his sister, and brought home a variety of friends, some suffering like himself from schizophrenia, who were an additional source of worry for a family already stretched to breaking point. He started to take 'street' drugs. During 1980, Jonathan's condition became worse. In 1981, Jonathan became entangled with the police, as a result of stealing; his relationship with his family deteriorated even more, and on February 2nd, during an acute psychotic attack, his mother rang the hospital for help. She is told to ring Crisis Care, who refer her to the police because her son is psychotic. The police refer her back to Crisis Care; when contacted again, they promise to come in two hours' time! Jonathan eventually agrees to go to hospital, but when the police ring to say that they are bringing him in, a doctor insists that there is no such thing as schizophrenia.

I think of the long night and the fear and anguish of Jonathan. I grab the phone from the policeman and begin talking, and don't stop until I have

30

convinced this idiot, this cretin, this man with his absurd textbook theories, that unless he does something there will be hell to pay. He gives in. Perhaps he decides he would rather face Jonathan than me.

When we get to the hospital, Jonathan says 'I'm sorry, sir,' to the doctor and I feel a sinking sensation as the doctor raises his eyebrows and says, 'Seems all right to me.' It's Mr Smarty-pants No-such-thing-as schizophrenia, but I am too tired for a fight. I put my head in my hands, and then I hear Jonathan.

'I think you've put me in here to punish me for my sins. Do not electrocute me, sir.' His voice trails away to a sigh.

I should have felt relieved. Instead I am unutterably sad. ...

I saw a social worker, who said in a syrupy voice, 'I know you are a very busy woman, but try to love your son'.

... Later, the social worker tells Brenda [Jonathan's probation officer] that it is obvious Jonathan missed out on affection as a child and that I loved the other two children more. Not long after that, another professional tells me that perhaps I have been overly involved with Jonathan ,'smother-love' it is called.

This is a no-win situation. I have lost the son I knew. My other two children are living under a fearful strain. My relationship with the architect [the author's lover] is fast disappearing. I am cursed and alone. I feel pain howling through every part of me. (ibid., pp. 88 - 90)

And so it continues. When Jonathan is floridly psychotic, he refuses to go into hospital and has to be forcibly taken there, usually by the police, adding to his terror and confusion. When he is less mad, it is impossible to obtain treatment for him because there are no grounds for hospitalising him; he is unable to acknowledge how ill he is, and as a legal adult, the authorities will not treat him against his will. His medication is only partly efficacious, and has unpleasant side-effects, so when out of hospital he does not take it and his psychotic symptoms return.

During the next five years, Jonathan is in and out of trouble with the law, spends time in prison, time in hospital leaves home, returns home - often breaking in and behaving violently - and continues to deteriorate. Nothing is effective in helping him; by now he is a drug addict, and in 1986, he takes drug overdoses four times. On Tuesday, June 10th., his mother rings a doctor and tells him 'I know that Jonathan is going to die soon. Get him into hospital.' She is told, 'I can't. He won't stay and we can't force him.' On Thursday, June 12, 1986, Jonathan died from a drug overdose at the Edward Eger night refuge in Sydney.

Anne and Jonathan Deveson's stories come from Australia, but many British families have experienced similar treatment. In 1987, *The Times* ran a three-part investigation into schizophrenia which included a selection of stories from sufferers' families. (Wallace, 1987). The same sad cycle of events that Anne Deveson catalogues so movingly are told over and over again by families who watched helplessly as a loved member deteriorated and, in many cases, died, as a result of neglect and lack of treatment, often justified by the argument that the sufferer was an adult and therefore the parents had no right to ask for treatment for him/her, even when he/she was far too ill to act at all rationally.

The 'benign neglect' model of treatment of the mentally ill might at first sight appear to be a more humane treatment model than the 'voiceless patient' model of treatment; this model results from one of two stances to the mentally ill. Recognising the appalling abuses that have resulted from denying the mentally ill any autonomy by virtue of their perceived irrationality, one stance treats the mentally ill as autonomous beings who have made the choice of behaving in the irrational way they do, but under the guise of respecting individual autonomy, then neglects them with frequently disastrous consequences. This is a debased version of the anti-psychiatry approach to the question of mental illness; it theoretically gives the sufferer from mental illness a voice, in that she can choose to reject help and treatment, but ignores the fact that for certain people with severe mental illness, as exemplified by Jonathan Deveson, the more ill they become, the less insight they have into their condition; thus their 'freedom' is no more than an illusion and the consequences of such 'freedom' are often fatal. Such an approach does, however, have the virtue of allowing those who espouse it the satisfying belief that they have upheld the individual's right to autonomy, and prevents them from having to make the frequently agonising decisions that otherwise arise in cases such as Jonathan Deveson's. But the price paid is excessive, to put it mildly.

The other stance acknowledges that the mentally ill may be irrational but values autonomy above all other values, to the extent that seriously mentally ill people may be left 'rotting with their rights on'. Both these models of treatment - the 'voiceless patient' and 'benign neglect' - raise the issue of the value that is placed on autonomy in comparison with other values.

Autonomy is valued by both deontologists and utilitarians, but the Kantian deontological perspective that restricting a person's autonomy is necessarily equivalent to dehumanising her is considerably stronger than the utilitarian perspective, which values individual autonomy because it is beneficial. The Kantian view rules out any justification for paternalism, which is what one might call the benign justification for the restriction of autonomy (as opposed to the malignant restriction of autonomy which may result from the perception of irrationality denying the mentally ill a common humanity with 'normal' members of society.) Thus, the relative value of autonomy and other values depends upon one's conception of autonomy. Dworkin (1988) argues that any notion of autonomy which makes it inconsistent with important values such as loyalty, commitment, benevolence and love is 'not one that has a claim to our respect as an ideal'. (p. 21). He goes on to argue that:

> There is an intellectual error that threatens to arise whenever autonomy has been defended as crucial or fundamental: this is that the notion is elevated to a higher status than it deserves. Autonomy is important, but so is the capacity for sympathetic identification with others, or the capacity to reason prudentially, or the virtue of integrity. Similarly, although it is important to respect the autonomy of others, it is also important to respect their welfare, or their liberty, or their rationality. Theories that base everything on any single aspect of human personality, on any one of a number of values, always tend towards the intellectually imperialistic. ... I believe that autonomy is both important normatively and fundamental conceptually. Neither of these precludes the possibility that other concepts are both important and fundamental. (p. 32)

If rationality is accepted as a necessary condition for autonomy, and all theories of autonomy do accept this, then it surely must be accepted, as I argued in the preceding chapter, that irrationality, if likely to lead to delusions that will harm either the person herself or others, constitutes a justification for the restriction of apparent autonomy, so that autonomy cannot necessarily rightly be considered to be the supreme value in cases of mental illness. Because the extreme view that the mentally ill have no autonomy is wrong, misguided and may result in cruelty does not mean that the other extreme, that the mentally ill must be regarded as completely autonomous, or even if not, that their autonomy must be respected above all other values, is correct.

The absurdity (and to varying degrees, inhumanity) of both these views of the mentally ill becomes blindingly obvious if we compare them with models of physical illness and ethical ways of treating the physically ill. Let us first consider the consequences of applying the 'voiceless patient' model to the treatment of a case of physical illness.

Let us imagine a patient, Ms X, a dancer with a foreign ballet company which is highly respected artistically, but extremely impecunious. Competition for work is intense, and no dancer can afford to be injured and drop out of the company even for a short time, as there is little likelihood of getting back in. Ms X is painfully aware - quite literally - that she has injured her leg, and knows she requires treatment. Reluctantly she finds her way to the nearest hospital where the medical staff realise she has a very serious injury which requires her leg to be immobilised in a plaster cast and to have no weight at all put on it for several weeks until it has healed. Unfortunately, Ms X speaks no English, and the staff in the hospital cannot even work out what language she is speaking; her colleague who brought her to the hospital speaks French, a language which at least one member of the

33

hospital staff is known to speak, but the staff take no notice of him and ignore his attempts to help.

Ms X is duly admitted to hospital, a decision with which she complies reluctantly because she has been told little about her condition, and although acknowledging that there is something wrong, is not sure whether she could not have been treated as an out-patient; her anxiety largely stems from her feeling that she has no say in the matter (which is effectively quite true as she shares no common language with the staff), and cannot even obtain any meaningful information as to what is going on. Once in hospital, her requests for information are ignored; she rarely sees a doctor and her complaints that her treatment, far from helping her condition actually appears to be worsening it, are ignored. By now Ms X is beginning to feel that there is some sort of conspiracy being enacted against her, and she is acutely anxious about her position in the ballet company, not even being sure whether she will have a job when her leg is better, or, indeed, if her leg will get sufficiently better to enable her to dance again. She is anxious, confused, lonely and very frightened. Eventually her French-speaking colleague manages to communicate to the staff that she can speak French, and some form of communication is established between patient and staff. When Ms X tries to voice her fears, she is told that this is a consequence of being ill in a strange country, and really all part of her illness and further proof that she needs continued treatment so that she can really rest and get better. As both a foreigner and an 'artistic' person she is considered by definition to be, at the very least, temperamental and prone to hysteria, so it is considered that her judgement is unreliable and therefore that it is far better for the staff to make all her decisions for her. Nothing is done to address Ms X's very reasonable fears, and she consequently becomes very depressed; by now the staff are considering the need for psychiatric treatment …

This scenario can be analysed by looking at the question of this patient's treatment in the light of the way her autonomy was respected and valued by the medical stag. Ms X is correctly identified as being in need of treatment, but from that point she is treated as a machine. No attempt is made to understand her or to communicate with her in any way. Because she is both foreign and 'artistic' she is stigmatised as hysterical; no attempt is made to communicate with her, or to understand what she is saying, and why she is saying it. There is no acknowledgement of Ms X's humanity, and certainly no idea of a shared humanity, therefore no empathy or sympathy with her situation, and absolutely no acknowledgement that her appalling situation might be leading to her distressed mental state. All Ms X's autonomy, and all respect for her autonomy, is denied her. The situation as described appears ridiculous, and the reason it appears ridiculous is because Ms X's complaint is physical, and it is not generally considered that being physically ill, by definition, removes all a patient's autonomy. Patients with physical illnesses often do have restricted autonomy, of course: they have to surrender a certain degree of their autonomy to those with expert knowledge, who use this knowledge to make decisions on a patient's behalf; and some physical illnesses whose meanings carry with them a stigma can effectively reduce a patient's autonomy. But no matter how stigmatising the meaning of a physical illness might be, it is not suggested that a patient automatically loses all her autonomy as a result of having a physical illness. Generally speaking, a person with a physical illness, when her situation and treatment options are explained to her, is usually considered competent to give informed consent to her treatment, and responsible enough to do what the experts advise regarding treatment; the whole situation is treated as confidential.

There are obviously exceptions to this, the most extreme case being that of a patient in a coma who obviously cannot exercise any autonomy; children also present a different case, as do the learning-impaired. But in general terms, patients with a physical illness are allowed a voice; they can make their wishes known, accept or refuse treatment, and opt for one form of treatment over another. In the majority of cases, patients bow to the greater knowledge of the experts treating them and accept their advice on treatment, sacrificing some degree of their own autonomy by letting the experts make decisions for them. The point is, however, that consciously to sacrifice part of one's autonomy - to have the autonomy to sacrifice part of one's autonomy - is a very different matter from having no choice. And having made the decision to delegate part of her autonomy to the experts, a patient suffering from a physical illness nonetheless expects to be able to discuss the effects and outcomes of treatment chosen by the experts, to be listened to and taken seriously if she complains that a particular treatment is not helping her, to discuss fears and worries and to be treated with the dignity that is generally considered to be her right as a human being. In short, she expects to have her right to autonomy respected, even when part of it is willingly surrendered to those treating her.

This is an ideal situation, of course. The profession of medicine has for many years been surrounded by the mystique and power that results from its members having access to specialist and highly valued knowledge; the ghost of Sir Lancelot Spratt has not yet completely vanished from the medical world, and the issue of paternalism is still very much alive. However, new, contractual models of doctor/patient relationships are being developed and the medical profession generally is becoming far more aware of the issue of paternalism and I think it is fair to say that one no longer loses all one's autonomy simply by virtue of suffering from a physical illness. Yet this is exactly what the 'voiceless patient' model of treatment of the mentally ill results in - by virtue of the illness being mental rather than physical, the patient is denied all autonomy.

Let us return to Ms X and consider the consequences of applying the 'benign neglect' model of treatment to her case. This time, let us imagine that after a few days her leg improves significantly, so she decides to leave the hospital and return to her company. Because of the language barrier, no-one is able to communicate to her the information that if she does this, she will in all probability damage her leg beyond repair and will never dance again. It is not possible to contact anyone in her company to ask them to impart this information to her, in the hope of persuading her not to take such a risk, or at least to keep an eye on her, because she is an adult, all her medical information is confidential and she has the right to discharge herself from the hospital if she chooses. This she duly does, returns to her role in the ballet, has a terrible accident and is taken back to hospital by her colleagues. Here she is told that if she is well enough to get to the hospital she does not require treatment! They will only treat her if she is totally unable even to stand and requires, in their opinion, a stretcher! And, as her friends have brought her to hospital might it not be the case that she is only there because they want her to be there? She cannot make herself understood in English, so is in no position to say what she perceives her situation to be. Ms X is sent away, her autonomy intact, her leg and her future destroyed.

I have used the fictitious example of the case of Ms X to illustrate how patently ridiculous it would be to treat someone suffering from a physical condition, unable to communicate adequately by virtue of a language barrier, in the way that many mentally ill people have been, and are continuing to be, treated. The fact that Ms X could not communicate properly would be unlikely, in the case of physical medicine, be considered as sufficient grounds for denying her all autonomy (except for extreme circumstances, such as a comatose state); neither would it be grounds for arguing that those who spoke for her were necessarily to be deemed to be infringing her autonomy. But the true stories I have described in this chapter illustrate that this is the way that many patients suffering from mental illness are treated; when these models are applied to a case of physical illness, their extreme crudeness and inappropriateness are highlighted. The crudeness of these models of treatment is a consequence, at least in part, of the fact that each takes a simplistic stance on autonomy and its relationship to irrationality and mental illness. These simplistic stances on autonomy ignore the complexity of the concept; they ignore the fact that autonomy is not an absolute state, but rather admits of degree, and may vary over time and according to circumstances, and may be restricted not only by others but by 'limitations in oneself'.

I have argued that irrationality may be considered to be a 'limitation in oneself' which consequently may result in what might be termed an 'internal' restriction on autonomy, which in turn may be a justification for an 'external' restriction of autonomy, particularly if the consequences of an individual's irrationality pose a threat to others, but also, in some cases, if they pose a threat to the irrational person herself.

This inevitably faces us with difficult and sometimes painful decisions relating to the treatment of the mentally ill, for there are no easy answers to many of the issues it raises. Notwithstanding the complicated issues relating to autonomy that are raised by mental illness, I take as read the assumption that it is morally right to attempt to maximise the autonomy of the mentally ill to the greatest degree possible. But the endeavour to find the most humane treatment for the mentally ill, and the best ways to maximise their autonomy will not bear fruit if we simply close our eyes to the complexities involved, and indeed, to the sometimes unpalatable and painful decisions that must be made, as the following chapters will demonstrate. It is therefore important to acknowledge at the outset both that autonomy admits of degree, and that there are other things which are highly valued, such as the right to be free from the violence of others, loyalty, love, commitment and benevolence, which may be argued to be either as important as autonomy, or at the very least, should be seen to be not inconsistent with it.

And it is appropriate to note at this point that language does us no service when considering mental illness: I have referred to *their* autonomy, *the mentally ill*, and the very terms used immediately set the mentally ill apart from the implied mentally well members of society. I am not indulging in the silly argument that the mentally ill are the 'sane' members of society and the so-called 'normal' members are 'mad'; nevertheless, it is perhaps appropriate to reflect that there but for the grace of God go many of us, and that the mentally 'well' share more characteristics in common with the mentally 'ill' than divide them: the acknowledgement of this shared humanity must inform all our deliberations on treatment and autonomy if we are to have any hope of achieving humane care and treatment for the mentally ill.

In the following chapters I propose to examine these issues as they relate to the specific areas of involuntary hospitalisation and treatment, psychotropic medication, ECT and psychosurgery, psychotherapy and community care, because all these areas frequently provoke knee-jerk reactions from both the 'pro' and 'anti' camps which may result in the inappropriate treatment models already discussed: the common factor that characterises both approaches is that such simplistic stances to complex problems may result in additional suffering for the mentally ill.

4 Involuntary hospitalisation and treatment

I have argued that in some circumstances it is justifiable to restrict the autonomy of the mentally ill; it is now necessary to consider what forms and methods of restriction of autonomy can be justified. The issues under consideration here are fundamentally those of involuntary hospitalisation and treatment. In England and Wales, the law relating to these issues is laid down in the Mental Health Act, 1983, and in Scotland, the Mental Health (Scotland) Act, 1984. (I shall only be concerned with the law relating to England and Wales.)

Mental illness is not the only illness that can result in medical intervention without the consent of the individual concerned: the 1984 Public Health (Control of Diseases) Act makes provision for the compulsory testing of carriers of certain infectious diseases such as cholera, typhus and typhoid, and for application to be made to a magistrate to order compulsory treatment. These powers were extended to cover those suffering from AIDS by the Public Health (Control of Diseases) Regulations, 1985; but they have been used only once in respect of an AIDS sufferer. This case occurred at Monsall Hospital in Manchester, in 1985, where an AIDS sufferer who was bleeding very heavily refused treatment.

The existence of this legislation has not provoked protest; the reason for this may be that it is rarely necessary to use it nowadays, as the infectious diseases it covers are relatively rare (though the situation could conceivably change if the threatened AIDS epidemic materialises). It could also be that these diseases, being seen as located firmly in the physical realm, are considered justifiable reasons for compulsory intervention in the case of sufferers considered to be behaving irresponsibly and consequently putting other people at risk of catching an extremely serious infectious disease.

Mental illness fails into a different category. It is not infectious, and because its diagnosis involves subjective judgements about rationality and behaviour it inevitably raises questions about civil rights which relate to its misuse for political ends or as a result of ethical bias. The nature of mental health legislation, and indeed the very need for it, reflects these two aspects of mental illness. Firstly, the nature of mental illness - the fact that it often involves decreased rationality and responsibility and that the sufferer may have little or no insight into her condition - has resulted in the power to decide to accept or reject treatment being removed, in

38

some cases, from the mentally ill person, and given to other, authorised, people instead. Secondly, the inescapable element of subjectivity involved in the definition of mental illness, the fact that its diagnosis is based on behaviour, and is therefore open to being abused, and the fact that treatment sometimes results in the sufferer's autonomy being restricted, result in a need for the rights of the sufferer to be protected. Mental health legislation therefore has the difficult role of protecting the right of patients to autonomy, the rights of others who may be adversely affected or even injured by the mentally ill person, and the rights of the mentally ill themselves to be protected from their own irrationality.

In England, the Mental Health Act of 1983 replaced the Act of 1959, which had repealed the 1890 Lunacy Act and 1930 Mental Treatments Act; its aim was to ensure that the care and treatment of the mentally ill became the responsibility of the medical and social work professions by removing the previous Acts' emphasis on the legal aspects of mental health care. The 1983 Act was intended to improve patients' rights and to counter the excessive medicalisation of mental illness, just as the 1959 Act was intended to soften the excessive legalism of the earlier Acts (Bean, 1988). The changes made by the 1983 Act seek to ensure:

> ... that except in particular circumstances people should not be admitted to detention for treatment in hospital if their condition is not treatable; [it also seeks to provide] the provision of much more frequent access to mental health review tribunals; the more stringent regulations of the use of treatment without the consent of the patient; the institution of a special health authority, with particular responsibility to oversee the powers to detain and treat patients under the Act; the institution of interim hospital orders, the powers to remand to hospital for assessment; and the limitations of the powers of a guardian to apply only to people over sixteen years of age. (Elton, quoted in Bean, 1988, p. 3)

English and Welsh mental health legislation has a wide base, and

> ... generally speaking, [is] concerned with two basic questions: first, how should patients and staff (that is, medical and allied workers) be regulated in the manner in which patients make contact with psychiatric services; second, how should patients and staff be regulated in the manner in which psychiatric treatment is provided. (ibid.)

These are fundamental questions about the treatment of the mentally ill; they could perhaps be paraphrased in layman's terms as: How does one get into the system; what might happen to one once one is in the system; and what degree of control over events does one have? The answers to these questions are, in one sense, contained within the 1983 Act, inasmuch as it attempts to define the relationship between the mentally ill patient, the law and psychiatry. But in reality, of course, the matter is far less simple than that because of the relationship between psychiatry, law and social control.

The claim that compulsory intervention in the care and treatment of the mentally ill is justified rests on two arguments: first, that of the 'police power' of the state, which claims its legitimacy from the need to protect others from the actions of the mentally ill. second, that of 'parens patriae', the paternalistic justification which derives its legitimacy on the grounds of protecting the mentally ill patient's own interests. (Cavadino, 1989). But because of the nature of mental illness, compulsory treatment inevitably raises the question of social control.

Law is an overt agent of social control - indeed, if there were no need for social control, there would be no need for a legal system. The criminal law has stringent safeguards incorporated into it to protect the rights of those charged under it; in the American legal system these are termed the rights of due process. In the English system, the term 'natural justice' is used. Natural justice has two basic requirements: these are, firstly, that a decision maker must act fairly, must assume that the defendant has full understanding of the case against her and must ensure that the defendant has proper opportunity to answer the charges and put her own case; and secondly, that the decision maker must be impartial and address her mind only to points of relevance in the case.

Criminal law also requires that offences be defined and that anyone proved to have committed an offence should receive a definite sentence, generally of a fixed term if custodial. (The exception to this is the life sentence, which does not have a fixed term.) When the sentence has been served, she will be considered, at least in theory, to have 'wiped the slate clean' and to have paid for her crime.

Mental health law deals with involuntary civil and criminal commitment, in Parts 2 & 3 of the 1983 Act respectively. Cavadino (1989) has pointed out that, as an agent of social control, mental health law can be more effective in some cases than the criminal law; it embodies no concept of natural justice; it is rarely necessary to prove that a specific offence has been committed before someone can be detained; once committed to hospital, drugs can provide an effective method of controlling deviant behaviour and finally, labelling behaviour as the product of mental illness can reduce or remove its legitimacy.

> All this means that there may be a tendency and a temptation to use psychiatric law as a means of social control in situations when, morally and politically, it would be more desirable to use the criminal justice system or no formal control at all. In other words, mental health law can be used to 'bypass' the criminal process. (Cavadino, 1989, p. 18)

I do not propose to examine the way UK mental health law works in practice; that is the province of others. Obviously, vigilance in the application of mental health law is essential; but as Cavadino also points out, mental health law is not only concerned with compulsory hospitalisation and treatment of patients; it can also permit, enable, encourage and require the provision of (non-compulsory) psychiatric provision as well as providing safeguards against the abuse of compulsory powers and infringements of patients' rights and civil liberties.

However, in relation to the treatment of the mentally ill, the law can only be regarded as a framework; it must be obeyed by mental health workers, which means observing its prohibitions and requirements: to do this, however, the law must be interpreted by those whose job it is to provide treatment, and there may well be a range of options to choose from, all or any of which would satisfy the law. This returns us to the consideration of what nature and degree of restriction of autonomy is justified in the treatment of the mentally ill, and who has the power to decide.

I have argued that the autonomy of the mentally ill should be respected and promoted; the problem that must be addressed is how this is best achieved for someone, who, by virtue of her illness, may be irrational and consequently unable to act autonomously, so that her short-term autonomy may have to be sacrificed in the interests of her long-term autonomy.

Autonomy may be restricted by compulsory hospitalisation and compulsory treatment, which may include physical therapies such as ECT and drugs and non-physical therapies such as individual psychotherapy, group therapy and behaviour therapy. All of these impose restrictions on an individual's autonomy, even if entered into voluntarily; if consent is not given, the restriction of autonomy can be considered to be total. There are also other, more subtle restrictions of autonomy which may not be so obvious. A psychotherapist to whom I spoke pointed out that his patients frequently know nothing at all about psychotherapy but often have to choose between individual therapy for which they may have to wait two years, and which will have a time limit imposed upon its duration or group therapy for which they will have to wait 'only' six months and which can continue more or less as long as wished. Ostensibly, their autonomy is being respected in giving them a choice, but in reality, how autonomous is such a decision in these circumstances?

Subtle restrictions of autonomy often occur at the interpersonal level; thus a patient maybe treated according to the letter of the law, may even be given choices concerning treatment but if the attitude of those around her is fundamentally contemptuous she may well be effectively deprived of some autonomy, because autonomy cannot simply be maintained by observing laws. A patient can be offered the choice of taking or refusing medication, but if those offering her the choice do not care what she chooses because they have no respect for her, can they truly be said to be respecting her autonomy? I would argue that they cannot be said to be doing so, unless one defines autonomy in extremely narrow terms. I shall return to this issue later, because I consider that it has particular relevance to cases such as Jonathan Deveson's and the thousands like him.

Let us begin consideration of what does and does not constitute justifiable restriction of autonomy with the most extreme case, that of compulsory hospitalisation. The issue is whether it is morally defensible to hospitalise someone against her will on the grounds of mental illness. The first justification for this is

41

the 'police power' of the state, the duty to protect the public from the possibility of danger from the actions of a very small minority of the mentally ill.

> Preventive detention in hospital or prison is intended to guard against a certain risk of grave harm; but in making use of these measures we unavoidably incur another risk - the risk of imprisoning or hospitalising an individual unnecessarily. Whatever we do, one or other of these risks will eventually be realised. (Floud, in Roth & Bluglass, 1985, p. 82)

Detaining a mentally ill person compulsorily on the possibility that she might do harm can be justified on utilitarian grounds by arguing that the consequences of any harm that she might do should be weighed against the harm she herself will suffer if detained; if there is a reasonable probability that a mentally ill person will do harm if not detained, it is justifiable to detain her in order to prevent that harm, given that the harm she suffers as a result of being detained is less than the harm that she would do if not detained. However, it is extremely difficult to predict whether or not someone is likely to do harm to others; predictions of dangerousness are notoriously unreliable. (Ennis & Litwak, 1974; Cocozza & Steadman, 1976). Results from the *World Health Organisation Collaborative Study on Assessment of Dangerousness in Forensic and Administrative Psychiatry* led to the conclusion that 'dangerousness' is neither a scientifically nor operationally valid concept. (Montandon & Harding, 1984). The following examples illustrate the immense complexities inherent in deciding whose rights are paramount when considering the problem of the conflicting rights of the public and potentially dangerous mentally ill people.

Janet Cresswell was sent to Broadmoor in 1976 for wounding a psychiatrist as a protest against the authorities' persistent refusal to give her an explanation for her original commitment to a psychiatric hospital; having been committed to Broadmoor, she is unlikely to be released until she can prove her sanity. I am not arguing that wounding a psychiatrist is justifiable, nor that such behaviour should not be punished. Neither am I in a position to judge whether or not this lady's action was the result of mental illness, and I am aware that I only have one side of the story. Nevertheless, for the sake of argument, let us take the information I have as correct. If this crime had been committed by anyone deemed mentally well, it would have resulted in a definite sentence, at the conclusion of which this lady would be free to pursue her life as she chose, providing she did not break the law. As it is, she is being detained for an unspecified, unlimited amount of time. It is possible that there is a risk that she would attack this psychiatrist again if released, or indeed any psychiatrist, or any member of the public. However, it could equally well be argued that criminals are quite likely to commit crimes again once they have been released from prison, but this does not result in their being detained for unspecified amounts of time. Similarly, one could argue that anyone found to be over the legal limit of alcohol whilst driving a car might do the same thing again,

42

but such an offence does not result in the driver being imprisoned for an indefinite period, nor, generally, even losing her licence forever, certainly not for a first offence. On the information I have, therefore, it seems hard to justify indefinite commitment for someone in Janet Cresswell's situation. We are all capable of irrational acts when provoked beyond endurance; that does not justify such acts, particularly when they involve harm to others, but it is surely something that one must bear in mind when considering what course of action to take. It is not possible to condone her action, but it is arguable that it is understandable - this woman vented her rage and frustration on the man she considered responsible for refusing to explain to her why she had been sent to a psychiatric hospital in the first place - she was not irrationally threatening all and sundry, and even if her action was that of an irrational person (arguably so, because one might expect someone who was rational to realise that there are more appropriate methods of tackling her problem), one must still ask whether indefinite detention is justified for such behaviour. As Janet Cresswell has said, 'I've been treated worse than rapists or child-murderers'.

The next case illustrates the other side of the problem. *Panorama* on BBC 1 on lst March, 1993, reported the case of Tracey Evans, who had been hospitalised for manic depression. Despite grave reservations on the part of her husband, Robert, she was released from hospital and one month later drowned their two young sons. She was convicted of manslaughter on the grounds of diminished responsibility and sectioned under the Mental Health Act.

In September, 1994, Lancashire County Council Social Services Department faced an enquiry into their handling of certain cases relating to children; one of these cases involved a woman who had been told that her children would be taken into care if she did not cease living with them, following a midwife's report that the woman had told her that she sometimes had an urge to kill her children. This woman had a long history of mental disturbance, but her husband claimed that she was now better, medical staff did not consider her to pose any threat to the children and therefore that it was unreasonable to deny her access to her children. These two cases starkly illustrate the problems facing the professionals who must make these decisions.

The third case, reported in *The Independent* on 27 January, 1993, is that of Pam Morrell, who was awarded £352,777 by the Criminal Injuries Compensation Board after suffering a frenzied attack by her schizophrenic son Jonathan, which has left her brain damaged and needing constant care for the remainder of her life. (Waterhouse, 1993). In April, 1988, her son battered her around the head with a motorcycle chain, almost killing her, and causing multiple fractures of her skull. The family had repeatedly appealed for help to members of the medical profession, social services and their local Regional Health Authority, and had told the psychiatrist that they considered that Jonathan was so dangerous that he might kill his mother. The County Council denied failing to help this family, saying in a letter that Jonathan could not have been subject to a compulsory hospital order because 'medical opinion indicated that [he] was simply not ill enough to warrant hospital admission' .Yet this young man had a ten-year history of illness which included terrifying delusions and, later, terrorising and beating up his mother and a sister. It was this sister who wrote to his psychiatrist of her fear that he would kill their mother if nothing were done to help him.

Given that Jonathan Morrell had threatened and actually beaten up his mother and sister and was diagnosed as suffering from schizophrenia, and that his sister was convinced that he would kill his mother if not helped, is it justifiable to argue that he should have been compulsorily detained on the grounds that he might cause harm to his mother? The same arguments apply as in the case of Janet Cresswell; prediction of harmful behaviour is notoriously unreliable, so he might not have harmed his mother but would have suffered the harm himself of losing his freedom. But he had already harmed his sister and mother, for which he could have received a criminal conviction which might have resulted in a custodial sentence. Presumably this did not happen because he was diagnosed as suffering from schizophrenia, and had been receiving treatment on and off for ten years. However, he did not take his medication, and when he stopped it, he suffered from delusions in which he heard imaginary people taunting him; he developed paranoia and began to carry weapons around with him to protect himself from the forces of evil. Then he began beating his mother and sister.

In this situation, I think one could have argued that the harm this young man would suffer from compulsory detention was likely to have been outweighed by the risk of harm to his family. It is always easy to be wise with hindsight, of course and so it is easy to say that this tragic event was entirely preventable, had the relevant authorities taken the step of compulsory hospitalisation of this young man. The 1983 Act certainly makes provision for this situation, and *The Code of Practice, Mental Health Act 1983*, 'offers much detailed guidance on how the Mental Health Act 1983 should be implemented'. (Department of Health and Welsh Office, 1993, p.v.) Under the heading *Protection of Others*, it states, in paragraph 2.8., that, 'Too high a degree of risk of physical harm, or serious persistent psychological harm to others, are indicators of the need for compulsory admission'. (ibid., p. 5). This appears straightforward, but of course it begs the question of what constitutes 'too high a degree of risk of … harm'? And who is to decide this? These are ultimately subjective judgements, requiring interpretation of behaviour, the weighing-up of information from a variety of sources and risk assessment. Presumably the experts did not consider that there was the necessary degree of risk of Jonathan Morrell harming his mother, because, despite his sister's warning and the fact that he had already been terrorising and beating up his mother and sister, they concluded that '[he] was simply not ill enough to warrant admission'.

This case highlights the issues raised by using the 'police power' of the state as justification for compulsory hospitalisation, which essentially are those of individual as opposed to collective rights. We are faced with the question of justice and specifically, comparative justice, which is concerned with balancing the competing claims of individuals, so that what one person deserves can only be judged in comparison with what another, or others, whose claims are in competition with hers, deserves.

Followers of Szasz would argue that there is no need for compulsory hospitalisation because mental illness is an invalid concept and the criminal law system can cope with those who harm others. However, if one accepts the concept of mental illness, and that there are situations where an individual's disturbed behaviour gives rise to serious concern that she is likely to harm someone, then the question that arises is whether or not one has a right to be protected in order to avoid being harmed, rather than merely accepting that the perpetrator of harm should be punished for her action.

In the case of Jonathan Morrell, the risk was to a specific person, his mother. But in the case of society generally, or the public, which is the expression often used, we are dealing with a collection of individuals, which raises the question of whether or not a collective right to protection exists, for the chances of any one individual amongst the public at large being at risk from a mentally ill person are probably very much smaller than the risk of harm such an individual would incur by driving along the M62 in the rush hour.

Can it be argued that there is a collective right to protection from the possible harmful actions of a tiny minority of the mentally ill? I think it can.

> The mere fact that the risk represented by a dangerous person is diffused over a population of potential victims, though it weakens individual claims against him by reducing the risk to which each is exposed, does not of itself rule out preventive measures. So long as the risk they collectively face is not diffused at source but is attributable to a specific individual, there is no reason to exclude the possibility of taking preventive measures against him. (Floud, in Roth and Bluglass, 1985, p. 85)

Indeed, the collective rights to what can be regarded as protection from various forms of harm are acknowledged in many areas of life - public health legislation is an obvious example. Certain medical conditions preclude sufferers from having a driving license. If someone is refused a driving license on the grounds of a medical condition which makes it unsafe for her to drive, it is not argued that the risk she poses to other road users is diffused amongst the whole population of drivers and therefore that because the chances of her injuring any particular individual are remote, all other road users must be exposed to the risk, no matter how slight, that she will injure one or more of them. Neither is it argued that as it is not her fault that she has this condition, to restrict her freedom to drive is unjust.

On the other hand, it has been decided that no action is to be taken against any HIV positive person who acts irresponsibly because it has been decided that it is not possible to frame a legal solution that would avoid us incarcerating someone when there is no treatment to be offered. There is a difference between the irresponsible actions of a rational person and the irrational actions of a seriously mentally ill person. however. Floud has highlighted the essential point that:

> Potential aggressors and potential victims, like actual aggressors and victims, are in a situation that is logically and morally asymmetrical. The victim would not harm the aggressor were it not that the aggressor would harm him; but the aggressor's inclination to harm the victim is unconditional. (ibid., p. 87)

It must be acknowledged that assessing the likelihood of an individual proving to be dangerous is an extremely difficult task; psychiatric expertise in this area certainly appears to be very limited and the consequences of making the wrong decision have extremely serious implications. In the absence of a foolproof method of predicting dangerousness, which is never likely to be achieved, we shall always have to contend with the risk of injustice resulting to someone in situations where dangerousness must be assessed. It is of note however, that there are currently being developed new approaches to risk assessment and management of potentially dangerous mentally ill people.

> The management of psychiatric patients who are potentially violent to others has moved away from the notion of 'dangerousness', an inflexible concept which implies wrongly that a patient has a static and unchallenging quality of personality, towards adopting the concepts of ongoing assessment of risk and risk-management, assuming that risk will changeover time and can be managed effectively. ... Risk assessment and risk management strategy are becoming much more familiar concepts across health and social services ... but the sound principles adopted by many hospitals in their attempt to manage their financial outcomes have, we regret, scarcely percolated to many psychiatric services. Surgeons and anaesthetists have embraced these concepts with more alacrity, as the spectre of medical negligence claims loom ever larger. Their potential clinical value in mental health practice is enormous, not for financial reasons but for sound clinical ones of producing better outcomes. All mental health services should now have a risk management policy. (Blom-Cooper, Hally and Murphy, 1995, p. 176. See also Crichton, 1995)

Given that 'an injustice is tolerable only when it is necessary to avoid an even greater injustice', (Rawls, 1989, p. 4), in situations where there is considerable risk of injustice resulting to someone, the only hope of achieving justice must surely be by treating each case individually, and attempting to weigh the relative risks to all concerned. Risk assessment and management would appear to offer a greater chance of equitable solutions being reached to the problem of potentially

46

dangerous mentally ill people, but it will not remove the difficult decisions relating to the restriction of liberty. And it will need much more efficient co-operation and communication between all involved with the patient than currently exists in many cases.

> Teams with the responsibility for managing a patient's risk must be sufficiently in touch with the patient and his or her carers to be aware of, and respond to circumstances which increase risk of violence. ... family members or other carers may see another side of a patient not seen by members of the clinical team. Information about their fears of an increasing risk of violence always needs to be taken seriously. ... When there is a high risk to members of the public, or family, or other carers, there will be some occasions when confidential information must be revealed to carers or the police. A positive duty to disclose rests uneasily with health care professionals' codes of confidentiality, but undue delay may itself increase risk and distress. (ibid., p. 181)

If such an approach had informed the treatment of Jonathan Morrell, it is possible that his mother would not have been violently attacked and injured. Problems will always be inherent in risk management and assessing dangerousness because in such cases we are trying to predict the largely unpredictable (although Blom-Cooper has argued that past violent behaviour is by far the best predictor of future behaviour), and so there will always be the risk of injustice to one side or another, because their interests are opposed. But the present situation, when relatives are deemed to have no rights concerning a mentally ill person who is a legal adult, and whose vital information about him or her often appears to be completely ignored, even when seriously irrational and/or violent behaviour is concerned, only exacerbates the situation and benefits no-one.

The issue in all these cases is the right to freedom - the freedom of the public not to be at risk from potentially dangerous mentally ill people and the freedom of the mentally ill not to be incarcerated on the grounds of their possibly being liable to harm others.

A right can be considered to be a justified claim that one individual can make upon another, and can be justified by different forms of rules, such as religious or legal rules. Moral rights are justified by moral rules (which in some cases may be similar to religious or legal rules). But the fundamental question that must be asked about rights is whether or not they can be regarded as absolute. I think that it is impossible to argue that rights can be absolute, and the right to freedom illustrates the case very well. It only makes sense to argue that an individual right to freedom exists if it is also recognised that such a right must be limited - and it is limited by the rights of other individuals to freedom. In other words, my right to freedom only exists to the extent that it does not pose a threat to the freedom of others. This is acknowledged by the legal system; I might sacrifice my right to freedom if in exercising it I commit a crime. And a right also entails obligations; my right to freedom places an obligation upon other members of society not to curtail that freedom, and similarly their right to freedom places an obligation upon me not curtail their freedom. If I ignore this obligation placed upon me, I may in the process sacrifice my corresponding right.

Thus I would argue that the exercise of any one individual's rights cannot be regarded as absolute and in some circumstances can be justifiably overridden by the claims of others to exercise their rights. The key word here, of course, is justifiably. If the existence of a right is acknowledged, its overriding must be justified by those with the legitimate authority. The debate then concerns the relative weights of the competing rights of the parties involved.

The approach I have argued for in considering the competing rights to freedom of the potentially dangerous mentally ill and the right to protection of members of their families and the general public can thus be approached from either a rule utilitarian or rights-based stance.

> ... the criterion of those who take their stand on human rights, rather than utility, is justice in individual cases; if preventive measures are permissible in certain circumstances, it is only because, in those circumstances, they are not unjust. However, those on the radical wing of the human rights movement deny that preventive detention on a presumption of dangerousness could ever pass this test. They denounce the notion of 'protecting the public' as a form of words with politically oppressive potential, and they raise fundamental objections of principle to the practice of making assessments of dangerousness. (Floud, in Roth & Bluglass, 1985, p. 83)

The extreme human rights perspective on compulsory hospitalisation values individual freedom more highly than any other considerations, and rejects the 'police power' of the state as justification for compulsory hospitalisation. This view appears to be fuelled at least in part by the belief that the majority of psychiatrists are engaged in a conspiracy with the state to deprive of their civil rights people who are in any way considered to be socially deviant, by incarcerating them in psychiatric hospitals. Notwithstanding the appalling misuse of psychiatry in the former Soviet Union, I find this an implausible argument in Britain. Indeed, from reading the many accounts of people who have been unable to obtain desperately needed help for their loved ones, I think it more plausible to suspect that any current conspiracy is aimed at preventing treatment of any kind, let alone expensive hospitalisation, probably in order to save money. Clare's comment on the notorious Rosenhahn experiment seems to me to be apt here:

> Such is the current demand for a psychiatric bed within the National Health Service and the prevailing emphasis on treating patients outside hospitals and in the community that the average admitting doctor in Britain is likely to find

himself under strict instructions to avoid admitting any patient who can see, speak, move and do all of these things without bothering himself or others to any significant extent. One suspects that in Britain, Professor Rosenhahn might well be advised to go home like a good man, get a decent night's rest, and come back in the morning (when he and another doctor could start all over again!) (Clare, 1980, p. 76)

It is indeed the case that in some periods of history many unfortunate people have been incarcerated in asylums who should not have been there, and this fact must never be forgotten if we are to avoid this ever happening again. Nevertheless, the sad fact that people have been incorrectly locked away in asylums does not mean that there are never any people so ill that they do not need hospitalisation. I am not, of course, arguing that those who need hospitalisation should be incarcerated, nor that the institutions where they are treated should be the inhumane asylums that so disgraced the treatment of the mentally ill in earlier (and unfortunately in some cases, contemporary) times. Nonetheless, I would argue that today there are significant numbers of mentally ill people who do, for some periods of their illness, need access to hospital treatment and asylum in the true sense of the word, and that the extreme human rights movement ignores this, ultimately to the detriment of those who are unfortunate enough to suffer from severe mental illness, and often, their loved ones.

The argument that freedom is so intrinsically valuable that it should be preserved at almost any cost is more plausible than the conspiracy argument; certainly freedom is a necessary condition for autonomy, but it is not a sufficient condition, for autonomy has as another necessary condition that one is not constrained by limitations in oneself, and it is my argument that the nature of mental illness frequently imposes a constraint in the form of a limitation in oneself. It all depends upon how one defines freedom; if it is defined merely as the absence of external constraint, then it can be argued that Jonathan Morrell retained his freedom, though not his autonomy; if however, the definition of freedom encompasses a wider meaning, to include the lack of internal constraints, which I would argue that it should, then simply not being subjected to compulsory hospitalisation did not ensure freedom for Jonathan Morrell. And although freedom is often conceived of in negative terms - freedom from interference with one's ability to choose - it can also be thought of in positive terms - the freedom to do certain things in the sense of having the ability to do them. So although there are no constraints imposed upon me which prevent me from being an international opera star - I have a voice, I can sing and no-one is threatening me, locking me up or taking any other coercive action that would prevent me exercising my freedom to do this, I unfortunately simply do not have the requisite ability to be 'free' to be an international opera star! And I would argue that anyone as disturbed as, for example, Jonathan Morrell, does not have the necessary freedom to function as an autonomous being by virtue of the severity of her or his illness. Jonathan Morrell's right to freedom was exercised at the expense of his mother's right to be protected from him and she paid a horrendous price for it. And it is arguable that what Jonathan retained - his physical liberty - was not freedom in any real sense because of the constraints imposed upon him by his illness.

However, consideration of the problem of the potentially dangerous mentally ill person can all too easily distort our perception of the nature of mental illness, for the vast majority of the mentally ill pose a threat to no-one other than themselves. This raises the issue of the other argument in favour of compulsory hospitalisation, that of 'parens patriae', the paternalistic duty to provide care and treatment for the mentally ill if they are too unwell to seek help voluntarily. Stone (in Roth & Bluglass, 1985) has noted that during the 1980s there were two images of mental illness prevalent in the United States, that of the 'violent, paranoid killer' and that of the 'bag lady'. (p. 9) The first image represents the failure of the state to protect the public, i.e. the failure of the 'police power' of the state; the second represents the failure of the state to meet its responsibility to the vulnerable. He continues by pointing out that there is a third image, which never makes headlines, that of 'a tragic set of private images known to those who have a child, a spouse, or a parent who is mentally ill'. (p. 10) Both these latter images illustrate the failure of the state's duty of 'parens patriae', and his argument applies equally well to the United Kingdom. The composite case he uses to illustrate this third, private, image of mental illness is also equally applicable to the United Kingdom, and indeed would apply to the case of Jonathan Morrell, which only became public because he very nearly murdered his mother.

Stone's case is that of a law student who begins to act oddly. His fellow students notice this because he begins to interrupt lectures with incoherent outbursts. His appearance becomes dishevelled and he smells. He rejects all suggestions from his fellow students that he should voluntarily seek help, and he cannot be treated involuntarily unless there is proof beyond reasonable doubt that he is mentally ill and a danger to himself or others, and it is unlikely, despite his increasingly odd behaviour, that these conditions would be met at this stage. The Dean of the law school calls in the student's parents, but there is nothing they can do to obtain help for their son unless he consents. His behaviour deteriorates so much that he is suspended from law school, which he refuses to acknowledge. The following week, during a severe psychotic episode, the student pushes the Dean, who is attempting to bar his way into a classroom. This enables the authorities to call the campus police and technically satisfies the requirements that this young man be mentally ill and dangerous; he can now be admitted against his will to hospital, for assessment at least.

This case, based on the author's experience of several cases he dealt with during the 1980s, is concerned with American law, which is somewhat different from English law. What might happen here is difficult to say, but there is very grave concern amongst organisations such as SANE and the National Schizophrenia Fellowship about cases very similar to this, where someone obviously seriously ill is refused treatment because she is 'not ill enough' or because parents have no rights to seek help for legally adult children, even if such a child is obviously too irrational to seek help for herself.

The question that must be answered in these cases is whether or not it is justified to make a paternalistic intervention and hospitalise someone against her will when the risk she poses is only to herself. Such a risk may be active, in that the ill person may be actively suicidal, or passive, in that she is incapable of caring for herself. Such cases rarely make the headlines but the individuals concerned can and do suffer terribly, and so do those who love them, as they watch helplessly while a loved one disintegrates before their eyes and they are not able, not allowed, to help; as Jonathan Morrell's family must have watched, and Jonathan Deveson's family and thousands of families like them.

Such suffering is the result of the attempt to protect the 'freedom' and 'autonomy' of the sufferer. But it is surely ridiculous to argue that we have preserved an individual's autonomy because we have prevented any external constraints, such as compulsory hospitalisation, from being imposed on her, when her own internal constraints, imposed on her by the illness she is suffering from, destroy her autonomy. Both utilitarian and deontological considerations of what constitutes morally appropriate action when considering an individual's actions assume that those choices are rational. In the case of a seriously mentally ill person, such an assumption cannot necessarily be made. If choices are not rational, then it is arguable that paternalistic intervention is justified.

I argued in the previous chapter that the position of justified paternalism with respect to the mentally ill is defensible, and I would argue that it extends to justifying compulsory hospitalisation for treatment if that is the only way to provide the necessary help. I do not accept as valid the argument that because being admitted to a mental hospital carries with it a stigma, which is unfortunately true, people should not be admitted even if their behaviour is deteriorating rapidly, because anyone behaving so oddly will rapidly acquire a stigma anyway.

There is also another dimension to the problem of compulsory hospitalisation that must be considered. Most people do not live their lives devoid of any relationships with others; it is often the case that it is a partner or member of a sick person's family who seeks help on her behalf if she has become too irrational to acknowledge that she needs help. However, if the person who is ill is legally an adult, the relatives are often told that there is nothing that can be done for their loved one unless she seeks help herself - but if she were well enough to do this, the situation would not arise!

So what rights (and corresponding duties) can a partner in a relationship claim with respect to overriding the wishes of a legal adult if she becomes mentally ill, irrational and consequently refuses treatment and help? And what would be the justification for any rights claimed?

In the UK a person is regarded as legally adult at the age of eighteen. From then, providing she observes the laws of the land, she is free to control her own life; her loved ones have no legal control over her. Personal relationships are thus to a certain extent regulated by the law of the land, insofar as those aspects of behaviour which are covered by the law also apply to behaviour within a purely personal relationship. But personal relationships are more generally conceived of in terms of an emotional relationship, based on love, and are seen as being regulated by negotiation between the parties involved; a formal legal code cannot therefore capture all the moral and psychological dimensions of relationships based on love. (I shall use the concept of 'love' here as a shorthand to denote relationships which are primarily governed by the feelings of those involved, rather than by legal rights and duties. This will include family relationships and those between 'consenting adults', whether sexual or otherwise. I am aware, of course, that love, in its ideal sense, is often not the predominant emotion in such relationships!) Love is a difficult area: Sir Walter Raleigh posed the eternal question :

> Now what is love, I pray thee tell?

His own answer acknowledged that:

> It is that fountain and that well
> Where pleasure and repentance dwell...
> It is a sunshine mixed with rain.
> It is a tooth-ache, or like pain;
> It is a game where none doth gain;
> (Sir Walter Raleigh, in Hands, 1976, p. 1)

In more prosaic terms, love can be a mixed blessing! Love rarely features in arguments about rights because it is an emotion and therefore seen as subjective and capricious, the antithesis of reason and rationality. Indeed, love is often seen as akin to madness:

> Love is merely a madness; and, I tell you, deserves as well a dark house and a whip as madmen do; and the reason why they are not so punish'd and cured is that the lunacy is so ordinary that the whippers are in love too. *(As You Like It*, Act III, Sc. 2)

Rosalind's comment in *As You Like It* expresses one view of love common throughout the ages (and, indeed, a common view of the appropriate treatment for the mentally ill). Another, more generous interpretation has been that of ideal love, self-sacrificing and ennobling, the province of saints and heroes, able to encompass, in the Christian ideal, all people. But in reality, love is more often focused on specific people: the Christian ideal may urge us to love our neighbours as much as we love ourselves, but it is an ideal rarely achieved and more often than not completely ignored, so love cannot be realistically regarded as having the

52

universality and impartiality required by morality. Thus we cannot legitimate claims to rights based on love. However, we cannot simply dismiss claims legitimated by love unless we deny that relationships based on love, rather than legal codes, are, in the 'real' world, seen as in some way special and privileged. The implications of doing this would be enormous, and pointless, for though we might choose to try and deny the importance of love in human life, the very fact that it is an irrational, powerful emotion means that such an attempt would inevitably be doomed to failure.

> ... a decent and humane society requires a shared language of the good. The one our society lives by - a language of rights has no terms for those dimensions of the human good which require acts of virtue unspecifiable as a legal or civil obligation. (Ignatieff, 1990, p. 14)

The obligations, duties and responsibilities associated with love cannot be specified as legal or civil obligations, but that does not diminish their importance. However, we cannot therefore simply remove the rights of the mentally ill to exercise choice in matters of treatment and invest those rights in those with whom they may have an emotional relationship. This would be morally indefensible, for emotional relationships do not necessarily entail love; even those that do are not necessarily good, for love is a complicated emotion, and does not inevitably ensure that the interests of the loved one are always paramount in the minds of those who care for her. Not all people have loved ones to care for them and some even have 'loved' ones who actively dislike or hate them: we cannot ignore the fact that many emotional relationships are abusive in some way or another.

Consequently, there must be a legal framework governing the relationships between people which ensures that rights and duties are specified and protected. If there were no such formal framework, and rights and duties were determined only within the context of personal relationships, the weak would always be at the mercy of the strong. This situation is well illustrated by the experience of women. For centuries in this country women have had inadequate protection under the law, being regarded primarily as the possessions of men. Consequently, they have been the victims of injustice, having little, if any, power to exercise self-determination and being condemned to dependence on men, a situation which still exists in very many parts of the world. Such a fate could all too easily apply to the mentally ill if they were denied the protection given by the laws acknowledging them as legal adults.

However, we may construct legal codes designed to ensure that the rights and duties of individuals are spelled out; we may value autonomy and seek to protect it; we may endeavour to build in safeguards to any laws concerning the mentally ill to try and ensure justice for them; we may try and do everything we can think of to protect the rights of the individual who is mentally ill; but very few individuals live their lives in isolation. A legal code cannot capture the complete moral and psychological dimension of personal relationships built on emotion. The vast majority of people are involved in personal relationships, frequently involving love and concern for each other, and if an individual in such a situation becomes mentally ill and irrational and refuses help and treatment to a degree that her life and well-being are perceived as endangered, those who love her will almost invariably claim a right to have a say in what happens to her by virtue of their love for her. Love now poses a considerable problem if the wishes of the ill person and her loved ones do not correspond.

We cannot simply argue that love confers rights to override another person's wishes, because just as it is unreasonable to claim that one can claim a right to the love of another person, so it is unreasonable to argue that love necessarily gives one the right to make decisions for another adult. To do this would be to throw away the vital protection of the law. Yet it is nevertheless the case that relationships based on love are held to be in some way special and privileged, and can be held to entail certain self-imposed moral duties and rights on the participants. How, then, are the rights of the individual - in this case an irrational, mentally ill individual - to self-determination to be reconciled with the 'rights' of those in a privileged relationship with her to demand help for her?

Although the protection of the law is necessary to safeguard the rights of the mentally ill, the almost paranoid reaction on the part of the authorities that the families of some very ill people have experienced is indefensible. It is as if the spectre of Mr Rochester's mad wife, safely incarcerated where she can cause her husband no embarrassment, her own rights and wishes ignored, haunts the civil rights movement to the exclusion of all other considerations when it comes to the issue of mental illness, reducing justified concern on the part of those who love the ill person to yet another part of the 'conspiracy' to deny the mentally ill their right to freedom.

It is difficult to resist the impression when looking at some of the cases of very ill people denied help because they are too irrational to seek it and loved ones do not have the right to seek help on their behalf that we seem to living in a society that is terrified of acknowledging any rights or responsibilities in emotional relationships.' Stone (1982) refers to 'The *assumption* of a conflict of interests between family and the patient ...' (p. 22, emphasis mine).

> They always made us feel it was our fault. We were the sick ones. ... If I tried [to help David] I was called a smothering mother. (Wallace, 1987, p. 5).

> When they did find help, Blanche [Green] was told she was the cause of [her adopted son's] illness. [He] was happy. It was she who was doing the crying. (ibid., p. 6).

Little wonder that this lady was reduced to tears by her son's illness and the unwillingness, in the name of liberty, of any of the 'experts' to help him:

It's a question of individual liberty. Some people prefer to live out the period of their illness in a disoriented state as free individuals in the community. The balance is between community care and policing. (ibid., p. 6)

Unfortunately for David Green, the balance did not swing in his favour. He died from carbon monoxide poisoning in the car in which he lived, on Bodmin Moor. His family claims that they warned the authorities of the risk he was in, but were ignored.

How might this dilemma between upholding the rights of a mentally ill person and the concerns of her loved ones that she receive help and treatment, even if against her will, be resolved? I would suggest that loved ones of a mentally ill person have a right to be heard, and to be listened to at length. They, perhaps more than anyone else, know that person; certainly they know her much more intimately than a stranger, for no matter how much expertise that stranger may have, the assessment of mental illness requires knowledge of the sufferer. Loving someone involves responsibilities, one of which is to care for the loved one if she becomes ill; in the case of mental illness, such care may involve seeking help for her if she cannot seek it herself, and as such I would argue that a right to be heard exists. However, such a right to be heard does not necessarily carry with it a right to have one's wishes regarding treatment carried out, for if a person's wishes and rights are to be overridden, there must be safeguards against abuse on the part of interested parties, and it is not inconceivable that cases could arise of relatives wanting an awkward member of the family 'put away'.

However, simply because some families or partners may abuse their relationship with a loved one is not sufficient reason for assuming that this is invariably the case when a relative seeks help for a seriously ill person too ill to seek it for herself. To operate in a climate where parents may be made to feel guilty for pleading for help for their child, where people have to watch helplessly as someone they love dearly disintegrates before their eyes in the name of 'freedom' and 'autonomy' makes a hollow mockery of those ideals. Allowing the loved ones of the mentally ill a right to be heard without necessarily having their wishes implemented could go a long way towards preventing the appalling consequences experienced in so many cases where autonomy and freedom were 'preserved' at the cost of dreadful suffering and even death.

The question of involuntary hospitalisation is inextricably involved with the wider issue of human rights, and questions of human rights:

... [presuppose] a moral choice... The moral choice is not as clear in... mental health matters for much depends upon what individual interest is intended to be protected: a person's health and well-being, or his self-determination and liberty. (Gostin, in Roth & Bluglass, 1985, p. 148)

I would argue that without a certain level of mental health and well-being, self determination and liberty are very likely to be unattainable, and therefore that there are situations where an individual's autonomy can justifiably be sacrificed in order to prevent harm to herself or others; in some cases, compulsory hospitalisation can therefore be justified.

As Gostin has pointed out, if one chooses to protect the human right to health and well-being, 'emphasis would be placed upon facilitating access to care without legal encumbrance' (ibid., p. 148); he concludes that:

> The absence of any general right to treatment continues to present the greatest dilemma for psychiatry and law. It is ironic that a human right can be fashioned from the concept of freedom from treatment, but that access to adequate treatment and care cannot. (ibid., p. 154)

If a general right to treatment for the mentally ill were to exist and incorporated the right to be heard of loved ones involved, it might also help to ensure that treatment were obtained earlier rather than later and avoid some of the horrendous situations that occur in the implementation of compulsory hospitalisation.

However, arguing theoretically that compulsory hospitalisation is sometimes justified is one thing; its implementation is quite another, as this experience told to me by an ex-patient demonstrates:

> I know I was very upset and disturbed at the time, and I'd just broken a window in my house. I was very frightened. The next thing that I was aware of was two large policemen and what seemed likes lots of strangers coming into the room, and trying to drag me outside into a car. No-one explained anything. The took me to hospital and injected me with something that made me feel awful. I think they sectioned me. I was there for five days, against my will. Then they suddenly let me go home. I can't understand why they let me go home so quickly if I was so ill as to need to be sectioned. If only someone had talked to me.

The young woman who told me of this experience was intelligent, articulate and understandably very bitter about her experiences. She knew she had needed help, and possibly that hospitalisation might have helped, if it had indeed been asylum in the true sense of the word, but at the time was incapable of seeking such help for herself and no-one else was able to seek it for her. By the time she had become acutely disturbed, she was considered an emergency case and subjected to this terrifying treatment; all that this awful experience achieved was to leave her more distressed and confused than ever.

The issue of rights in relation to the mentally ill is a very complex one; compulsory intervention in care and treatment can be justified by appeal to the argument of the police power of the state if it is felt that the behaviour of a mentally ill person is a threat to others members of society, because they can claim the right not to be harmed; in this case there is the possibility of a conflict of interests between members of society, claiming the right to be protected, and the mentally ill, claiming the right to preserve their autonomy to accept or reject treatment, or, in the case of compulsory hospitalisation, claiming the right to not to have their freedom restricted on the grounds of the possibility that their future behaviour might pose a threat to other members of society. A right to refuse treatment can therefore be fashioned from this argument; but I would suggest that this is a simplistic approach which frequently results in disastrous consequences for the mentally ill and their loved ones. The rights of all those involved with mental illness - patients, professionals, loved ones and other members of society as a whole must be respected, but this does not mean that everyone's wishes can be met; deciding whose rights should be regarded as paramount in any given situation is extremely difficult, because the information upon which decisions have to be made is not the sort of information which can be considered to constitute hard facts; it involves weighing probabilities and possibilities and must accommodate large numbers of variables for which there may not be any proven method of assigning weighting., we are not dealing with an exact science in this situation. However, simplistic attitudes which ignore rights, for example, the right not to be put at risk by the irrational behaviour of a seriously mentally ill person, are a travesty of justice, and in so far as they usually also result in hurt for the mentally ill, ultimately protect nobody's rights. Consequently, the best that can be done in the immensely complex situations that so often occur when dealing with people who are mentally ill is to use common-sense informed by humanity to assess the risks and the scale of possible harm that may result from different courses of action to endeavour to decide upon action that will best protect the rights of all concerned, in the realistic knowledge that it may not be possible to protect everybody's rights.

I would argue that the emphasis should be on a right to care and treatment for the mentally ill; I would suggest also that there should also be a right to be heard (though not necessarily to have one's wishes acted upon) for interested parties when the question of seeking help for an adult who is too irrational to seek it for herself arises. If we say that there is an absolute human right to freedom *from* treatment and no right at all *to* treatment, the result is that undeniably difficult and painful decisions are avoided, under the facade of preserving a right to freedom, at enormous cost to those unfortunate enough to suffer from serious mental illness, and to their families. And it is only with extremely serious illness that the issue of compulsory treatment arises; cases where, as a result of mental illness, serious danger is posed either to the sufferer herself or to others.

A shift in emphasis from the concept of an absolute right to freedom from treatment to a right to treatment requires both a change in attitudes and a change in the formal procedures associated with the treatment of the mentally ill. One might argue that perhaps the obsessive emphasis on legal rights to the exclusion of other considerations, even in cases where this results in great suffering for the mentally ill, is a subconscious acknowledgement that the equally obsessive emphasis on the individual that is increasingly the model for western industrial societies is promoted at the cost of any real concern for each other. In such an environment, even those who truly love a mentally ill relative or friend are at risk of being regarded in an adversarial light. Thus we may fight to protect the autonomy of the mentally ill, but if we are not prepared to finance the necessary practical measures that are required in order to best promote true autonomy, we are merely being hypocritical. It is therefore necessary to change attitudes and to acknowledge that simply fighting for the legal rights of the mentally ill to exercise what in fact is often a spurious autonomy may be a comfortable abnegation of responsibility.

A start could be made by making overt the assumptions that often seem to be taken for granted about the nature of the autonomy that is being defended when the right to refuse treatment is promoted. In the current situation the assumption often appears to be that autonomy is regarded simply as the freedom from external constraint, with no acknowledgement of the internal constraints imposed upon autonomy by mental illness. It is these internal constraints, I would argue, that justify the claim that those near to the mentally ill have a right to have their concerns about their loved ones acknowledged and acted upon if this is necessary to procure the help that the mentally ill person may be unable to seek for herself. But if it is acknowledged that the situation regarding the mentally ill and autonomy is more complicated than any legal code can address, there must nevertheless be adequate procedures set up in order to avoid the other extreme, that of those near to the mentally ill acquiring the right to decide their futures irrespective of what they themselves might wish.

What must be avoided is a system that might more adequately be considered to be crisis management rather than treatment. It should be possible for someone close to a person whom they are concerned is or might be developing mental illness to voice that concern to the professionals involved in the treatment of the mentally ill, and for the professionals to be able to follow up the matter. However, in order to avoid any risk of someone being coerced into unnecessary treatment or inappropriately treated, if anyone other than the mentally ill person herself seeks help for her, then there should be an independent advocate appointed for the potential patient immediately any action is taken, because it must be remembered that the assessment of mental illness cannot be an objective science. This may appear to be a threat to the rights of the individual to decide her own future, and the risk must be acknowledged and adequate protection built into the procedures; but it must also be acknowledged that to let a seriously mentally ill person exercise her 'autonomy' and perhaps as a result suffer terribly is equally an assault on her right to be cared for when she cannot care for herself.

However, such a change in attitude to the autonomy of the mentally ill will not ultimately prove to be of any benefit if treatment is not designed to enhance their autonomy as far as it is possible to do so. It is vitally important that the implementation of care and treatment should be conducted in such a manner that the patient is kept informed about proposed treatment and wherever feasible should be consulted; consent to treatment should be gained if at all possible, and where this is not possible, then treatment should be administered in as humane a manner as possible; and she should have an advocate whose role it is to see that her rights are not being abused.

Intervention in order to provide help and treatment for a seriously ill, irrational person who does not want to be helped will always be a situation fraught with risks and difficulties. However, to ignore such people until they become acutely ill emergency cases can only make the situation worse; emergency treatment of a sick person by medical staff who may not know her can only ever be crisis management, and such an approach cannot possibly lead to optimum conditions for treatment: being hauled off to hospital or a cell by large policemen would be terrifying for anyone; it must be the final straw for a disturbed, frightened, irrational individual. It may be the case that such situations can never entirely be eliminated, but in many cases it is arguable that if relatives had been listened to and more realistic concepts of freedom and autonomy had been constructed than simply equating them with the maintenance of physical liberty, and a positive right to help and treatment constructed, such appalling methods of intervention as many seriously disturbed people experience could be avoided.

A right to treatment does not mean, however, that the ethical issues raised by different forms of treatment can be ignored, whether it be administered in hospital or in the context of community care. There are currently four mainstream therapies offered to the mentally ill; these are drug therapy, ECT, psychosurgery and psychotherapy. Of these, it is the so-called physical therapies - surgery, drugs and ECT that are the major causes of concern, both to patients, their carers and the civil liberties movement, and in the following chapters I shall be considering the ethical dilemmas which they pose.

5   Psychotropic medication

Concern about the treatment of the mentally ill is currently at a high level in the contemporary developed world, fuelled by stories of murder and neglect resulting from policies of community care and by the concerns of the civil liberties movement that individual freedom is being threatened by proposals for Community Treatment Orders, which they see as coercive and authoritarian. Amongst the professionals whose job it is to provide care and treatment, mechanistically oriented psychiatrists argue for treatment with physical therapies whilst psychotherapeutically orientated practitioners protest at the use of what they consider to be largely inappropriate therapies. In the middle of the chaos and confusion that permeates so much of contemporary mental health care are the patients themselves and their families, whose already worrying situations are often compounded by problems in obtaining appropriate help and treatment. This is hardly surprising, given the complex issues that surround treatment for mental illness, and yet it is hard to avoid the conclusion that a difficult situation is made far worse by the attitudes of many involved in the care of the mentally ill.

The treatment of mental illness has always provoked controversy. Its history contains many examples of practices that nowadays would be considered barbaric; at various times, physical methods - straitjackets, manacles, whips and chains; hot baths and cold showers and a variety of drug therapies - have all been used to treat the mentally ill. They have been subjected to drugs to sedate them, stimulate them and purge their systems of 'poison'. 'Calomel, saline draughts, antimoniacs, cathartics, valerian, blisters, purges - all had their particular advocates.' (Porter, 1990, p. 184)

Such 'treatments' are ridiculed now, evaluated as useless at best and positively harmful at worst, the products of mistaken faith rather than objective scientific evaluation, from ages not blessed by the greater scientific knowledge we now possess. Yet twentieth century practice is not necessarily more scientific; insulin coma therapy, for example, an extremely dangerous form of treatment introduced in the mid 1930s, was not scientifically evaluated until a study carried out in 1957, which showed that it was not an effective treatment for schizophrenia. (Ackner, Harris and Oldham, 1957). Occurrences such as this (and there are many others) cast doubt on the claims of modern psychiatric treatments to be 'scientific'.

The treatment that the majority of people diagnosed as suffering from mental illness will be offered is drug therapy. The drugs that are used in such treatment are the so-called psychotropic drugs; these drugs affect mood, and include the categories of major tranquillisers, (also called neuroleptics or anti-psychotics), minor tranquillisers, anti-depressants and anti-mania drugs, all of which are the subject of controversy. The areas of concern include efficacy, appropriateness, costs and benefits and the question of whether compulsory treatment can be justified. (For a summary of the effects of psychotropic drugs, see the appendix.)

In 1990, MIND conducted a survey, the results of which were published under the title *Experiencing Psychiatry* (Rogers, Pilgrim and Lacey, 1993); they found that in the qualitative data there were more negative than positive spontaneous comments about the effects of taking antipsychotic medication (the major tranquillisers), despite the fact that in statistical results twice as many people described the drugs as helpful. Comments included:

Dull the senses and hide the problem.

I feel that people should not be forced to take them because of the side-effects.

I find twice in my life being turned into an overweight zombie, harmful and objectionable. The medication did clear up my symptoms (delusions, voices, etc.) but I feel I need this short term, i.e. I feel psychiatrists have a tendency to keep me on major tranquillisers too long.

They were used as a punishment and to control my emotions.
(Rogers, Pilgrim and Lacey, 1993, pp. 133, 134)

The efficacy of antipsychotic drugs is varied; Leff and Wing (1971), in a study of the outcome of maintenance therapy with anti-psychotic drugs for patients diagnosed as schizophrenic, found that 7% had no positive response and 24% of patients who took the drugs regularly relapsed within one year. Crow et al (1986) found that 78% of patients receiving a placebo relapsed within two years, compared to 58% of those receiving neuroleptics. How such findings are interpreted will depend to some extent on the attitude of the observer to the issue of drug treatment; thus an anti-drug observer may well argue that in Crow's study there was only a 20% difference in relapse rate between those on medication and those taking a placebo, whereas those of a pro-drug orientation might well argue that a difference of 20% is very significant. And the problems of definition and measurement in such research have already been noted.

Some people do find these drugs helpful:

Felt very much better. Altered mood completely. Brought back appetite.

Helped me to see things in perspective.

Helped me to get back to normal life and feelings.

I don't know - but I expect they did some good.

Did not really find anti-depressants all that helpful. Perhaps they would have been more useful if I had gone for treatment earlier.

Felt they did little good.

Though the side-effects were mild, the anti-depressants had no positive effect because they did not alter the original circumstances which had led up to it, and the current frustration I was experiencing, caused by those original events. I stopped taking anti-depressants long before my GP and the psychiatrist were aware that I had, and they noticed no difference. (Rogers, Pilgrim and Lacey, 1993, pp. 138-140)

Lithium is an anti-mania drug, used in the treatment of manic depression, which is characterised by extreme mood swings from deep depression, where the sufferer may be suicidal, to mania, where she may be euphoric, sexually promiscuous and liable to make ridiculous and irresponsible decisions about financial matters because she inhabits a fantasy world where she 'knows' she has the most amazing opportunities available to her. Lithium is used to stabilise these mood swings. According to Lacey (1991), it is very successful in treating about 70% of sufferers from manic depression. It is, however, an extremely toxic substance; there is a very fine line between a toxic and a therapeutic dose; care is needed to ensure an adequate salt and fluid intake and regular blood tests are necessary to establish the correct dose for the patient.

There are considerable drawbacks associated with taking psychotropic drugs, and overlooking the drawbacks of any dangerous drug can only be justified if its efficacy is such that the costs of taking it are outweighed by its benefits. However, it is extremely difficult to reach any conclusion as to the efficacy of psychotropic drugs; extreme positions are taken by the pro-drug and anti-drug movements, both of which tend to present the issues in simple black or white terms. Those of a strongly anti-drugs persuasion such as Peter Breggin present the view that drugs are uniformly bad: referring to neuroleptics, for example, he states that:

In summary, the neuroleptic drugs are chemical lobotomising agents with no specific therapeutic effects on any symptoms or problems. Their main impact is to blunt and subdue the individual. ...Thus they produce a chemical lobotomy and a chemical straitjacket. ... The drugs are also the cause of a plague of brain damage that afflicts up to half or more of long-term patients. (Breggin, 1993, p. 83)

An equally firm stance is taken by those who strongly believe in the efficacy of psychotropic drugs. It is generally considered that their advent heralded the process of the closure of mental hospitals in favour of care in the community, a view not shared by all (see, for example, Warner 1985; Scull, 1984). Certainly the assumption of the efficacy of drug treatment for mental illness influenced official policy on the provision of mental health services:

Psychiatry is to join the rest of medicine... since the treatment of psychosis, neurosis and schizophrenia has been entirely changed by the drug revolution. People go into hospital with mental disorders and they are cured, and that is why we want to bring this branch of medicine into the scope of the 230 district general hospitals that are planned for England and Wales. (Sir Keith Joseph, 1971)

The same attitude to the miraculous effects of drug therapy in the treatment of mental illness can be seen if one glances through journals such as the British or American Journals of Psychiatry. Here the efficacy of drug treatment for mental illness is presented as fact; page after page of advertisements show happy, affluent people who have apparently been restored to a utopian state as a result of treatment with drug X or drug Y. Indeed, reading these advertisements one could be forgiven for wondering why there were any problems with the treatment of mental illness: it is only when one turns over the page and reads the often very small print that one is made aware of the problems involved in taking these drugs.

If the treatment of mental illness were as simple as Sir Keith Joseph's remark makes it appear to be, there would be few problems - simply take people into hospital, administer the appropriate drugs and cure will follow! This is patently not the case. Equally, however, some people are helped by drugs: Stuart Sutherland experienced a variety of treatments and different drugs during his experience of severe mental breakdown which lasted, with periods of remission, for ten years. He was eventually treated with lithium:

I waited to see if I would become hypomanic the following winter. I did not - the lithium was working. Moreover, I was lucky in its side effects. It gave me a permanently runny nose and a massive thirst. ... This is a small price to pay for freedom from those slow swings of mood that disrupted my life and that of those around me for ten years. ... over the last five years I have been free from the agony of depression and the folly of hypomania. (Sutherland, 1987, p. 88)

Commenting on the eventual breakdown of his marriage, he states:

I am convinced that without the lithium the break-up of the marriage would have thrown me into a deep depression, which would eventually have been succeeded by extreme hypomania. (ibid., p. 89)

Lacey, a psychotherapist, and as such presumably not likely to be biased in favour of drug therapy, writing for MIND, an organisation similarly not actively pro-drug, states:

When properly prescribed the drugs used in psychiatry can relieve the misery of depression or terrifying hallucinations and delusions. They can help people lead lives which would otherwise be impoverished by profound despair or mental torment. (Lacey, 1991, pp. 13, 14)

The key phrase here is 'when properly prescribed', however, and there is considerable evidence to suggest that psychotropic drugs are frequently not properly prescribed. Particular concern has been voiced about polypharmacy, the practice of prescribing a cocktail of psychotropic drugs for patients. Edwards and Kumar (1984) noted evidence of polypharmacy, incorrect prescribing and incorrect doses in their study of a Birmingham psychiatric hospital, where nearly half the patients on medication were taking two or more drugs, minor tranquillisers were being prescribed in conjunction with major tranquillisers and anti-depressants; a third of the patients prescribed major tranquillisers were taking two at once, having both pills and depot (long-term, slow release) injections and half the patients who were prescribed major tranquillisers were also prescribed anti-Parkinsonian drugs; all these practices considerably increase the risk of serious side-effects from the various drugs. (See also Sheppard et al, 1969; Herxheimer, 1976; Hemmenki, 1977; Michel and Kolakowska, 1981; Clark and Holden, 1987) Sutherland describes how:

At one stage I was simultaneously taking two tranquillisers (chlorpromazine and Valium), [i.e., a major and a minor tranquilliser], an anti-depressant (amitriptyline), and sleeping tablets. I asked [my doctor] if this was not too many drugs at once: I feared I could never be weaned from them. He said: 'We are well aware how dependent you become on people and things ... but don't worry, none of them are addictive and we'll withdraw them from you gradually when you are ready for it'. (Sutherland, op. cit., p. 50)

64

William Styron has described a conversation he had with a psychiatrist:

> When he asked me what I was taking for sleep, and the dosage, I told him 0.75 mg of Halcion; at this his face became somber, and he remarked emphatically that this was three times the normally prescribed hypnotic dose, and an amount especially contraindicated for someone my age. ... I don't recall Dr Gold once questioning the overly hefty dose which he knew I was taking., he presumably had not read the warning data in the *Physicians' Desk Reference*. (Styron, 1991, pp. 70-71)

Warner (1985) has argued that antipsychotic drugs:

> ... have emerged as a routine, almost automatic, remedy in psychosis and relatively little effort has been made in psychiatry to use these medicines selectively. One might search a long time to find a diagnosed schizophrenic who has never been treated with a neuroleptic drug. It may be better, however, to avoid the use of antipsychotic drugs in the care of substantial numbers of these patients, but the existence of such subgroups of schizophrenics has not been well recognised. (p. 239)

Warner is not anti-drugs, but he argues that there are numerous cases where drugs may be unnecessary or even harmful. He identifies the 'good prognosis' schizophrenic, whose illness typically begins suddenly in later life, who has had a history previous to the onset of illness of good work and social functioning and who has not been ill for long as one type of patient for whom a trial period of drug-free treatment may be appropriate. Another group is that of the non-responders - patients who do not respond well to neuroleptic medication:

> Interestingly enough, it may be possible to predict which schizophrenics will respond poorly to treatment with the neuroleptics. Different groups of researchers have independently shown that patients who find the first dose of these drugs particularly unpleasant are most likely to show little benefit from their use and to relapse early. Such 'dysphoric responders' react to a small amount of the drug with depression, anxiety, suspiciousness and immobilisation symptoms which are not alleviated (in one study, at least) by the usual antidotes to the extrapyramidal side effects of the neuroleptics. (Extrapyramidal side effects - rigidity, tremor and restlessness - mimic the symptoms of Parkinson's Disease and may be relieved by the drugs used to treat that condition.) (Warner, p. 241)

He argues that it is reasonable to treat patients who show no short-term benefit from neuroleptic medication, and many patients who relapse whilst on medication, without drugs. He goes on to cite a number of research studies which examine the effects of different forms of treatment on good and poor prognosis schizophrenics. Some of the results appear to contradict each other, although it is difficult to draw definite conclusions because of the differences in research design; nevertheless, there is significant evidence to support the view that good prognosis schizophrenics do better without drug treatment, (and indeed may even do less well with it) whilst poor prognosis patients do better with drug treatment Warner also argues that intensive dynamic therapy, which is extremely expensive, is not necessary for schizophrenics; what good prognosis patients need to have a chance to recover without drug treatment is an environment which is 'warm, protective and enlivening without being smothering, overstimulating or intrusive', and where they can stay 'long enough for their condition to improve and to be free of urgency to move on' (p. 262); he gives as an example of such an environment a project at Soteria House, in San Francisco. Warner offers a convincing argument for a more subtle, individual approach to treating schizophrenics, and given the considerable problems with neuroleptic drugs, it is surely the case that it is justifiable to adopt such an approach. However, as he acknowledges, it does not work for all schizophrenics and drug treatment will be the appropriate and necessary treatment for many. (For a hypothesis as to why some schizophrenics respond better to neuroleptic drugs, and the complexity of drug treatment, see Warner's exposition of the dopamine hypothesis of schizophrenia in Warner, 1985).

An enormous quantity of research into the efficacy of psychotropic drugs has been carried out, and is still being undertaken, but it remains the case that it is impossible to reach any hard and fast conclusions about their effectiveness. What is certain is that psychotropic drugs are potentially extremely dangerous, may be abused, may have side effects ranging from mild to extremely severe, are not always predictable in their outcome and the mode of their operation is poorly understood. It must be accepted that far from being magic bullets, psychotropic drugs could more accurately be likened to sledgehammers; and unfortunately many psychiatrists appear to wield them as such, often with disastrous results. In view of this, is the use of psychotropic medication in the treatment of mental illness unjustified? Despite these problems, the answer to this question must be 'No'.

The admittedly very serious drawbacks associated with psychotropic drugs are not sufficient reasons alone for arguing against their use. To begin with, it is undoubtedly the case that many people are helped by psychotropic drugs. Some people experience very few side-effects; others are prepared to tolerate the side-effects because the benefits outweigh them, and if the help they receive from medication is sufficient to outweigh the drawbacks, it cannot be justifiable to deny them this. The consequences of not taking medication can be horrendous: a Manchester court recently heard the case of a man who had murdered two of his children. He was a voluntary psychiatric patient who suffers from schizophrenia and who ceased taking his medication. He heard voices telling him to kill his children and so took a hammer and battered to death his son and one of his daughters, whom he was looking after while his wife was at work. His neighbours reported that he had seemed quite normal and cheerful that day when they saw him in the street. His children have lost their lives; his wife has lost two of her children, and, effectively, her husband. He has lost two of his children and his freedom and must live forever with the remorse he suffers from committing this terrible act whilst insane.

We accept a cost-benefit analysis of other drug treatments. Certain drugs used to treat cancer, for example, have the most appalling side-effects and are extremely toxic; their effects vary from patient to patient, they cannot be guaranteed to work for everyone and there is a great deal about their use that is poorly understood. Nevertheless, cancer sufferers often judge it worth suffering the misery of their side-effects in the hope of a cure, if it is considered that there is no viable alternative. And there are significant drawbacks to almost any drug: even 'everyday', over-the-counter drugs such as aspirin and paracetamol can have serious side-effects for some people, and used inappropriately can cause serious illness and even death. What these problems mean is that the costs and benefits of their use must be carefully weighed up; if a patient consents to treatment, having made the judgement of relative costs and benefits, and decides that the benefits outweigh the side-effects, there is no problem. Contemporary western society has an ambivalent attitude towards the use of drugs generally and the use of drugs which affect mood and behaviour particularly. Relatively few people oppose the use of antibiotics, painkilling drugs or anaesthetics; the use of drugs such as caffeine and alcohol to alter mood are socially acceptable, and although nicotine is far less so nowadays, it is arguably not the substance but its method of consumption that is unacceptable. Were it not for the dangers associated with smoking generally, and passive smoking in particular, there would possibly be far less of an outcry over its use.

Yet all these examples have potentially serious side-effects; alcohol, particularly, is a powerful drug whose use can lead to addiction, extremely undesirable behaviour changes, a variety of unpleasant and potentially lethal illnesses and even in quite small quantities can so much impair judgement that driving or any other task requiring a lot of concentration becomes very dangerous. And the concept of using some form of drug at times of stress or crisis is a commonplace, socially sanctioned aspect of life. It is socially acceptable to consume large quantities of the stimulant caffeine in the form of coffee and equally so to use alcohol to relax; brandy is used 'medicinally'; the English tendency to offer tea (which contains caffeine) during almost any conceivable form of crisis is a standing joke and people are even sometimes offered aspirin if they are upset. Other forms of social drug use are strictly prohibited, and many of them do have undeniably dangerous side-effects, which are the ostensible reason for them being prohibited except for medicinal use.

Veatch has made the point that:

> Ultimately, we must confess that *all* drug-use choices depend upon and reflect a philosophical choice of a value system or life style even if such choices may seem trivial or "common sense" - at least until we are confronted with a patient who is a Christian Scientist or Jehovah's Witness. (Veatch, 1974, p. 69)

Nevertheless, psychotropic drugs are in a different category, because they affect aspects of functioning that are seen as specifically human, even the *essence* of being human; things such as emotions, behaviour, mood and experience. Consequently,

> ... decisions about the use of chemical agents to control behaviour, mood and experience are ultimately decisions about what constitutes a humanising life style or world view. (Veatch, 1974, p. 80)

Klerman (1972) argued that there is a conflict of values regarding the use of drugs, which he has classified as *pharmacological Calvinism and psychotropic hedonism:*

> The pharmacological Calvinist view involves a general distrust of drugs used for nontherapeutic purposes and a conviction that if a drug "makes you feel good, it must be morally bad". ... It is of note that mental health professionals, especially in the field of psychotherapy, have their own variant of these Calvinist views. ... The conviction is often held that the use of psychotropic drugs in psychiatric treatment is morally wrong, because it promotes gradual dependency. Drug therapy is thus a secondary road to salvation; the highest road to salvation is through insight and self-determination. (Klerman, 1972, p. 3)

He argued that the prevailing Calvinist view of drug-use in the USA was gradually weakened by the exclusion of drugs such as nicotine, alcohol and caffeine from the restrictions that governed other mood-altering drugs, and by the emergence of youth culture, which places greater value on the immediacy of experience than on achievement. He also drew attention to:

> ... the use of psychotropic agents by relatively normal or mildly neurotic persons with anxiety, tension, depression, insomnia, and related symptoms often associated with the stresses of everyday life in modern industrial society. (p. 3)

as another factor in the debate about drug use. Klerman's point about pharmacological Calvinism and psychotropic hedonism, and the issues they raise are well-illustrated by the controversy over Prozac, (Fluoxetine hydrochloride), one of a new breed of anti-depressants known as SSRIs - selective serotonin re-uptake inhibitors. This drug is claimed to have no side-effects, to be safer for suicidal patients because it cannot be overdosed on, and generally to be a major breakthrough in the treatment of depression. The controversy over its use has been generated by claims that it can make non-depressed people function far better, turning pessimists into optimists, shy, introverted people into socially secure extroverts and losers into winners. It is claimed that it can fundamentally alter personality for the better; perhaps unsurprisingly, a large number of lawsuits have now been filed in the USA by people who claim that the drug indeed had a profound effect on personality, but in ways that have proved devastatingly detrimental to them. (See Appendix).

It could be argued that if one reaches salvation, however that may be defined, it hardly matters what sort of help one needed on the journey. And exponents of psychological Calvinism regarding the treatment of mental illness do not argue that help is not needed by the mentally ill; indeed, they generally insist that help is needed. It is the form of help with which they disagree; drug help is wrong; psychotherapeutic help is right. Drug treatment of mental illness conjures up a fear of a *soma* induced oblivion to any psychic pain being achieved at the cost of real humanity. This quasi-mystical 'world view' of humanity can be quite alluring, but it ignores a great deal of evidence that drug treatments may, for many people, alleviate the suffering caused by mental illness.

If someone were suffering the misery of severe depression or a psychotic schizophrenic state, would it not be kinder at least to admit that there may well be something to be gained by trying physical treatment, rather than leave the person suffering? Does the essence of humanity demand that some people should suffer the torments of mental illness because we must not interfere with the mystical properties of the mind? This smacks of the same kind of arrogance as was found in the nineteenth century debate on the use of anaesthesia in childbirth - the opponents of which argued that it would be contrary to the law of God as the Bible decreed that women should endure suffering in childbirth.

It would also appear to be the case that this quasi-mystical view of humanity which classifies drug use in the treatment of mental illness as morally wrong is fuelled by a fear that admitting any form of relationship between what might broadly be termed 'psychological events' and neural functioning must be reductionist and tantamount to admitting to a simplistic determinism that would destroy cherished beliefs about Homo sapiens' capacity to exercise free will.

Consequently, if a relationship between psyche and brain is denied, the argument can be made that drug treatment for mental illness cannot address the 'real' problem, which in this view is located in the psyche; any 'cure' or alleviation of the problem as a result of drug treatment must therefore be 'inauthentic'. This raises the spectre of the mind-body problem again, consideration of which is outside the scope of this book. However, in order to refute this argument, a brief consideration of the relationship is necessary.

The complicated brain and nervous system of Homo sapiens frees it from a restricted, simple stimulus-response behavioural repertoire; it made possible the development of those aspects of Homo sapiens broadly termed 'mental events' such things as intelligent thinking, planned behaviour, emotions and consciousness. With consciousness comes self-awareness and ultimately the need to impose meaning on an otherwise random, chaotic world: without meaning, Homo sapiens disintegrates psychically. This means that Homo sapiens is dependent on its external environment not only in a physical sense, such as needing food and shelter, but also in a psychic sense, in that it has the problem of satisfactorily marrying its internal perceptions of reality with the external signals it receives from other members of the species to construct a coherent, meaningful world.

All these functions evidently depend upon underlying physiological, brain functioning; dead people do not function psychically (or physically) and brain damaged people are often psychologically impaired. But is equally evident that psychological functions can influence physiological ones - for example, hypnosis can stop bleeding in some subjects; grief can lead to loss of appetite; paralysis and blindness can be caused psychologically, with no underlying physical lesion. There would therefore appear to be a two-way interaction between psychological and physiological events; (but that does not mean that the mechanisms of functioning of the brain can be deduced from the mechanisms of functioning of the psyche, or vice versa.) It may be that the psyche is greater than the sum of its underlying physical mechanisms, but it is certainly not independent of them. The mechanisms of both brain and psyche are very poorly understood, but neither operate in a random fashion; both are organised systems, interdependent, and I would therefore argue that common-sense suggests that both are vulnerable to stresses of their own or from each other - in other words, the brain can obviously be affected by physiological factors because it is a physiological organ; but equally, psychological factors can influence it. Similarly, psychological functioning can be affected by underlying brain dysfunction or by external environmental factors which cause disruption to the fundamental human psychic search for meaning. Thus it would seem reasonable to accept that a variety of treatment methods will be appropriate in the case of mental illness, amongst which will be some forms of drug treatment. As knowledge of the relationship between brain and psyche develops, it is possible that such treatments will be greatly improved.

Another powerful argument levelled against the use of drug treatments for mental illness is that they diminish or remove an individual's autonomy, an issue which I have considered in detail in Chapter 3. Twentieth century western culture places great value upon autonomy and freedom as essential components of being human; we are considered to have the freedom of will to make choices about our lives; this power is perceived as valuable and indeed, it is considered that individuals should control their own lives - both in the sense of being allowed to

70

and in the sense of being expected to, and thus anything that is seen as diminishing autonomy is regarded as diminishing authenticity as a human being. But if someone experiencing the misery of mental illness *chooses* to take psychotropic drugs to alleviate or cure her illness, we cannot argue that her autonomy is being diminished. However, the issue of choice in relation to the acceptance of psychotropic medication is not always as straightforward as it might appear to be.

A straightforward case of voluntarily choosing to take psychotropic drugs might be where the patient acknowledges her illness, is anxious to receive help and trusts her doctor's judgement as to what is the best course of treatment. If she is correctly informed about the risks of treatment and the possible side-effects, as well as her doctor's assessment of the probable benefits of treatment, then there can be no cause for concern (given that she is in exactly the same situation that she would be were she to be suffering from any one of a large number of medical conditions where it is accepted that the patient and doctor must weigh up the costs and benefits of treatment and make a choice whether to accept or reject it.) But what about the patient who is pressurised into accepting drug treatment with an oblique threat being made that if she refuses, she may be compulsorily hospitalised; or the patient who consents to drug treatment but is not adequately informed about its possible side-effects, whether deliberately or through ignorance on the part of the prescribing doctor?

The situation in the former case is complicated. If a doctor genuinely believes that without drug treatment a patient's condition is likely to deteriorate so greatly that she will require hospital treatment, and that if she refuses hospitalisation she will have to be compulsorily detained, then she surely must have a duty to explain the situation to her. The possible costs of drug treatment must be explained fully, as well as the expected benefits, and the possible consequences of non-treatment. As the law in England stands at the moment, medication cannot be imposed upon someone who is not hospitalised; so, if the patient continues to reject her doctor's advice, that is her right. If she decides to accept drug treatment when everything has been fully explained to her and discussed with her, then I do not think that it is arguable that she was coerced into 'consenting' to treatment. It is, however, arguable, that if there are no viable alternative courses of action open to her doctor, such as the chance to spend time in some form of real asylum, to see how she progresses, that this is not a real choice; in such a case, I think it is arguable that the doctor is not at fault, but rather those who are responsible for the system of provision of treatment for the mentally ill.

It is quite likely, however, that there are cases where patients are coerced into 'consenting' to drug treatment with the threat of hospitalisation, and in such a situation it cannot be argued that consent has been given and therefore this is a travesty of consent. It may be the case that compulsory medication can sometimes be justified (and I shall discuss this shortly) but that is a different issue from gaining 'consent' by coercion.

The case of a patient who consents to treatment on the basis of inadequate or incorrect information is different. In general medicine, a patient may only be given treatment if she gives informed consent, having been told what it is that she is consenting to; consent obtained from a patient in the absence of reasonable explanation is not adequate. (Chatterton v. Gerson and Another, 1980; Robertson, 1981). She must be capable of giving such consent. If treatment is given without consent it is a battery, which is a form of legal trespass to the person which may result in action in both criminal and civil courts; treatment given without enough information to ensure that consent is informed may be regarded as negligent. These conditions regarding treatment also apply to voluntary psychiatric patients, who have the right to refuse treatment. A patient who consents to treatment with psychotropic drugs when she has not be adequately informed of all the issues involved cannot therefore be said to be consenting to such treatment.

Ensuring that a patient is fully informed about the consequences of treatment is not a simple matter because the issues involved in assessing costs and benefits are often so complicated that even the experts cannot agree on what constitutes the best course of action. People react differently to drugs, and it may not be possible to predict accurately what the consequences of treatment will be; perhaps most importantly, once treatment is commenced it may be the case that what the doctor considers to be an insignificant side-effect may be considered to be totally unacceptable by the patient.

Klerman and Schechter (1984) consider that the following principles must be observed when the issue of medication is considered: first, that the psychiatrist is 'duty-bound' to be as informed as he possibly can about the advantages and disadvantages of the drugs he uses; secondly, that the benefits of any drugs prescribed are   likely to outweigh the hazards and thirdly, that the patient must be fully informed, even if the situation is complicated. They also acknowledge that in some cases it might even be detrimental to the patient to bombard her with too much technical information, not all of it scientifically proven.

There are no simple solutions to any of these issues relating to how truly informed consent can be achieved; it would undoubtedly improve matters, however, if the medical profession were to be far better trained in communicating with non-medically trained people. It seems most unlikely that the average psychiatrist would consider that a mechanic should not explain to her why her car needed major repairs, and the possible and probable consequences of ignoring them, on the grounds that engines are complicated, there are a lot of decisions involved which could only be assessed by an experienced mechanic and therefore she will in all probability not understand and should simply do as she is told. To assume automatically that this is the case with the mentally ill in relation to understanding the pros and cons of proposed drug treatment is patronising and ill-judged. What is necessary is that the professionals should learn how to present information in as accessible a manner as possible, and be willing to share it.

It must be acknowledged, however, that there will be cases of seriously ill people who are unable to make a reasonable judgement regarding treatment, which raises the issue of compulsory medication. Some of those who are compulsorily detained in hospital will fall into this category, and the law is different in relation to them. Although it should not be assumed that a patient who is compulsorily detained is unable to give informed consent to treatment, in cases where this is judged to be the case, the law allows compulsory treatment to be administered, subject to the rules laid down in the Mental Health Act, 1983. These state that medication may be given without the consent of the patient, and without requiring a second opinion, for up to three months. After this it is necessary either to obtain the patient's consent or the endorsement of an independent psychiatrist for the treatment to continue. If a patient who has given consent withdraws it, an independent psychiatrist must give approval for the treatment to continue without consent. If urgent treatment is required which in other circumstances would require either consent or a second opinion, these requirements may be waived and the treatment administered.

Those who oppose compulsory medication argue that to compel someone to take a powerful drug which affects behaviour and which may have extremely unpleasant side-effects removes their freedom and autonomy, and that this is morally unjustified. At one end of the scale of objections on these grounds lies the conspiracy theory of state control of deviant behaviour; at the other end lies concern about the paternalism of the medical profession. I have already argued that there is no evidence to suggest that the members of the psychiatric profession in this country are all engaged in a conspiracy with the government to control behaviour deemed deviant. (This does not exclude the possibility of individual members holding views on the treatment of the mentally ill or others whose behaviour is considered deviant that would be considered morally indefensible in a society that values the freedom and autonomy of the individual, of course, but the existence of such individuals would not constitute a psychiatric conspiracy with the state.)

The issue of paternalism has more substance; in a society apparently obsessed with individualism and individual autonomy, paternalism is almost a term of abuse. And unchecked paternalism can undoubtedly be a horribly oppressive force. Nonetheless, it must surely be accepted that some mentally ill people, at certain times in their illness, are not capable of making rational decisions, in which case someone has to decide what appears to be the best method of helping them. There is evidence, as I have shown in the first part of this chapter, to suggest that some people in this state are helped by drug treatment, if it is used properly. Therefore, if these drugs are helpful in some cases, is it morally justified only to allow their use for those who consent to take them, particularly when it is often the case that the nature of the patient's illness is the cause of her refusal to take them, simply to avoid the accusation of paternalism? The following example illustrates the problem:

Mrs A. the youngest of four children, was raised in a deeply religious family from South America; she had difficulty with the move to the United States in her teens and had never really learned English. Her diagnosis of paranoid schizophrenia was based on her paranoid delusions, auditory hallucinations, her feelings that others could control her thoughts, and her increasing social isolation over the two years following her first hospitalisation. Her first psychosis had responded to hospitalisation and fluphenazine [a major tranquilliser] in about a month. The second admission a year later was related to the family's emotional abandonment of the patient; an increase in medication was found to be helpful. In the summer the patient stopped taking her medication, broke off all treatment, and slowly deteriorated over the next six months.

In the winter the patient was readmitted on a voluntary basis for treatment of her third psychosis in three years... There was some question of a mild tardive dyskinesia involving the tongue. After discussion with the patient and her family, it was decided that the benefits outweighed the risks and treatment with fluphenazine was started.

Over the next four weeks the patient's psychosis slowly improved to the point that she was permitted an increased range of movement on the ward. Eventually, however, this patient refused her medication and began to deteriorate very significantly:

... after one month of only sporadic medication, she was feeding cigarette butts to the "snakes" on the ward and felt the medication was poison.

For the next month the staff had to watch helplessly while the patient slowly deteriorated until she was "crazy" enough to be declared legally incompetent. In other words, for the patient to be found incompetent to make decisions about her treatment ... she first had to become more psychotic, despite the availability of a treatment of proven efficacy in this very patient. (Gutheil et al, 1980, p. 348)

[The law in the United States is different from English law regarding compulsory medication, in that compulsory medication can only be administered if the patient is declared legally incompetent, at which point a guardian must be appointed by a court to decide whether it is justified. This generally takes a considerable time.]

Despite the difference in the law, the ethical issues raised by this American case are equally relevant here. (I shall take the facts as given whilst acknowledging that issues such as the determination of the severity of illness and the criteria for measuring improvement would normally be open to discussion).

This patient's condition improved considerably while she was taking her medication, although at a price - the mild tardive dyskinesia of the tongue. In fact, she improved sufficiently to be considered legally competent to refuse medication. However, when she ceased taking her medication, she deteriorated greatly and became severely psychotic again. This situation occurs too in this country, particularly when patients who have been discharged from hospital into the community cease taking medication; the only difference is in the legal situation. The ethical problem lies in the fact that if the patient is well enough to be considered competent to refuse medication, how can it be justified to impose that medication on her, even if experience has proved that without it she will become very ill again?

Let us consider the case of diabetes. Suppose I am a stabilised diabetic, with my condition controlled by insulin, which I have to inject twice daily. As a result of taking the insulin, I am functioning fairly well and I feel fine. However, the twice daily injections are painful and are leaving my body bruised and sore, which is causing me considerable distress, and problems with adjusting the dose of insulin that I require are causing me to suffer the occasional attack of hypoglycaemia, which is extremely unpleasant. Nonetheless, I know that the alternative to suffering this discomfort is a painful death, and I have no hesitation in accepting that the injections are the lesser of two evils.

Now let us suppose that I do not really believe that my doctor is correct when he says that I really need these injections, so I decide to put it to the test and give them up. After I have been treated in hospital and recovered from the diabetic coma which resulted after I ceased taking the insulin, I realise that the doctor was right, and I continue with the treatment, despite its unpleasant aspects.

In the first instance, I reasoned rationally that the consequences of refusing treatment, although it is not very pleasant, is death, and I made a rational decision to continue treatment. Had I reasoned that I would, in fact, prefer death to a life dependent upon painful treatment, although many would undoubtedly have tried to persuade me otherwise, I would have been free to allow myself to die, because as a legal adult, in full possession of all the facts, and quite rational, that would be my right.

In the second example, I acted extremely foolishly, but although I learned the hard way that the doctor was correct in his insistence that I needed insulin, I was able nonetheless eventually to use my powers of reason to accept that the consequences of refusing the insulin would be death, and that notwithstanding the unpleasant side-effects of treatment, I had no choice but to put up with them if I wished to stay alive.

The essential element in both these examples is that I have ultimately been rational enough to accept the need for medication and to accept that its unpleasant aspects are the lesser of two evils. The problem in the case of a mentally ill person is that it is not always the case that, when improvement occurs as a result of medication, the patient is able to make the same rational assessment of cause and effect that the diabetic patient makes. There are a number of explanations for this;

to begin with, improvement is a relative term; it does not necessarily mean that the patient is fully restored to normal functioning. And as in the case of insulin and diabetes, the drugs that bring about improvement in some patients suffering from mental illness do not necessarily cure the disease, they only control, to some extent, the symptoms. And as many diabetics discover, the drugs used to control the symptoms of the illness frequently have undesirable side-effects. Just as the insulin that saves the life of a diabetic can also kill her if the dose given is too large and she lapses into a hypoglycaemic coma from too little sugar in her blood, so the drugs which can, for example, control the horrors of hearing voices ceaselessly can also cause awful side-effects, a situation graphically described by Carol North in her book *Welcome, Silence* (1988).

So there is a problem, given that physical treatments for mental illness almost invariably have side-effects and are often not fully effective, which is that of whose costs and benefits are being taken into account when these treatments are compulsorily administered. In the example given, I think it fair to argue that the patient did benefit from treatment, and despite the mild tardive dyskinesia of the tongue, was better off taking the medication than not taking it - because it must be borne in mind that her delusions were extremely unpleasant and causing her considerable distress. In these circumstances, therefore, it would seem that compulsory medication was justified because although her autonomy was diminished by virtue of medication being administered against her will, her autonomy was even more restricted by her untreated illness. If one is suffering from mental illness severe enough to cause severe irrationality, then one's autonomy will inevitably be severely diminished. Thus to argue that compulsory medication is unjustified on the grounds that it removes an individual's autonomy is a ridiculous argument:

> The truly incompetent lack full autonomy, and so that quality cannot be violated by imposing treatment. If there is a reasonable likelihood that their autonomy can be preserved or restored by medication, then forced treatment of such patients is warranted. (Macklin, 1982, p. 340)

I would argue that arguments against use of psychotropic medication in the treatment of mental illness based on variants of *pharmacological Calvinism* or based solely on the premise that psychotropic drugs remove autonomy are insupportable; I would also argue that in some situations their compulsory use may be justified. However, although I have rejected such arguments as sufficient reasons for rejecting the use of psychotropic medication in the treatment of mental illness, I am not simply arguing for the uncritical acceptance of its use: there are very serious reasons why drug treatment should be treated with reservations.

Drugs may be incorrectly prescribed to subdue misery; this was very obvious when the medical profession finally acknowledged the appalling consequences of long-term tranquilliser use. These drugs, often referred to as 'mother's little helper', were routinely prescribed by some doctors (mainly to women) to treat conditions caused by living problems - poverty, poor housing, isolation, for example - which did not require medication but social action.

Concern has also been justifiably expressed about the role of the pharmaceutical companies in promoting psychotropic medication in order to make huge profits. This has led to claims that the determination of drug companies to find a market for their products has led to a search for problems which their products can be claimed to alleviate:

> According to the drug companies, the psychiatric applications of chlorpromazine were an instance of scientific serendipity. A less charitable view of evidence available on the development phase in the United States suggests an at times almost frantic search for therapeutic applications with which (a) to convince the Federal Drug Administration to allow marketing of the drug; and (b) to persuade American physicians to prescribe it.
>
> Chlorpromazine originated from research "seeking to produce a phenothiazine derivative with a high degree of central nervous system activity primarily for use as an anaesthetic potentiator" ... and much of the early testing of the drug was done with this in mind. By 1953, efforts to find a commercial use for the compound had been extended to include attempts to demonstrate its value as an anti-emetic, controlling nausea and vomiting; as a treatment for itching; as a general sedative; and as a help in cases of dramatic and acute psychosis. A Smith, Kline, and French internal memorandum dated April 8, 1953 indicates that "nausea and vomiting are still felt to be the most appropriate indications on which to conduct rapid clinical testing to try to get marketing clearance by the FDA." Reflecting this emphasis, by the end of 1953, only five months before it was to be marketed, chlorpromazine had been tested on only 104 psychiatric patients in the United States. Thirteen months later, it was being given to an estimated two million patients in the United States alone; and by 1970, US pharmaceutical manufacturers sold $500 million of "psychotherapeutic agents" - of which phenothiazines accounted for $116,500,000. (Scull, 1984, p. 80)

I have already noted concerns about the inappropriate use of drugs and polypharmacy. This issue could be addressed by better education and monitoring of doctors; and improved education of doctors should not only relate to knowledge about drug treatments and their correct prescription; it should include teaching about listening to patients and that the answer to the question 'What works?' is not necessarily a simple one.

When the treatment of illness with a clear physiological dysfunction is undertaken it is relatively easy to know what it is that is being treated, so the question 'What works?' can be used as a pragmatic approach to the question of treatment options. It is generally the case that a pragmatic approach is also taken to the treatment of mental illness, again simply posing the question 'What treatment works?', but it is difficult to reach any firm conclusions regarding the efficacy of drug treatments for mental illness. Consequently, as Sider has pointed out, although:

Many believe that the question, "What ought to be done for the patient?", is transcribable into the empirical inquiry, "What works?"

we must acknowledge that:

... the demonstration of treatment efficacy is always in reference to a specified outcome. (Sider, 1984, p. 391)

The 'specified outcome' in the case of mental illness is fraught with difficulty because mental illness largely expresses itself through beliefs and behaviour which are considered deviant by the society of which the sick person is a member. The laudable aim of relieving suffering can then become inextricably bound up with moral issues relating to what constitutes 'mad' behaviour as opposed to that which would be more appropriately classified as 'sad' or 'bad', because if the different forms of deviant behaviour are not differentiated between the possibility exists that any form of deviant behaviour that is socially unacceptable may be labelled as mental illness and the 'specified outcome' of treatment for mental illness could then be the control of 'bad' behaviour. We must always acknowledge that the question of whose costs and whose benefits is involved in the specification of the desired outcome of treatment for mental illness, and in the consideration of which treatment methods are appropriate, and the degree to which they are successful.

The complex questions relating to how we define 'works' in terms of treatment for mental illness, and its costs and benefits and the ethical issues involved in weighing them up are clearly illustrated in this letter, sent to me by a man who considers himself to have been mad, and who would, I think, have been be judged so by the world at large. Certainly the medical profession considered him to have been very ill indeed. He now takes the minimum dose of Melleril to stabilise his condition and remain 'sane'. (Melleril is the trade name for Thioridazine, a phenothiazine antipsychotic drug used to control the symptoms of schizophrenia.)

The drug side effects I have suffered from as a result of Melleril ... are as follows: Apathy (the worst), drowsiness, trembling hands (very minor), skin rashes (also minor), nasal stuffiness (minor), lack of sex drive, pigmentation of skin around the eyes (though this may be age!), poor memory, lack of mental alertness, slow thought, weight gain, paucity of ideas, poor conversational skills, lack of general drive and wit and dry mouth in the mornings. All these side effects are worth the general feeling of control that I now have over myself. I am, however, a different person from the person I was prior to illness and the hardest part of life post hospitalisation has been coming to terms with this. What I regret losing most is my intellect.

From the point of view of the medical world I am a success. I feel a total failure. Don't get me wrong, however, I am not suffering from depression. I feel this in a rational way.

Consultant A, at the hospital, told me in October 1988 that what had happened to me was not as a result of purely exterior environmental causes. He said, or implied, that there was an innate predisposition to the illness. I do not agree, though I appreciate it is debatable as to how one can separate self from environment anyway. I believe that it is innate in the sense that it is innate in all of us. This consultant knew little of my history. ... The consultant also said I had been really ill and had been through trauma.

In July 1989 Consultant B told me that it wasn't the drugs that made me slow and stupid. He said it was more likely the effect of my illness. [This does not agree with what the pharmacopoeia says or indeed the 'May cause drowsiness' message that is stuck on my box of drugs every time I get a prescription.] I think there is a tendency amongst consultants to put the side effects of drugs down to the patient. They are concerned that if they blame the drug you will stop taking it and therefore become psychotic again.

The main problem, inside myself, now is apathy. I am trapped by my medication but also dependent on it. The alternative to being sane and slow is to be mad and quick but unable to concentrate on anything, with the added danger that I might harm myself or others.

An interesting point is this. What happens if I stop taking the drug, because of its side effects, and then kill someone? I made the decision to stop taking the drug whilst rational. Is it not therefore my fault as a rational person rather than an insane one?

This man told me his story in thirty six A4 pages of eloquent, lucid prose; it is a story which is profoundly moving and profoundly distressing, and raises all the questions relating to mental illness and its treatment that medical textbooks on the subject seem determined to ignore.

Despite the help which his medication affords this man his problems are exacerbated by the appalling social conditions in which he lives - his flat is regularly vandalised and he is subject to abuse by gangs of local children. He is extremely lonely, and his attempts to find any worthwhile employment have been unsuccessful. He has effectively been left to survive on his own; the medical professionals treating him consider him to be a success; this is possibly accurate in terms of his medication reducing the worst of his symptoms. In terms of helping the whole person, however, it is a very limited measure of success, equivalent to operating to remove an irremediably damaged leg and pronouncing the treatment a success but leaving the patient with no means of walking and no help to achieve this.

Drug treatment in mental illness has a varied success; for some, it will prove to be very helpful; for others, it will not help; and for some, drugs will be inappropriate. For the vast majority of mentally ill people treated with medication, drugs alone will not be sufficient; other forms of help and support will be required in addition. The greatest dangers from drug treatment seem to me to be that it is too easy to see it as *the* treatment, particularly in cases where it is relatively successful, rather than as a possibly useful element in a more comprehensive treatment programme, and too easy to employ it as the first treatment option. An automatic reaching for the prescription pad can lead to an insensitive and unsophisticated use of drugs which alienates patients and some mental health practitioners, and achieves very little in the way of positive results. It is these issues which should be addressed rather than adopting totally negative stances to the use of all forms of psychotropic medication, which could lead to a great deal of unnecessary suffering for the thousands of people who are helped by its use.

The need for drug treatment does not exclude the necessity for help being given with social and personal problems; even if the root of mental illness were proven to be biological this would still be the case. Nobody seriously argues that the treatment of a physical illness should ignore the patient's social and personal situation; it is not good medicine to mend a broken leg and send the patient home to negotiate three flights of stairs daily before the leg is fully mended. Equally, however, nobody would argue that because the patient has the problem of living in a flat at the top of three flights of stairs her broken leg should not be mended! (it must be acknowledged that, unfortunately, certain doctors do take an extremely limited view of intervention in physical illness, and some psychiatrists are equally, and arguably even more inexcusably, limited in their approach to the treatment of mental illness. This is a weakness in the training and selection of the medical profession, rather than in particular forms of treatment.)

The greatest chance of success in the treatment of mental illness will surely result when simplistic either/or approaches to treatment are abandoned, and patients are treated as people, not cases, and all their needs and problems are considered. Drug therapy, used skilfully and sensitively, will form one element of such an approach to treatment for some sufferers from mental illness. Even MIND, an organisation not noted for supporting a medical model of mental illness, has stated:

> Major tranquillisers are the single most important and effective treatment for serious mental disorders such as schizophrenia ... Many people with serious mental disorders are able to lead a worthwhile life in the community thanks to major tranquillisers. ...All treatments have advantages and disadvantages. For many people with serious mental disorders, any problems caused by the side-effects of major tranquillisers are outweighed by the good they do. (MIND, 1986)

However, in cases where it is considered necessary to impose medication upon patients, there *must* be a more subtle approach adopted than is often the case. I would suggest that when the question 'what works' is posed, the specified outcome of treatment should be made overt, and if possible agreed with the patient; drug treatment should not be automatic; prescribing doctors *must* be better educated in the use of drugs, their effects must be monitored and patients' assessment of their effects listened to; it should not be automatically assumed that the administration of drugs will necessarily be beneficial. Equally, it must be acknowledged that in some cases there will be no ideal solution and that some outcomes will inevitably be the lesser of two evils.

6 ECT and psychosurgery

Drugs are the most commonly used physical therapies for the treatment of mental illness, but there are two others, ECT, which is in common use, and psychosurgery, which is now very rarely used. These raise even more emotive issues than does drug therapy because it is impossible to ignore the fact the brain is being directly manipulated, and the brain is accorded a unique status amongst all our organs. Interfering with the brain is often regarded as interfering in some way with an individual's essential being, the 'I' that makes each of us unique, for the brain is seen as integral to the self in a way that an arm or a kidney is not, despite their importance. The relationship between the brain and self-consciousness is extremely complex and poorly understood, but that there is a relationship is indisputable. There is overwhelming evidence that the brain is intimately linked with our humanity through its neocortical development which distinguishes Homo sapiens from other animals. It is the nature of the relationship between brain function and self-consciousness that causes the problems and we must accept that in our present state of knowledge all we can reasonably assert is that the elusive quality of Homo sapiens which we call self-consciousness is undeniably influenced by very complicated neural processes operating within the brain. In the broadest sense, of course, and ignoring the philosophical problems that the relationship raises, all mental functions can be argued ultimately to depend upon brain function: if the physical organism is indisputably dead, there can be no form of mental functioning.

Therefore, the brain has a special status in relation to self-consciousness, and consequently, while severe damage (or even loss) to an arm or a leg may well have a considerable impact on the way I feel about myself, and may alter my perception of myself, it does not entail the loss of my total sense of identity, whereas damage to the brain, if severe enough, may cause exactly that. However, not all damage to the brain causes loss of identity or destruction of the self; it is possible to interfere with it to quite a considerable extent without this occurring; and we must acknowledge this, and also that such interference is sometimes justifiable. Otherwise, if the brain is accorded a sanctity which makes it regarded as untouchable by virtue of its unique role in self-identity, we would be forbidden to perform procedures which have the potential to save life or ameliorate suffering, such as the removal of brain tumours. Nevertheless, the limitations of our current state of knowledge about the brain and its functioning must also be acknowledged; there is therefore a balance to be struck between undue reverence for the brain and foolhardy interference with it.

The special status accorded to the brain makes descriptions of procedures used in its manipulation seem barbaric; certainly descriptions of ECT, particularly before it was administered under general anaesthetic, are unpleasant. But the same could be said of any surgical procedure if described in detail, and also, for that matter, to a perfectly natural event like childbirth. It is important, therefore, not to let such emotive factors influence decisions about the justifiability of these forms of treatment; if they work, it might be justifiable to employ them.

The first ECT treatment was administered in 1938 in Italy, by Professor Ugo Cerletti; the treatment basically consists of passing an electric current through the brain, which causes a seizure. It is still not known how ECT works. A standard course of treatment consists of between four and twelve shocks, administered a few days apart. The MHA (1983), section 58, requires either valid consent or, if consent is withheld, a second opinion recommending the treatment, before a detained patient can be treated with ECT.

There is a huge amount of literature relating to experiments to assess the efficacy and safety of ECT, but the results are confusing, and much of the research, certainly from the early days of treatment and research, is of very poor quality; ultimately it is hard to avoid the conclusion that whatever stance one adopts on the question of the efficacy of ECT as a treatment for mental illness, somewhere there will be a record of research which appears to confirm that one is right. (See, for example, Bruce, et al, 1960; MRC, 1965; Sainz, 1959; Lambourn & Gill, 1978; Ottosson, 1979; Watt, 1979; Wilson et al, 1963; Costello, 1976; Cronholm & Ottosson, 1960; Price et al, 1978.) The 'official' view is that ECT is a useful form of treatment for some forms of mental illness; this is reflected in the more discerning use of ECT for specific conditions for which it is claimed that there is evidence of its beneficial effect, rather than the indiscriminate use for all sorts of conditions which was characteristic of the early implementation of ECT. The Royal College of Psychiatrists issued a memorandum on the use of ECT in 1977 which stated that there is:

... substantial and incontrovertible evidence that the ECT procedure is an effective treatment in severe depressive illness [and that it] is at least as effective as the most effective antidepressant medications, and exerts its effects more rapidly. (RCP, 1977, p. 266. See also Johnstone et al, 1980)

Granville-Grossman has concluded:

The best results [of ECT] are obtained in cases of severe depression with retardation, arising suddenly in patients with good premorbid personalities, where guilt feelings and delusions are prominent, where the symptoms are much worse in the mornings and where there is early wakening. (This clinical picture corresponds to that of classical "endogenous depression"). (Granville-Grossman, 1971, p. 9)

Opponents of ECT argue that far from being beneficial, ECT causes brain damage, is dehumanising and is frequently used as a punishment.

> To the extent that it works at all, shock has its impact by disabling the brain. It does so by causing an organic brain syndrome, with memory loss, confusion, and disorientation, and by producing lobotomy effects. For a few days or weeks the patient may be euphoric or high as a result of the brain damage, and this may be experienced as 'feeling better' .In the long run the patient becomes more apathetic and 'makes fewer complaints' .(Breggin, 1993, p. 245)

It is generally acknowledged that memory loss is a side-effect of ECT, but attitudes to the importance of this vary:

> [ECT] produces a transient memory difficulty which may upset a patient who is already concerned about himself and may feel that his memory is specially vulnerable; it is not infrequently followed by a severe headache... [this] occasionally produces in patients a pronounced fear of the treatment that is unexplained and is out of all proportion to the triviality of the procedure. (Hays, 1964, p. 98)

Faced with a believer in the efficacy of ECT who displayed such gross insensitivity and ignorance, it would hardly be surprising if patients reacted with a 'pronounced fear' of ECT. The memory loss resulting from ECT may persist for a number of weeks after treatment, and memories of events immediately preceding the treatment may be lost for ever, although there is no evidence that memories of events that took place in the years preceding treatment are permanently affected. However, a *Task Force Report* of the American Psychiatric Association, considering the issue of the effects of ECT on memory, noted that:

> ... a fully satisfactory study of this issue with maximally sensitive tests has not yet been accomplished. (American Psychiatric Association, 1978)

Mortality rates from ECT have been reported to be as high as 2.9 deaths per 10,000 patients or 4.5 deaths per 100,000 patients (NIMH, 1985, quoted in Rogers, Pilgrim and Lacey, 1993). These death rates are said to be comparable to those resulting generally from the use of short-acting barbiturate anaesthetics, such as those given to patients receiving ECT. Any anaesthetic carries with it a slight risk of side-effects or even death, and ECT cannot therefore be regarded as a trivial form of treatment, on these grounds alone, even before the possibility of brain damage is considered.

The responses of patients treated with ECT vary greatly:

ECT is the most frightening experience. I have had over 50 and still am very afraid.

ECT is inhuman.

Terrible loss of memory of considerable duration. I had to retrain my brain to remember things. Mainly the worrying aspect was long-term memory loss where I could not remember things which I knew that I knew. (Rogers, Pilgrim and Lacey, 1993, pp. 144, 145)

Nevertheless, ECT does appear to be an effective treatment for some mentally ill people, as these accounts testify:

Worked - very effective; returned to work within three months.

Depression lifted very quickly after six treatments.

[I would like to try and] dispel the erroneous belief that ECT is a terrifying form of treatment, crippling in its effects on the memory and in other ways. The technique is today so refined that the patient suffers a minimum of discomfort, and the therapeutic benefits are so great in those cases where it is indicated that it is a great pity to withhold it from mistaken ideas of kindness to the patient. (Anonymous, 1965)

This account is from a psychiatrist who was treated with ECT for severe depression. However, one of the major problems with ECT appears to be ascertaining 'where it is indicated' - i.e., which people it will help. Rogers, Pilgrim and Lacey have observed that there is a wide variation in the rates of ECT treatment both between different NHS regions and within regions, depending on the clinical team, leading them to conclude that the most likely explanation for this lies in the treatment preferences of particular consultants rather than differences between patients. Thus it may well be the case that whether or not one receives ECT depends upon the stance of one's consultant as much as on scientific indications of its efficacy as a treatment. Such an approach does little to dispel fears about ECT being used as a punishment, or its side-effects outweighing any benefits. The APA Task Force Report (1978) concluded that the weight of evidence supported the view that ECT is an appropriate treatment for severe depression where there is a high risk of suicide and other forms of therapy will take too long to be effective or where a severe, life-threatening, catatonic state exists that has not responded to medication; and in severe manic illness where medication is contra-indicated by other medical conditions which require that the manic state be alleviated promptly. It concluded that ECT should not be used to control violent behaviour unless there is clear evidence that there is an existing condition for which ECT is indicated, and was sceptical about its efficacy as a treatment for schizophrenia. It also concluded that ECT had not been proved to be a useful treatment for children, reactive depression or people with long-standing character disorders. A British enquiry into ECT (Committee of Enquiry, 1976), set up following allegations of maltreatment of patients at St. Augustine's Hospital, Kent, in 1976, recommended that the Royal College of Psychiatrists should issue guidance on the use of ECT. This resulted in the Memorandum on the use of ECT (Royal College of Psychiatrists, 1977). Its conclusions were essentially the same as those of the APA Task Force Report.

ECT poses the same problems as are posed by psychotropic medication, with the added emotive element of direct manipulation of the brain to contend with, an issue which I have argued is irrelevant, philosophically speaking. However, it may not be irrelevant from a practical point of view, for whatever one may argue logically, it remains the case that many people are even more frightened by the idea of having an electric current passed through their brain than they are by the thought of taking psychotropic drugs. This is hardly surprising, given the special status that is reserved for the brain and the fact that we are taught, quite sensibly, to treat electricity with caution and respect, as it is capable of killing us. The juxtaposition of these two elements, perhaps flavoured with Frankenstein overtones and a lack of understanding about the brain, electricity and the nature of the procedure is guaranteed to produce extreme fear in anyone, let alone one who is unfortunate enough to be suffering from mental illness. And the necessity for general anaesthesia, which has made the administration of ECT much more humane, nonetheless turns the procedure into a major event for the patient, with the added fear of being unconscious and out of control at the very moment when people who are fundamentally strangers are interfering with her brain.

Given the above, the compulsory administration of ECT is extremely hard to justify. In general surgery, it is acknowledged that patients who, whilst consenting to an operation, are nevertheless reluctant to do so, tend to do badly; it seems quite illogical to expect a person who is already in a very fragile mental state to benefit from ECT if she is terrified and refuses her consent.

I know that ECT is a reasonable suggestion to be made in a case such as my own, when I had seemingly failed to respond to drug therapy and had side effects from it. ... While I respect the right of others to agree to it, I realise the improvement in techniques over the years and the greater restraint with which it is used, I could never agree to have it myself. Involuntary ECT is an invasion of man's last barrier of freedom - his mind, and hence of greater moment than invasion of his body. The medical aspect of a problem is one aspect only ... sometimes a patient would rather live through the illness than accept a particular line of treatment. I doubt [whether] I could have psychologically survived a course of ECT and continued to regard myself ... as ever again being authentically myself. Whether this is logical or not, it is the way I feel [and] I believe these feelings of repugnance and great anxiety regarding ECT would have militated against any useful outcome of the treatment. (Human Rights & Equal Opportunities Commission, 1993, p. 249)

This patient's acknowledgement that her attitude to ECT may be illogical does not diminish the fact that if someone feels this strongly opposed to ECT there is little likelihood of her condition being improved by its forcible administration. In such a situation, if it be the case that expert opinion strongly suggests that ECT will prove beneficial, then it is the task of the experts to convince the patient of the need for ECT - even enlisting the help of patients who have benefited from the procedure, if need be. (Given the frequently appalling communication skills of many in the medical profession, it is entirely possible that the approach taken by psychiatrists may contribute to patients refusing to give consent for ECT, and then facing the prospect of compulsory treatment, a situation which is hardly likely to engender a therapeutic relationship between doctor and patient.) A psychiatrist who believes in the efficacy of ECT has summed up the situation thus:

We [psychiatrists] are in an embarrassing position, because we do not know how [ECT] works... and so it is difficult to defend our position... The problem is we have got a bad press and we are in a situation where we can't defend ourselves. (ibid, p. 250)

There may be some truth in this, but it still seems to be rather simplistic to rely on the 'bad press' argument without asking why ECT has received a bad press; such an attitude illustrates the gulf between professional attitudes and the fear many patients experience when confronted with ECT.

Most consumers expressed a deep personal fear and rejection of ECT - even when it had been administered as a last resort and *when it was accepted by them as an effective treatment* Most psychiatrists who mentioned it viewed it simply as a 'treatment option' or an 'appropriate next step' in a limited number of cases. The evidence suggests that the depth of consumers' negative feelings about ECT is often discounted, overridden or misunderstood by their treating doctors. (ibid., emphasis mine.)

In view of this, I would suggest that the compulsory administration of ECT to patients who are rational enough for their relationship with those treating them to be seriously adversely affected would be likely to be counter productive, and therefore unjustified except in extreme situations where the alternative to ECT would almost certainly be death; such a situation may arise in the case of severe and intractable depression, where the patient has already attempted suicide and other treatments have proved to be ineffective.

Even more contentious than ECT is psychosurgery. There are three objections to its justifiability as a treatment for certain forms of mental illness: firstly, what I have already called the 'sanctity' of the brain argument; secondly, the argument that it is ineffective; and thirdly, in contrast, that it is effective, but so open to misuse that it should never be used. In England, under Section 57 of the MHA (1983), psychosurgery requires consent and a second opinion before it can be carried out. (Bluglass, 1984).

I have already argued, when considering the case of ECT, that although great caution should be exercised when considering treatment that directly affects the brain because the extent of our knowledge about its functions is still extremely limited, arguments against neurological interventions on the grounds that the brain is sacrosanct are not sufficient to prohibit such interventions. The remaining two arguments, though in fact opposed, frequently appear to be confused with each other, and the debate is not helped by the often intransigent positions adopted by the protagonists. As Clare illustrates, the debate about psychosurgery has frequently not been conducted objectively: he cites the case of an article in the British Journal of Psychiatry, which as he points out, is 'a journal famed internationally for its normally stringent academic standards'. (Clare, 1980, p. 308). The article in question is by Walter Freeman, 'the doyen of American psychosurgery', and was published when the journal's editor was Eliot Slater, who co-authored a textbook which advocated the practice of leucotomy for schizophrenia.

> ... here we have a paper which on the basis of four pages of casual anecdote, potted history, and amateur statistics argues for more frequent use of a most serious, indeed arguably the most serious method of treatment that can be employed in schizophrenia and indeed insists, in the absence of any objective evidence, that it can be *more dangerous not to operate than to do so* - and the *British Journal of Psychiatry* publishes it. (Clare, 1980, pp. 309-10)

Clare then goes on to criticise the 'blatantly one-sided and tendentious' analysis of psychosurgery offered by Peter Breggin, one of the harshest critics of physical treatments of mental illness.

> ... he dismisses the role of psychosurgery in relieving intractable physical pain and seems uncertain ... whether psychosurgery should be banned

because it does not work or banned because it does work and may be abused in a sinister and fearful fashion. He ruins his case by his tendency to wild exaggeration and, on occasion, a somewhat cavalier approach to the use of facts. As perhaps befits a contemporary assailant of psychiatric orthodoxy, Breggin mounts his attack with a series of sweeping assertions, selected quotations, and random examples which together constitute an indictment of such staggering proportions that it leaves the casual reader stunned and in disbelief that anyone professing himself to be a physician would indulge in such shameful practices. (ibid.)

Such approaches do nothing to help ascertain the efficacy of psychosurgery and appear to have little to do with the interests of sufferers from mental illness, but a great deal to do with the determination of the participants in the debate to prove that their viewpoint is the 'correct' one.

The US National Commission for the Protection of Human Subjects of Biomedical and Behavioural Research (1977) defined psychosurgery as:

... brain surgery on (1) normal brain tissue of an individual who does not suffer from any physical disease, for the purpose of changing or controlling the behaviour or emotions of such individual, or (2) diseased brain tissue of an individual, if the primary object of the performance of such surgery is to control, change or affect any behavioural or emotional disturbance of such individual.

This definition differentiates psychosurgery from brain surgery, which is surgery on damaged or diseased brain tissue; unlike psychosurgery, brain surgery is not regarded in principle as any more ethically problematic than any other form of surgery. Kleinig (1985), considers that this differentiation is itself problematic. He argues that a simple differentiation between structural normality and abnormality is simplistic and unrealistic:

The reference to [normal] brain tissue, if not tendentious, is at least misleading. What is properly intended in this characterisation is histological or structural normality: the absence of anatomical damage or malformation. However, it is commonly inferred from this that psychosurgery involves the destruction of brain tissue with which there is 'nothing wrong'. This cannot be assumed. Structural normality is only half the story, for it may be accompanied by functional abnormality. This is almost certainly the case with movement disorders (such as Parkinson's disease and Sydenham's chorea) and sometimes with temporal lobe (or psychomotor) epilepsy. ... If, instead of distinguishing grossly between brain surgery and psychosurgery, we seek to distinguish between neurosurgery and psychosurgery, we are confronted by a continuum or overlapping of procedures, rather than a clear differentiation. It

89

has become increasingly common for advocates of psychosurgery to claim that metabolic or electrochemical abnormalities are associated with conditions for which psychosurgery is most successfully indicated. Although the significance of this association can be questioned, it indicates a certain 'question-beggingness' or at least misleadingness of appeals to 'healthy brain tissue' as one of the differentia of psychosurgical operations. Structural normality needs to be understood. (p. 2)

Kleinig acknowledges that 'psychosurgery has often been performed without evidence of or even belief in brain abnormality, structural or functional', and that claims of functional abnormality have often been speculative, and even claims for functional abnormality that are evidentially based often do not stand up to scrutiny. He also makes the point that even evidence of brain pathology does not remove the problems raised by the destruction of normal brain tissue, as the site of the pathology may not correspond to the site of the surgery. Another problem with the distinction between brain surgery and psychosurgery, according to Kleinig is that the simple delineation between the primary and secondary objectives of such surgery is inadequate:

An operation to remove a tumour might have as an important object the alleviation of undesirable mental states and/or behaviour caused by the growth. Indeed, if the growth is benign, the only reason for intervention may be to ameliorate the patient's psychological condition. It is not clear why the presence or absence of some structural abnormality should make so much difference, when the effect on mental states may be intended or foreseen and considerable in either case. (p. 3)

Gaylin (1975) has also made the point that the distinction between organic and non-organic is not a simple matter, and that an organic lesion may well be located in an as yet unidentified chemical system rather than an obvious anatomical one. He also argues that there are various procedures that are carried out on healthy organs/tissues in order to improve the functioning of a damaged or unhealthy part of the body. He gives as an example the shortening of a healthy eye muscle in order to improve vision where there is weakness or paralysis in the other eye which cannot be corrected. His point is that we are concerned with the *functioning* of the individual, not organic integrity.

The presence or absence of structural abnormality is an important issue for some, because if a brain lesion can be identified, it can be argued that one is primarily operating on the body and not interfering with the mind, as would appear to be the case if no lesion has been identified. Thus in these circumstances it can be argued that one is altering the brain only in the sense of removing an abnormality in order to restore it to normality, rather than altering one's sense of self or being. This is a simplistic approach, although it can be argued that in such a situation at least it is known what is causing the problems and therefore what intervention is appropriate, whereas in the case of psychosurgery, intervention may be largely speculative. Given that:

> ... the 'disordered mental states and/or behaviour 'which psychosurgery has been employed to alter ranges between intractable pain and obesity, between hyperactivity and endogenous depression, and between anorexia nervosa and compulsive gambling. (Kleinig, p. 4)

it is hardly surprising that it is easier to justify neurosurgery for behavioural problems where an identifiable lesion is considered to be the cause of the problem. The range of conditions for which psychosurgery has been argued to be effective is not necessarily a valid objection to its use; there are many different problems which require, for example, abdominal surgery, and it is not reasonable to argue that abdominal surgery is invalidated because it is employed for many different purposes; similarly, the term 'psychosurgery' does not refer to a uniform procedure; (for a history and description of psychosurgery techniques see Clare, 1980, and Valenstein, 1980).

However, psychosurgery must still be regarded as experimental, it is irreversible, and the definitions of normal or improved functioning that are adopted to ascertain its success may be extremely limited. Gaylin has also made the very pertinent point that there is a considerable difference between what he describes as an intrapersonal disease, where the person who suffers most is the victim of the disease, who therefore potentially benefits most from treatment but also bears any adverse consequences of it, and an interpersonal disease where, for example, the perpetrator of violent behaviour who is subjected to treatment bears any adverse consequences, but society as a whole may reap considerably greater benefits than the patient. This raises the spectre of the possible large scale social control of deviant behaviour through brain surgery:

> We are in danger of creating a society in which everyone who deviates from the norm will be in danger of surgical mutilation. (Breggin, 1972, p. 1608)

A little thought surely shows this to be a most unlikely situation. Brain surgery is difficult and expensive, and as brain surgeons and psychiatrists are generally paid considerably higher salaries than executioners and gaolers, it would surely be far more effective to execute or incarcerate those considered deviant, options which it seems to me would be unlikely to bother a government prepared to lobotomise its dissidents and deviants. Finally, if we are dealing with fears of mass control, we must remember that there are tried and proven methods of social control such as indoctrination and the exploitation of fear by propaganda which sadly have all too often proved their efficacy in the past, which would seem to render psychosurgery as a method of social control largely irrelevant. So if behaviour control through psychosurgery is a serious fear, we are likely to be considering a small number of cases, which does not in any way reduce the importance of the issues, of course.

The issue of psychosurgery being used as a means of social control often focuses on the fear that particular groups are more likely to receive it. Valenstein (1980), however, surveying the American evidence, has noted that the great majority of patients referred for psychosurgery were referred by psychiatrists in private practice, a fact which he argues indicates that they were more likely to be members of the middle-class rather than the members of deprived minority groups. Investigating data relating to the race of recipients of psychosurgery, he argues that it indicates that 'the incidence of psychosurgery performed on blacks is very significantly below their proportion in the total population' .(Valenstein, 1977, pp. 82-88). He also notes, however, that the information on race is not totally adequate, as the race of the patient is not always cited; where it is, the most frequent comment is 'the patients were all Caucasian.' (Valenstein, 1980, p. 101). He mentions a personal communication from Bridges, at the Geoffrey Knight Psychosurgical Unit at Brooks General Hospital in London, regretting that not a single black person has been able to benefit from psychosurgery; Bridges also asserts that because of the system of NHS referrals, British psychosurgery recipients are proportionately spread throughout the socio-economic range.

The evidence relating to women patients is more complicated: Valenstein conducted a review of all published articles on psychosurgery in the US between 1971-76 in an attempt to analyse the distribution of surgery by sex, which showed that 59% of psychosurgical patients in the 'other' category, which comprised all groups except those classed as 'aggressive 'were female; in the 'aggressive' category, 61% were male. In total, 56% of psychosurgical patients were female. (Valenstein, 1977). Whether this reflects an unfair bias towards treating women with psychosurgery or the greater proportion of women in mental hospitals is unknown.

On the basis of this evidence, I think it is difficult to argue that there is a conspiracy to subject any group to psychosurgery as a means of social control; I have already dismissed the 'slippery slope' argument that because something is open to abuse and misuse, it must necessarily be banned. This does not mean that vigilance is not necessary, however, and the possibility of the abuse of a treatment as potentially damaging as psychosurgery must always be acknowledged, and its use strictly controlled.

But abuse of psychosurgery need not result from a conspiracy to control the deviant; it may result from arguably well-intentioned, but insensitive, simplistic approaches to difficult problems, as the following cases illustrate.

A woman of 38 suffered from tension and anxiety since childhood. Following *marriage to a sadist* ... she developed multiple jerks and sweating, so severe that she had to change her clothes several times a day, and obsessional tidiness and depression. The effort to tidy her wardrobe was exhausting. She was unable to face meeting people. Strong suicidal impulses developed. Following operation [a subcaudate tractotomy] 9 years ago she was immediately improved. Within two months the jerking, sweating and suicidal ideas were gone; she was able to put things away in the wardrobe and forget all about abnormal tidiness. "Formerly it had taken me ages to get away from it - I seemed glued to it" .She has maintained this complete cure. (Knight, quoted in Clare, 1980, p. 313)

And presumably she lived happily ever after. I find it almost impossible to believe that even the most mechanistically orientated psychiatrist can seriously extol the virtues of an operation on the brain of a woman to cure her of the effects of her *husband's* cruelty! Surely in such a case, if anyone's brain were to be operated on in order to change behaviour, it should have been the husband's ?Lest incredulity leads us to think that such a case must surely be an isolated aberration, Clare cites another case from an influential textbook by Sargant and Slater (1972):

Another type of depressive illness that may be helped by leucotomy is the reactive depression in which environmental factors of an irremediable kind are involved. A depressed woman, for instance, may owe her illness to a psychopathic husband who cannot change and will not accept treatment. Separation might be the answer but is ruled out by other ties such as children, by the patient's financial or emotional dependence or by her religious views. Patients of this type are often helped by antidepressant drugs. But in the occasional case where they do not work, we have seen patients enabled by a leucotomy to return to the difficult environment and cope with it in a way which had hitherto been impossible. (ibid p. 313)

God help any unfortunate woman who falls into the hands of Messrs Sargant, Slater and Knight and their ilk for treatment; she would be well advised not to keep an appointment without a good lawyer and possibly a large Rottweiler if she wished to emerge with her brain intact. It is impossible not to wonder whether these 'experts' would prescribe psychosurgery for depressed men rendered ill by nagging wives. I am not suggesting that any devious intention lay at the root of such treatment decisions; it is possible that they were motivated by a genuine desire to help the women concerned, but informed by ignorance, insensitivity and a narrow model of human psychological functioning. It is situations like these which give all of psychiatry a bad name, and cause people to reject physical treatments outright. It *cannot ever* be justified to take an extreme step such as psychosurgery to cure the psychological misery that a woman suffers as a result of living with a violent man. Such problems require social intervention - the provision of accommodation, for example, to enable her to leave him, and psychological support and help - but not removal of a section of her brain in order that she will be less bothered by her awful situation. Such an approach is the equivalent of giving the starving appetite suppressant drugs so that they will not feel hungry as they starve to death.

If neither fears of social engineering nor the sanctity of the brain are sufficient to argue against the use of psychosurgery, the deciding factor must surely be the question of its efficacy - does it work? Valenstein has pointed out that:

> Whether they start over legal, ethical or social issues, most psychosurgery debates ultimately come down to conflicting opinions about the outcome of psychosurgical operations. If these operations always accomplished what their most enthusiastic advocates claim and never resulted in any impairment, most of the controversy would evaporate. If the converse were true - that is, if the worst results were typical, psychosurgery would not be performed at all. Obviously, the truth is somewhere in between these extremes, and therefore there is controversy. Of course, even if it were possible to state the precise statistical probability of various outcomes, there would still be disagreement over the course of action. Clearly, personal judgements are involved in any consideration of a trade-off between, for example, a loss of motivation or affect and a gain in "peace of mind". Important as these judgements are, it is first necessary to obtain evidence as objective as possible - on the outcomes of psychosurgery. (Valenstein, 1980, p. 141)

Obtaining objective evidence on the efficacy of psychosurgery is easier said than done. Assessing the efficacy of psychosurgery is extremely difficult; in a study of the scientific merit of 153 empirical studies of psychosurgery which were published between 1971-76, Valenstein (1977) concluded that almost 90% were so badly designed that if they had been animal studies, no reputable scientific journal would have published them. The definition of efficacy depends upon what criteria are used to define success, and who chooses them; success for a doctor may not equate with success for a patient. (For a review on the literature on postoperative evaluation of psychosurgery, see Valenstein, 1977; 1980; National Commission for the Protection of Human Subjects of Biomedical and Behavioral Research, 1976.) Kleinig has identified four interpretations of 'success' in the evaluative literature on psychosurgery; these are: success as symptom removal; success as manageability; success as test mastery and success as restoration. (Kleinig, 1985).

Kleinig suggests that in the early days of psychosurgery a simple approach to success defined as symptom removal was taken by many practitioners, which focused on the removal of given, specific symptoms and ignored any undesired side-effects. As he says, such an assessment of success is seriously inadequate, because:

> It operates with a model of treatment in which the objects of treatment are disorders or their symptoms, and not the people who are their bearers or sufferers. (Kleinig, 1985, p. 98)

94

Side-effects cannot be discounted because the success of treatment is often a cost-benefit analysis between side-effects and symptom removal or alleviation, and the decision as to whether the benefits outweigh the costs cannot be made by a doctor using an extremely limited set of criteria, but should be made the person who is ill; it is her well-being, after all, which is ostensibly the reason for treatment. It would be naive, however, not to acknowledge that it is quite possible to address other criteria for success under the guise of concern for the patient's welfare; the criterion of success as manageability is one such.

A closer look at manageability shows it to be anything but a surgical triumph: quite the opposite. What manageability requires is a certain kind of passivity on the part of the managed party. It does not imply an equality of standing in social relations, but submissiveness and a general compliance with the will and purpose of others. When Walter Freeman wrote that 'on the whole, lobotomised patients make rather good citizens' ... he was not thinking of their creative and stimulating contribution to social life. The emphasis was quite different. As he was later to put it: 'lobotomised patients seldom come into conflict with the law precisely because they lack the imagination to think up new devilries and the energy to perpetrate them.' ... Life in *Brave New World* may be more pleasant for all, but only John the Savage is fully human. (ibid., p. 99)

Lest there be a temptation to think that the world might be a better place with some of our 'fully human' capacities subdued, it should be remembered that it is John the Savage who can appreciate:

On the white wonder of dear Juliet's hand, may seize
And steal immortal blessing from her lips,
Who, even in pure and vestal modesty,
Still blush, as thinking their own kisses sin.

(Though it must also be acknowledged that the 'fully human' John the Savage is also unable to realise that Lenina is no Juliet!)

The evidence regarding the efficacy of psychosurgery does not offer any clear-cut answers to the question, 'Does it work?' The nearest to an answer to this question appears to be, 'it depends' .It depends upon whom one asks and how one measures success. From this it might appear to be justified to argue that psychosurgery should be discontinued However, there are patients whose suffering is so great that it is arguable that if they are able to consent to psychosurgery then it should at least be considered. Valenstein gives a representative case-study of a patient suffering from a severe obsessional state who would be considered a good candidate for psychosurgery.

Her day was totally occupied with checking and re-checking actions such as washing, dressing and household tasks. She had, for example, to wash her face in a special order - starting with the left side, nose, right side, forehead - up to thirteen times. A similar elaborate system was involved in her bathing, which took her over an hour each day. After washing clothes she had to squeeze them a certain way, repeating the proceedings twenty-two times, the bottom of the bowl was then examined, checking the maker's mark numerous times to make sure the bowl was empty. Cleaning her teeth was a major task, taking over half an hour. Making a bed, with checking at each stage that the sheets and blankets were exactly symmetrical, might take over half an hour. … The patient felt extreme guilt at her disruption of the family's existence and, at times, felt very depressed and that life was not worth living. (Valenstein, 1980, p. 90)

No other form of treatment had any significant effect on this patient's illness. In the face of a life of unmitigated misery such as this patient must have suffered, maintaining a 'sanctity of the brain' approach which forbids even the consideration of psychosurgery may enable the holder of such a view to feel morally superior but it is a position bought at the expense of any hope for the sufferer.

Let us consider the issues raised by this patient's situation further. Let us assume that all possible forms of treatment have been tried to alleviate this woman's condition, including psychotherapy, and that they have been ineffective. Let us also assume that this patient is competent to discuss her treatment and make a rational decision as to whether her situation is so intolerable to her that she is prepared to try anything that might have the slightest chance of offering her some relief from her suffering, no matter how experimental. Assume that she has had all the risks explained to her, all the known statistical evidence regarding the likelihood of success or failure of treatment explained to her, and has also considered, with the doctors treating her, what would constitute success for her. After due consideration, she decides that she does not wish to undergo psychosurgery. This poses no ethical problems; without consent, psychosurgery cannot be carried out, and this patient's wishes (and, it could be argued, her autonomy) will be respected.

Now let us consider a different scenario; this time, the patient decides that she does wish to undergo psychosurgery as a last resort, even accepting the risk that surgery might worsen her condition. Those who argue that psychosurgery is never justified would deny this patient the option of psychosurgery. Would this be justifiable? I do not think that it would be. This patient's autonomy is severely restricted by the uncontrollable obsessions imposed upon her by her illness. If we wish to respect her autonomy, we cannot forbid her to subject herself to psychosurgery in the hope that it will enhance her capacity to exercise her autonomy. Denial of treatment in such a situation denies autonomy just as much as forcing a patient to have treatment does. Therefore, if we respect the patient's decision not to have psychosurgery, we must surely respect her decision to have it, if all the assumptions made are the same in both cases. The problem, of course, remains that it is one thing to base an argument upon a constructed situation, and quite another to deal with real - life situations which are inevitably not tidy and controlled in the way that constructed ones are. In real life, it is impossible to ignore the multitude of problems which have been artificially 'solved' in my hypothetical example: how likely is it that patients will have received a thorough trial of all available alternative treatments; would all possible consequences of psychosurgery have been explained, along with the risks; would the criteria for success have been considered with the patient; would the patient be capable of understanding all this and making rational decisions - bearing in mind the great difficulty that is encountered by those who could be considered experts in the field of assessing the efficacy of psychosurgery, what possible chance is there that a lay person, and a very seriously distressed lay person at that, could possibly make an informed, rational judgement about the pros and cons of psychosurgery?

It is possible to go on forever considering the ifs, buts and maybes involved in this issue, because every individual case is different, the evidence of the efficacy of psychosurgery is so difficult to interpret, the brain is a poorly understood organ and, ultimately, psychosurgery is irreversible, and so any undesirable consequences which might have severe implications for the patient will be there forever. And it must be acknowledged that the doctor/patient relationship is not one of equals; it cannot be, no matter how ethical the doctor, because one partner in this relationship is severely disadvantaged by virtue of being ill, and the other has the power that inevitably comes with the possession of valued knowledge. All these factors, and there are many more that might occur in specific cases, conspire to make the ethical issues that must be addressed when considering the justifiability of psychosurgery extremely complex, to such a degree that the easy answer would be to argue that in view of these considerable problems this treatment should be banned. I do not think that such an approach can be justified, because the nature of the problems that psychosurgery seeks to alleviate or cure is so great and the effects are so devastating for the individuals unfortunate enough to be afflicted by them that we owe it to them to try and find a way of confronting these issues that allows them hope without this hope being bought at the expense of others' rights. To do this requires that safeguards be built into the procedures that determine who receives psychosurgery. In the UK, the safeguards against misuse of psychosurgery are limited to requiring consent from the patient and a second medical opinion; in view of the complexity of the problems relating to psychosurgery mentioned earlier, this seems to be a rather limited approach to safeguarding against abuse, however caused. The approach taken by the State of Victoria in Australia would appear to offer greater safeguards. There, the Psychosurgery Review Board, established by section 56 of the Mental Health Act, 1986, provides that the Board should consist of five members, men and women, and must include:

a person who is, or is eligible to be, admitted as a barrister and solicitor of the Supreme Court: and

a person who is a neurosurgeon nominated by the Royal Australasian College of Surgeons; and

a person who is a psychiatrist nominated by the Minister; and

a person who is a psychiatrist nominated by the Royal Australasian and New Zealand College of Psychiatrists; and

a person who is a member of the public nominated by the Victorian Council of Civil Liberties Inc. (Psychosurgery Review Board, 1993, p. 82)

The function of the Board is to decide whether psychosurgery should be allowed to be performed on any member of the State of Victoria; any psychiatrist who proposes psychosurgery as treatment for a patient must apply to the Board for permission for the procedure to be carried out; psychosurgery performed without the authorisation of the Board is a criminal offence. The report sets out the information that must accompany any application to perform psychosurgery, and sets out its powers and procedures. Section 60 of the Act provides, amongst other criteria, that the Board is bound by the rules of natural justice, the two most pertinent to the Board's functions being considered to be that:

… no member of the Board should be biased and that, in the absence of good reason, the patient is entitled to hear and question all oral evidence given to the Board and to examine and challenge all written material placed before the Board. (ibid., p. 84)

If permission to carry out psychosurgery is granted, the name of the practitioner, the nature of the surgery, the hospital where surgery is to be carried out and the period of time within which the surgery must be carried out must all be specified by the Board.

If the following criteria are all met, the Board must consent to any proposed psychosurgery being performed:

a) the person in respect of whom the application is made has the capacity to give informed consent;
b) the person in respect of whom the application is made has in fact given informed consent;

98

c) the proposed psychosurgery has clinical merit and is appropriate;

d) any person proposing to perform the surgery is properly qualified;

e) the hospital or psychiatric hospital in which it is proposed to perform the psychosurgery is an appropriate place;

f) all other reasonable treatments have already been adequately and skilfully administered without sufficient and lasting benefit;

g) notice of the hearing has been given in accordance with Section 59 (2) of the Act.

If the Board is not satisfied that these conditions have all been met, it must refuse to authorise the application for psychosurgery, the exception being that the Board can substitute its own consent regarding (a) and (b) if it considers that it is in the patient's best interest to undergo surgery but the patient is not capable of giving informed consent.

There are considerably greater safeguards against inappropriate use of psychosurgery built into these procedures than exist in the Mental Health Act (1983) which operates in England and Wales; if psychosurgery is to be allowed, then this level of safeguards should be demanded.

And despite the complexity of the problems that must be confronted when addressing the question of whether or not psychosurgery should be allowed, I do not think that the arguments advanced against its use are sufficient to justify banning it. This is not an argument for simply leaving it to the professionals to decide on its use, however; the doctor /patient relationship, as I have previously argued, is not one of equality. Acknowledging this is not tantamount to accusing the medical profession of being part of a conspiracy to suppress deviant behaviour by devious means, but rather a statement of a fairly obvious fact; and members of the medical profession are as likely to be incompetent, poorly educated or simply blinkered in their approach as any of the rest of us; consequently we cannot rely only on an internal system of checks and balances to ensure that a treatment as serious as psychosurgery is always used wisely. To deny this (as some members of the medical profession undoubtedly would) is arrogant.

Those who would ban psychosurgery outright adopt an equally arrogant attitude; such an attitude is evidence of a degree of paternalism, of knowing what is best for the severely mentally ill, that is as reprehensible as the extreme medical paternalism of 'the doctor knows best' type, because it has not been proven that psychosurgery never helps anyone, and neither has it been proven that psychosurgery is used as a means of social control.

Direct manipulation of the brain is an awesome prospect, both in terms of the practical problems encountered when interfering with the most complicated organ in the body, and about whose functions little is understood; and in terms of the moral implications of interfering with the organ that is in some sense thought to contain the essence of our humanity. As a result, any interference with the brain for the purposes of altering behaviour or personality must be the subject of scrutiny and control. We must be constantly aware of the possibility of the abuse of such treatment, and also the possibility that it might be discovered that it simply does not work. The former can be best achieved by instigating more rigorous safeguards, such as those used by the State of Victoria in Australia; to ascertain the effectiveness of psychosurgery much more research will be needed, and such research should listen to what patients say about the results of treatment, as well as using so-called objective measures of success (or lack of it); how can a sick person measure their state of being by objective performance measuring tests? We must listen to what patients have to say when assessing progress and improvement, and not restrict ourselves to simplistic, inadequate models of human functioning against which to measure the efficacy of treatment.

If psychosurgery (and possibly ECT) is to be banned it should be because the evidence clearly demonstrates that it is ineffective, not because of vague notions of the sanctity of the brain, or because it might be abused or simply because the situation is so complex that it is easier to ignore it by banning contentious procedures. We must remember that the problems for which psychosurgery is suggested are truly incapacitating and result in a quality of life so grim that it is arguable that any technique which offers hope of alleviation should be considered:

> ... what if [psychosurgery] is effective, if in a number of highly selected, chronically distressed, and intractable cases it is found to provide considerable improvement and relief? ... Let us take as an example the crippling obsessive disorders. ... Those patients who suffer from severe forms of this condition experience terrible psychic agony. ... To date, treatment for the severer varieties of such states is far from impressive. Drugs have a limited value while psychotherapy has not proved particularly effective. In a number of patients ... psychosurgery, allegedly has provided some relief.
>
> It is this criterion, namely the relief of severe and disabling symptoms, that serves as a justification for psychosurgery for many British psychiatrists. (Clare, 1980, pp. 326, 327)

If all other forms of treatment have been tried thoroughly and proved ineffective, if the patient's misery is such that she is prepared to try a drastic remedy as possibly the lesser of two evils (and the operative word here is misery - we are not talking about the mild anxiety that may afflict anyone as to whether they have left the gas switched on as they depart for a week's holiday) and if sufficient safeguards have been built into the system, as outlined above, then to ban psychosurgery for the wrong reasons is to deny hope to a small, but greatly suffering number of people who have as much right to treatment as they have to refuse treatment.

All three forms of physical treatment for mental illness - drugs, ECT and psychosurgery - may offer hope for some sufferers, but equally they are none of them without risks and side-effects and consequently safeguards need to be built into the procedures employed in cases where compulsory administration is proposed Despite the arguments of those like Breggin, that drugs are the equivalent of a chemical lobotomy, it seems reasonable to demand the highest level of safeguards for psychosurgery, because this is completely irreversible. Psychosurgery should therefore remain a treatment that may only be administered with the patient's consent, and I would argue for the implementation of the procedures outlined earlier in this chapter that are employed by the Australian State of Victoria in cases where psychosurgery is proposed.

In the case of drugs and ECT, where there is evidence to suggest that merely ceasing the treatment will not necessarily remove any deleterious effects it may have had, I would suggest that although the power to prescribe these treatments against the patient's wishes should not be removed because of the extremely serious consequences of some forms of mental illness if it is left untreated, there should nevertheless be greater safeguards built into the procedures for compulsory administration because there is a considerable amount of evidence that suggests that ECT is often inappropriately used: it appears all too easy to get the required second opinion from a colleague whose views support the prescribing doctor's so that from the patient's point of view, there may be the feeling that the process is merely a formality:

> … according to Liz Sayce, MIND's policy director, 96 per cent of second opinions agree with first opinions, "so the patients are saying the safeguards are not good enough." *(The Independent,* 6 November 1994)

I have already suggested safeguards for the compulsory administration of drugs, and these should be extended to ECT. However, it would be futile to create a system where lengthy delays are involved in this process, because in cases where a patient unequivocally needs treatment, lengthy delays will only result in the unsatisfactory situation described in the case of Mrs A occurring. Therefore, a 'rapid response' system would be required, where an independent patient's advocate could be appointed quickly; loved ones should also be allowed to make their contribution, and the opinions of any professionals who know the patient well should be given more weight than those who may only just have become involved. In the event of ECT not proving beneficial, or its costs seriously outweighing any benefits, it should not be repeated interminably against the patient's wishes. It seems highly unlikely that the majority of the medical profession will be in favour of outside intervention in their professional decision making, but when contentious, potentially damaging treatment may be imposed upon the patient without her consent all possible safeguards must be implemented, because such a course of action must be seen as a last resort; in such circumstances, the interests of the patient must come before the pride of the professionals.

7 Psychotherapy

The final treatment for mental illness that I wish to consider is psychotherapy, often classed as a 'talking cure'; the term was coined by Bertha Pappenheim, one of Freud's patients, as the method of helping the patient is carried out through the medium of talking.

Psychotherapy occupies a somewhat confusing position in the treatment of mental illness because there is a divergence of opinion as to its uses. For those whose model of mental illness denies the validity of any possibility of a physical component, it is the only valid method of treatment; those who adopt this view would consider psychotherapy to be useful in all cases of mental illness. Others regard it as the appropriate form of treatment for some types of mental illness, but as inappropriate for those which are physically based, though even in these cases its use may be encouraged as a form of supportive help for the mentally ill in addition to physical treatments, and indeed, for those suffering from some particularly unpleasant physical illnesses. Thus a common model of the employment of psychotherapeutic treatment regards physical treatment as the first approach to the treatment of mental illness, with psychotherapy employed in a supportive but secondary role. The argument advanced for this approach is that irrespective of the causes of mental illness, a certain level of ability to communicate is required before there is any point in engaging in psychotherapy; in some forms of mental illness this state may not be achieved without medication. Therefore, it is argued, common sense dictates that even though it may well be the case that a patient must acknowledge and be helped to sort out her problems, she first needs medication to help lift her depression or control a manic state..

The confusion is added to by the fact that increasingly psychotherapy of some sort is also advocated, in addition to its use as treatment for mental illness, for those who are often referred to disparagingly as the 'worried well' .Such cases might be considered to be part of what Lasch has described as 'the culture of narcissism' .He has made the point that:

102

Medicine and psychiatry - more generally, the therapeutic outlook and sensibility that pervade modern society - reinforce the pattern created by other cultural influences, in which the individual endlessly examines himself for signs of ageing and ill-health, for tell-tale symptoms of psychic stress, for blemishes and flaws that might diminish his attractiveness, or on the other hand for reassuring indications that his life is proceeding according to schedule. (Lasch, 1991, p. 49)

Irrespective of the uses to which psychotherapy is employed, however, the fundamental issues it raises remain the same.

Further confusion results from the varied nature of psychotherapy itself. Although psychodynamic therapies may all be considered to owe their origins to Freud's development of psychoanalysis, both as a model of human psychological functioning and as a method of treatment for certain forms of mental illness, the diversity of therapies currently on offer makes definition extremely difficult - *The Psychotherapy Handbook* (Herink, 1981) lists over three hundred different types of therapy. There is also a problem in differentiating between 'therapy' and 'counselling', and the terms are often used interchangeably. The British Association for Counselling considers that:

It is not possible to make a generally accepted distinction between counselling and psychotherapy. (British Association for Counselling, 1984)

However, it is generally considered that therapy involves exploring a patient's problems in greater depth, identifying and exploring patterns in long-term problems, whereas counselling is more concerned with specific, current problems a patient may be experiencing.

Psychotherapy must therefore be considered to be as varied as drugs are; if we take as an analogy painkilling medications, at one end of the scale there is aspirin, which, though potentially lethal and capable of producing severe side-effects, is nonetheless freely available over the counter; at the other end are opiate derivatives, whose prescription is very strictly controlled. We might consider the psychotherapeutic equivalent of aspirin to be Alexander's (1957) definition of psychotherapy:

Everyone who tries to encourage a despondent friend or to reassure a panicky child practices psychotherapy (p. 148)

This is quite straightforward, and acknowledges what has long been known, that talking may help those suffering various forms of distress; certainly the healing powers of talking were recognised long before formal theories were articulated. Shakespeare wrote:

Give sorrow words; the grief that does not speak
Whispers the o'erfraught heart and bids it break...
(Macbeth, Act IV, Scene iii.)

But psychotherapy is more than this; Sutherland has defined it thus:

> By *psychotherapy* I refer to a personal relationship with a professional person in which those in distress can share and explore the underlying nature of their troubles, and possibly change some of the determinants of these through experiencing unrecognised forces in themselves. (Sutherland, 1968, p. 509)

It might seem, therefore, that psychotherapy is a particularly appropriate form of treatment for mental illness, involving, as it does, a relationship between people that uses the medium of language to explore the patient's negotiation of the relationship between her 'reality' and the rest of the world's 'reality' .Consequently, it is argued that psychotherapy takes people and their problems seriously and may therefore get to the heart of a patient's problems, rather than merely seeing her as a series of problems to be fitted into a diagnostic category and treated with drugs, which, if they work at all, will only alleviate symptoms. This may result in the view that psychotherapy is a route to 'salvation' superior to drug therapy, because it involves insight and self-determination. The issue of compulsory treatment may also be thought to be largely irrelevant, because psychotherapy cannot be effectively administered under duress (although it may be made a condition of a probation order). Psychotherapy is thus considered by those who support it to be more enhancing of a person's autonomy than other treatments, and consequently more humane.

If it were the case that psychotherapy were merely sympathetic listening, as Alexander defines it, this could be argued to be true, inasmuch as sympathetic listening offers support to someone to enable them to make their own decisions. It is difficult to imagine anyone seriously objecting to this; indeed, unless one takes a totally mechanistic medical model of mental illness and ascribes every type of condition that is currently included under that heading to biological dysfunction, it is difficult to imagine how there could be any objections in principle to trying to help the mentally ill by talking to them. And even if a totally mechanistic, biological model of mental illness were adopted, there could still be no objection to helping the mentally ill by talking to them in addition to any physical therapies employed in their treatment; nowadays it would not seriously be suggested that those requiring treatment for any form of illness might not be helped by sympathetic listening and talking.

But there is a great deal of evidence which supports the view that psychotherapy is not merely sympathetic listening, and therefore I would take issue with the simplistic notion that psychotherapy is necessarily more enhancing of the autonomy of the mentally ill than physical treatments. Sutherland's definition makes clear that psychotherapy as a professional discipline and practice is significantly different from sympathetic listening and concerned advice and support; this is moving away from the 'aspirin' end of therapy, towards the more specialist, and I would argue, inherently more dangerous end of the spectrum of talking as therapy. (And the analogy with drugs now breaks down in one very significant area; for whilst the use of dangerous drugs is strictly, if increasingly ineffectively, controlled by law, psychotherapy is not. Anyone may practise as a therapist and those official bodies which purport to control the practice of therapy have no statutory powers to enforce standards and codes of practice.)

A key term in Sutherland's definition of 'psychotherapy' is professional. It is professionalism which distinguishes between friendly support and care, and psychotherapy. It has been argued that professions have two core characteristics. These are:

> a prolonged specialised training in a body of abstract knowledge, and a collectivity or service orientation (Goode, 1960, quoted in Freidson, 1970, p. 77)

The 'body of abstract knowledge' is one of the means by which professions derive the legitimation of their authority; this immediately differentiates psychotherapy from sympathetic listening to, talking with, and support, because psychotherapy claims to be and to do more than these 'ordinary', layman's interventions. As a result, psychotherapy must be open to the same theoretical scrutiny as any other form of treatment, and simplistic stances which regard it as necessarily more humane or better than physical treatments simply by virtue of being carried out through the medium of talking are naive at best and dangerous at worst.

The claim that psychotherapy, or indeed, any other form of treatment, is based upon a 'body of abstract knowledge' implies that it is based on fact, rather than belief, and this in turn implies a certain degree of objectivity. The most objective form of knowledge is considered to be scientific knowledge; Freud considered that psychoanalysis was scientific, a claim which has generated considerable debate (see, for example, Clark & Wright, 1988; Farrell, 1981). The degree to which types of psychotherapy can, or do, claim objectivity is both variable and debatable, but that it is even considered an issue is a consequence of the overwhelming strength of scientific objectivity - its claim to moral neutrality. There is debate as to what 'science' is or means, but in broad terms, science is generally considered to concern itself with definite, causal relationships which deal with facts, demonstrable probabilities and correlations and which may lead to universal generalisations rather than opinions. If any form of psychotherapy could legitimately claim this level of objectivity, it would greatly strengthen its claims to be a valid method of treatment for mental illness because it could be argued that the premises upon which it operates had been demonstrated to be true, and not merely dogma.

But the dichotomy between 'hard', objective science and 'soft', subjective disciplines oversimplifies a complex situation. To begin with, even in the 'hardest' of science a creative element is often involved which results in intuitive leaps beyond demonstrable facts and causal relationships, and thus to some extent even science cannot claim to be totally objective. (Nevertheless, the fact that a theory may be arrived at intuitively does not mean that it is necessarily untrue; the truth or otherwise of a theory can only be determined or estimated by testing.) Secondly, any discipline is influenced by the a priori views of the world which its practitioners inhabit, because nobody lives in a cultural vacuum - we are all influenced by the world and the tradition within which we operate. Thus if one is engaged in a sub-atomic quest for the secret of life and the universe, one might be engaged in the pursuit of the Higgs-Boson, apparently an extremely small and elusive sub-atomic particle whose existence, it is argued, it is necessary to prove to explain these mysteries. To this end, £1.3 billion and 14 years of effort are being expended by CERN, the European Laboratory for Particle Physics, on the construction and operation, in Geneva, of the Large Hadron Collider, in order to find the Higgs-Boson. It requires a certain view of the world to engage in this pursuit, even if one does not believe that the Higgs-Boson holds the key to the mysteries of the universe, and engages in the project with the intention of proving that it does not exist because the real key to everything is the Bloggs-Watson. Such a view of the world is very different from a view which holds, for example, that the answer is not to be found in sub-atomic particle physics at all, but will only be revealed when the mythical unicorn is found and captured; and depending upon which view one holds will be the direction in which 'objective' scientific research is pursued. If one's world view is that the answer to life, the universe and everything will be found in sub-atomic particle physics, one is unlikely to go and seek the unicorn, and vice versa. And it is not entirely accurate to consider science to be ethically neutral; the decision to spend £1.3 billion on the Large Hadron Collider when a large percentage of the world's population is starving involves ethical issues and decisions. Thus any scientific theory may be argued to be subjective to the extent that certain things are picked out for study. It would therefore arguably be more fruitful to see things in degrees of objectivity, and to accept that even science is not totally objective, rather than to set 'objective' science in opposition to non-objective non-science. So if science is less objective than we might like to think, perhaps psychotherapy can be argued to be more scientific than its opponents might like to think it.

If this approach is adopted psychotherapy can be argued to be objective to the degree that it seeks to identify connections and causal relationships between ostensibly random events and to find meaning in the apparent chaos of mental illness. To find meaning in the chaos of mental illness is the first step along the road to helping the patient negotiate a different, and presumably 'better', relationship between her 'personal narrative' and the outside world.

I have argued that any scientific theory may be argued to be subjective to the extent that the decision as to what warrants study and explanation is subjective, and this is particularly so in the area of human psychological functioning. Different types of psychotherapy choose to focus on specific aspects of psychological functioning, and whatever their perspective, all eschew the exploration of physical determinants of behaviour. But as is the case with 'hard' science, explanations result in general theories, which may or may not be true. However, given the infinite variety amongst human beings, it is far harder (if not impossible) to accommodate all the possible forms of their behaviour in a general explanatory theory, than, say, it would be to explain all the behaviours of birds, even if all species were included. Notwithstanding the problems raised by the claims of 'hard' science to be objective, it is nevertheless difficult to regard the bodies of 'abstract knowledge', which various forms of therapy use to legitimate their professional status, as objective. Different therapeutic systems have different perspectives on mental illness, and there is consequently a danger that patients' problems may be interpreted to fit the arguably limited theories employed by one particular therapeutic school, rather than being approached as individual problems.

Some supporters of psychotherapy argue that it adopts a hermeneutic approach to mental illness, and hermeneutics, its supporters would argue, is fundamentally simply a different kind of science which involves '*methodological* self-reflection' (Habermas, 1972, p. 214, emphasis mine). This self-reflection is concerned with the interpretation of subjective experience, forcing the patient to consider that reality is not necessarily as she perceives it; thus therapy may be regarded as a demystification process which demonstrates the essentially false character of consciousness.

Interpretation is an integral part even of science, for facts on their own are of little interest. The fact that the earth is round, not flat, may have little significance to me; but if I wish to sail around the world, matters change, because I can interpret the fact that the earth is round to imply that I shall not risk failing off the edge of the world. Similarly, it is a fact that the M62 runs east to west across the British Isles, linking Hull in the east with Liverpool in the west. But the significance of this fact is depends upon a number of factors. If I simply wish to travel by road from Liverpool to Hull, the fact that the M62 exists will be very useful to me. If, however, in attempting to find the M62 I become lost and when I finally find it I have lost all sense of direction, I might find my initial euphoria on getting onto the M62 rapidly diminishing if I cannot work out which direction I am travelling along it; in order to work this out, I need other information, which I must interpret. If I do not know where I am, I cannot work out if a sign to Leeds means I am travelling east or west; if, however, the sign says Leeds and Manchester, I can interpret this information, providing I have sufficient knowledge of geography, to mean that I am travelling west, and am therefore going in the wrong direction. And even if my geographical knowledge is wrong, and I believe that Leeds is further west than Manchester, a time will come when I will quite simply be proved to be wrong - when I arrive in Liverpool instead of Hull!

In this example I can test my interpretation of the facts against universally agreed explanations. Travelling east to west along the M62, one reaches Leeds before Manchester. Psychotherapeutic theory does not have an agreed body of accepted facts, far less facts which may be tested against demonstrable probabilities and correlations. Therefore, we must ask how one person's 'demystification' of consciousness is any more valid than another's; different schools of psychotherapy use significantly different explanatory models of human nature and psychological functioning; none of them have any significant evidence to support their claims over any other school's. Is there therefore not a risk of creating in any therapeutic interpretation a situation akin to that which occurs when two mirrors are placed opposite each other, producing an illusion of an infinite number of identical images? We know that this is not an accurate reflection of reality, but only an illusion created by a clever optical trick. How does a patient know that the therapist's 'demystification' of her reality is no more than a clever trick, with no more substance than the endlessly repeating images produced by two mirrors? Why should the therapist's 'reality' be any more 'real' than the patient's? Who is to 'demystify' the therapist's interpretation? When do the reflections cease and when does 'reality' appear? And whose 'reality' is it to be? It is surely inevitable that it will be the therapist's 'reality', because the therapist claims to possesses specialist expertise; otherwise, what can legitimise her professional intervention?

> In dynamic psychotherapy there is a hierarchy, just as there is in psychiatry. The psychotherapist is superior, the patient inferior. The psychotherapist, by virtue of his knowledge, training and special insight has access to truths above and beyond the capacity of the patient's. The psychotherapist's truths have a higher truth value than the patient's truths. The psychotherapist interprets the patient's truths and tells him what they really mean. (Rowe, in Masson, 1989, p. 13)

Whatever the specific nature of any form of psychotherapy, the therapist must have an underlying ideology, i.e., a system of beliefs, concerning the nature, causes and possible means of curing and/or alleviating, mental illness, for it is this ideology which legitimises and authorises her professional role as therapist. As a result, psychotherapy may present as fact what is really only one way of looking at the world; or hypotheses may be presented as fact, an example of which, frequently in the news nowadays, is Recovered Memory Syndrome, where a patient 'remembers' being abused by a parent at the instigation of the therapist, who takes child abuse to a be a 'fact' in the causation of certain conditions, rather than one possible causal explanation for them. A case in point is that of the Schwiderski family, in the USA, where Recovered Memory Syndrome is rapidly becoming an extremely contentious issue amongst therapists, families and patients alike. This case was reported in *The Independent* of 17 November, 1994. The Schwiderski family were a prosperous Texan family until they were:

> ... destroyed, persuaded by therapists that they were the victims and perpetrators of sexual and physical abuse as members of a murderous, cannibalistic, satanic cult. (p. 21)

Kathryn Schwiderski, the mother, felt mildly depressed in November, 1985. She sought therapeutic help, and over the next few years was in and out of hospital. Her mental state declined, and in 1989 she was diagnosed as having 'multiple personality disorder, repressed memory syndrome and ritual abuse'. She was said to be. and indeed was convinced of the truth of allegations that she was, a member of a satanic cult and had participated in rape, torture, drugging, human sacrifice, cult programming organised crime, physical and sexual mental abuse, cannibalism, kidnapping, murder and 'other nefarious activities' - although it is difficult to imagine what other nefarious activities there are. Her husband Dennis was investigated by a grand jury on allegations of abusing his son, but the case was not pursued; their elder daughter still believes that she was a member and victim of a cult; the younger daughter has rejected this idea but is estranged from her parents. Kathryn Schwiderski is claimed to believe now that her 'recovered' memories were false, implanted by therapists using hypnotism and drugs; she is now claiming $35 million in damages for what she claims were erroneous diagnoses by her therapists, and for their assurances that their therapy would help her. The defendants have filed a lawsuit denying the allegations.

It is easy to dismiss this case as yet another example of some of the bizarre practices that we may smugly characterise as typical of American 'psychological society'; it is, of course, impossible to tell what the truth of the matter is from a newspaper report. It must not be forgotten, however, that there have been much publicised claims of satanic and ritual abuse made in the UK which have resulted in children being summarily removed from their families, and which have been hotly disputed and in many cases dismissed in court.

What such cases illustrate is the dangers inherent in simplistic claims that the theoretical basis of psychotherapy is objective. A therapist may be able to take a more objective view of someone's problems and situation than somebody more closely involved, such as a friend or loved one; and the theoretical basis of psychodynamic therapy could be argued to be more objective in its stance in that there is more possibility of creating order out of the apparent chaos of much mental illness and producing a coherent and plausible causal story than if, for example, one ascribes it merely to possession by the devil. But objectivity is still to some extent a question of degree, and it cannot be argued that psychodynamic therapy possesses a very high degree of objectivity because it still depends on essentially subjective interpretations of, for example, patients' words and behaviour.

Simplistic claims about the objectivity of psychotherapeutic theories may also be used to legitimate claims to ethical neutrality, and may as a result legitimate positions which are really ideologies, (and all ideologies have moral values built into them). Indeed, it is the moral values built into ideology that influence both the way the therapist views her client's needs and her therapeutic methodology; they determine her definition of treatment, cure and even inform her definition of reality. Therefore, all therapies must embody moral values, and consequently the therapist cannot escape being a moral agent: even the stance of moral neutrality is itself a moral position.

There is a great difference between suggesting a possible alternative explanation or interpretation of reality and maintaining an ideological perspective which allows one person to dominate another. Ricoeur has argued that one feature of:

> ... all ideology is simplifying and schematic. It is a grid or code for giving an overall view, not only of the group, but also of history and, ultimately, of the world. The 'codified' character of ideology is inherent in its justificatory function; its transformative capacity is preserved only on condition that the ideas which it conveys become opinions, that thought loses rigour in order to enhance its social efficacy, as if ideology alone could mediate... systems of thought themselves. Hence anything can become ideological; ethics, religion, philosophy. 'This mutation of a system of thought into a system of belief', says Ellul, 'is the ideological phenomenon'. (Ricoeur, 1988, p. 226)

As a result, therapists may subscribe to a particular explanatory dogma to the exclusion of all other considerations, with potentially disastrous consequences for the patient; even biological medical models, simplistic though they may be at times, allow practitioners to evaluate a given diagnosis and treatment, and if treatment does not work, to reassess either or both treatment and diagnosis, and try something else.

The claim that the 'body of abstract knowledge' which legitimates psychotherapeutic practice is fundamentally objective legitimates the claims made by the practitioners of some forms of therapy that it is, and indeed, must, take an ethically neutral stance to patients' problems. I have already mentioned some objections that may be made against this claim; and there are others. Therapy is concerned with changing behaviour in order to promote greater autonomy; it therefore starts from the assumption that certain aspects of the patient's behaviour and/or thoughts, feelings and desires are undesirable, and, indeed, that autonomy is desirable. As it is change that is sought, this presupposes that any change aimed for is for the better; there is therefore a moral dimension implicit in therapy before it even begins. And it seems somewhat paradoxical to argue that therapy is value-free, because surely the logical extension of this claim is to deny that the patient receiving therapy has any value in the eyes of the therapist, in which case, why is the therapist engaged in therapy with the patient at all, unless it be to effect a form of brainwashing upon her in order to make conform to the dictates of the rest of society - in which case, therapy cannot be argued to be value-free! Stone (1984) has argued that therapists inevitably include moral instructions in their treatment, even though they may not be aware of doing so and that this is unavoidable because patients coming for treatment are bringing with them problems which include a moral dimension, and concepts such as 'better', 'improvement' etc. have implied 'oughts' embedded in them.

But does it matter if therapy cannot claim to be ethically neutral? The answer must be no, *providing that its ethical bias is recognised and acknowledged.* Very few things are ultimately ethically neutral. Even the M62, whose existence may be considered to be an objective fact, has an ethical dimension. Ethical issues arose when the decision to build it was taken - as the many protests currently being made about the expansion of the road-building programme illustrate. It is a social decision to call it the M62 and designate its use as carrying cars and lorries; it is possible, for example, that the Transport Minister could decree that it should no longer be used as means of enabling motorised traffic to travel from Liverpool to Hull; its use could be restricted to cyclists, for example, or it could be designated a 'leisure resource', for the use of roller skaters and skateboarders only.

The acknowledgement that therapy cannot claim to be objective and ethically neutral means that the claims made by different schools of therapeutic practice regarding the mechanisms by which they operate to enable people to change their behaviour in order to increase their autonomy must always be examined. Smail (1987) has argued that:

> There are... three main strands to be identified in the accounts theorists of psychotherapy have put forward of the basic factors involved in change. These suggest that psychotherapeutic change may be brought about through the operation of (a) insight, (b) learning, and (c) love... (p. 81)

I would argue that to make these claims is to lay oneself open to the charge of distorting what is really being done under the name of therapy. These claims inform the theoretical approaches of various types of therapy, but although basing treatment on a specialist therapeutic ideology may be comforting for the therapist, there is no evidence to suggest that any particular form of therapy is any more effective than any other; theoretical orientation appears to be irrelevant to therapeutic outcome. (Luborsky, Singer and Luborsky, 1975; Pilkonis, 1984). Evaluating therapeutic outcomes is notoriously difficult because the methodological problems are considerable, but what does appear to be a critical variable is the therapist; research suggests that irrespective of theoretical orientation, some therapists consistently produce better results than others (Luborsky et al, 1975).

This might appear to suggest that love is a more important agent of change than theoretical perspective, and that a more 'loving' therapist will be more successful. It is upon the claim of love as the modus operandi of therapeutic intervention, which informs some humanistic therapies, that such claims as 'unconditional positive regard' for patients on the behalf of the therapist, and love as a 'corrective emotional experience' are most plausibly made, and there is evidence to suggest that therapists who posses qualities such as empathy, non-possessive warmth and honesty are more effective, not surprisingly, than those who are cold or aloof (Luborsky et al, 1975).

However, the claim that this is love is open to debate. The question of the nature of love is raised once again: in an earlier context I argued that, as Raleigh put it rather more elegantly so many centuries ago, love may be a mixed blessing! It certainly is not an easy quality to define; however, whatever love is, it is a sufficiently special, and some would argue, rare, capacity in humans that it cannot be produced to order. Yet this appears to be what many therapists do claim they are able to do. Therefore, it seems to me that if therapists claim to be offering love as the modus operandi of therapeutic change, they must be referring to it in the sense that some religions do, defining it in the sense of a universal concern for all humankind, irrespective of their 'sins'. I find this a rather worrying attitude. Short of possessing divine characteristics, can one really claim to love every stranger who enters one's office? It might be possible to give 'unconditional, positive regard' to a stranger for an hour (although I would still challenge the universality of this claim), in a very 'unreal' world, lacking many of the qualities of the 'real' world that make life, and the people in it, often so difficult; but in the 'real world, love is not limited to fifty-minute-hour bursts. And it is surely a fundamental attribute of love that it cannot be bought - yet therapy is bought, whether directly by the patient or by the health authority which offers the treatment. Whatever therapy may offer to the mentally ill, it cannot be called love:

> For all the technical mystique psychotherapists have managed to erect around themselves, for all the reverential awe in which they have, sometimes rather sentimentally, managed to intone their rhetoric of love, for all, even, the draining and dedicated effort they put into what is often a very demanding job, they are still but weakly allies. Unlike (in ideal circumstances) family or friends, therapists play an only temporary role in the lives of their patients, and their commitment to help is strictly limited in terms of their actual involvement in patients' lives (were this not so, the job would become demanding beyond endurance). To talk of love in these circumstances is to edge close to hypocrisy... (Smail, 1987, p. 86)

To call what therapists offer their patients 'love' is a distortion of their role. I am not denying that the majority of therapists care about their patients, nor that they do not offer them something which may indeed have a profound effect on them. As a result, this may enable patients to gain self-esteem and confidence, thus possibly greatly altering their lives for the better. This may be provided in a warm, caring environment, where respect is shown for people irrespective of their problems, and support and help is offered to them. But I would argue that even such a situation fails short of being accurately described as 'love'. Love implies a great deal of responsibility; how can someone who sees each patient for perhaps only an hour a week, in very unreal circumstances, and who has the security of knowing that her responsibility has very definite limits to it, truly claim to love her patients? I would argue, therefore, that claiming that therapists can offer all their clients something as complicated and profound as love is unethical; at the best it is a form of verbal inflation, using 'love' where what is really being offered, although very valuable, is only professional care, concern and attention, not love; or else it is just simply immoral. Either way, claiming to offer love runs the risk of raising unrealistic expectations in people who are very vulnerable, and consequently exposes them to the risk of great disappointment, hurt and confusion. Indeed, there appears to be a strange paradox emerging in some areas of mental health orthodoxy, in which those close to the mentally ill, who may well love them are denied any right to seek help for them or be involved in the consideration of treatment and care options because of a conspiracy model of family relationships, while at the same time a stranger with a purely professional relationship with the ill person, and whose claim to legitimacy as a professional may be based on spurious theoretical foundations, may 'legitimately' offer 'love' as a therapeutic mechanism. This situation has elements of *Alice in Wonderland* about it.

The claim that insight into the nature and causes of one's problems is a necessary, and in some cases, sufficient, prerequisite for a patient to be able to effect fundamental changes in her behaviour, rather than simply treating symptoms, as it is argued, physical therapies do, is also open to question. Ryle (1982) has argued that it achieves this by enabling people to reduce the compulsive element that fashions their behaviour and consequently enhance those aspects of their lives that they actively choose to experience, but the extent to which insight gained through psychotherapy enables people to change is debatable. Smail (1987) has made the point that if it were as possible to alter people's behaviour as therapeutic ideology would have us believe, then those in political power would establish the norms of functioning that best suited their needs, and see that people's behaviour was modified to conform with these requirements. He argues that in fact politically dominant groups try to do exactly this, not by changing behaviour but by standardising the environment, because they have a more sophisticated understanding of what 'makes people tick'. It is far easier, he argues, to control what goes into people's heads than it is to alter what has already been entered.

Television is a much more powerful means of ensuring uniformity of belief than was the Inquisition. (p. 87)

113

Consequently, he argues that:

> ... the kind of help [that psychotherapy] offers cannot accurately be seen as one constituting a technology of change. (Smail, 1987, p. 80)

Given that love and insight are not appropriate terms for whatever it is that is the effective element in therapy, it might be more honest to consider that perhaps there is greater currency in the claim that therapy has more in common with magic or religion than anything else. Ellenberger (1970) has argued that the origins of dynamic therapy can be seen in exorcism, where healing was expected to take place when the evil spirits thought to be its cause had been driven from the sufferer; Dicks (in Lowe, 1969) argues that the behavioural sciences are set apart from physical sciences by virtue of having the attributes of a secular priesthood or therapeutae, and likens the concern with achieving mental health to religious concepts of salvation.

Fromm (1950) defined religion as:

> ... any system of thought and action shared by a group which gives the individual a frame of orientation and an object of devotion (p. 21)

It is not difficult to imagine that a distressed person who may at last have found someone to listen to her and apparently take her seriously could come to be part of the 'religion' of therapy, and to regard a therapist in a quasi-mystical light, an 'object of devotion', having at last been provided with a 'frame of orientation' for her life. It could be argued that it is at least as likely that this might prove to be the agent of change for a patient as any of the claims made by psychotherapeutic doctrines.

It is arguable that this is no more reprehensible than bona fide religion; but there is a significant problem, however, and that relates to the nature of God and religion. These are extremely difficult and contentious areas, but however one defines the nature of God, one of her fundamental attributes must surely be that of infallibility, and this confers authority on divine prescriptions. But whilst God may be infallible, therapists are not; indeed, I am not suggesting that the majority of therapists ever consider themselves to be so. Nevertheless, given that theoretical perspectives appear to make no difference to therapeutic outcome, but that the personal attributes of the therapist do, perhaps it is time that therapists ceased to legitimise their professional status by claims to spurious ideologies, and admit that something else is at work in the therapeutic relationship. The pretence of being morally neutral or the practice of presenting hypotheses as verified truths distort the nature of therapy and such dishonesty ultimately does nothing to enhance its status, and may even obscure the good done by realistic, honest practitioners who do not make such unsubstantiated and inflated claims for what they do.

To summarise, therefore, I would argue that psychotherapy cannot justify claims to be ethically neutral because there is a moral aspect involved in all forms of therapy, and that claims that psychotherapy effects changes in patients through insight or love cannot be justified. I would suggest that any form of treatment which may, as some forms of therapeutic practice do, insist on excluding those who perhaps really do love the patient from any information about her treatment, or involvement with those treating her, irrespective of the circumstances, is employing a dangerously simplistic approach to mental illness. I think it is also arguable that psychotherapeutic practitioners are involved in advising their patients, even if such advice is not overt, because whatever may be argued to be the effective agent of change in therapy, it remains the case that the fundamental element in the process is the relationship between therapist and patient. As a result, therapists may exercise considerable authority over their patients. Authority can be considered to be:

> ... the capacity to evoke compliance in others on the basis of formal position and of any psychological inducements, rewards, or sanctions that may accompany formal position. The capacity to evoke compliance without relying upon formal role or the sanctions at its disposal may be called *influence*. When formal position is not necessarily involved, but when extensive sanctions are available, we are concerned with *power*. ... Authority, power and influence are often interlaced in operating situations. (Presthus, 1962, p. 123)

It is not difficult to see how a therapist may exercise any or all of these means of 'evoking compliance' from a distressed patient, depending upon her situation. Thus an NHS therapist may have authority invested in her by virtue of her formal position in a large, powerful organisation, as well as the professional expertise she claims from the theoretical ideology that informs her practice; and the psychological state of her patients may mean that she is able to exert a great deal of influence over them without the need to invoke formal sanctions. Equally, an untrained, self-employed therapist with no formal authority or sanctions may be able to exercise great power over patients who by virtue of their emotional distress and consequent dependency may become very susceptible to the therapist's stronger personality.

The fact that therapists are in a position to exert considerable power and influence over their patients raises issues relating to dependency and exploitation and the consequent diminution of autonomy that may result for some patients. These two issues are closely interrelated, for it is the patient's emotional dependency upon the therapist that leaves her vulnerable to being exploited.

Psychotherapy claims to have as its ultimate goal the promotion of autonomy, but it is often the case that the influence which the therapist may exert over patients reduces their autonomy and leads instead to dependency and the exercise of a considerable degree of paternalism on the part of the therapist. This is not a criticism limited to therapy alone, of course. Neither is it necessarily an indictment of therapy. I have argued throughout this book that a definition of autonomy that restricts it merely to the absence of external constraints acting on the mentally ill is a moral opting-out on the part of those who have the responsibility of providing treatment and care for them, because the internal constraints operating on the sick person may be so great that she effectively has little or no real autonomy. Someone suffering from agoraphobia, for example, who cannot leave her house even though she both wants and needs to, can hardly be said to be autonomous. Illness may therefore justify paternalistic intervention; such intervention would satisfy Komrad's (1983) view that paternalistic intervention is a response to incapacity rather than a negation of an individual's rights. The question is, however, what degree of paternalism is justified, and what type.

Any treatment for illness of any kind may involve a temporary reduction in a patient's autonomy, part of which will result from the unequal distribution of power which is a characteristic of all professional/layperson relationships, but it is arguable that psychotherapy raises particular problems which derive from the intensity of the relationship. However, when the therapist is nurturing and supportive, developing and strengthening the patient's self-esteem, with the ultimate aim of creating a greater capacity for independent, emotionally self-reliant living, a temporary loss of autonomy is not cause for concern. Indeed, such a temporary loss of autonomy may be necessary to enable progress towards regaining full autonomy. It may also be the case that a patient's problems are so great when she enters therapy that she has little real autonomy, and thus dependence on the therapist may be no worse than the loss of autonomy she experiences as a result of her condition, and at least therapeutic help offers the possibility of bringing about an improvement in her condition. Therefore, the temporary restriction of autonomy is not a sufficient argument against therapeutic intervention. But nonetheless, as with all forms of treatment for mental illness, it is necessary to be aware of the potential for abuse; there is a great deal of justifiable concern about the diminution of autonomy that may result from paternalistic attitudes in mainstream psychiatry; the possibility of loss of autonomy from negative paternalism on the part of therapists must be considered to be equally worrying. Paternalism that is expressed in a negative form is a particularly destructive form of abuse; a therapist who appears condescending, who relies too heavily on her specialist, 'superior' theoretical knowledge and denies the validity of her patient's perception of her experiences may destroy any latent self-esteem a patient has and completely remove her capacity for autonomous action.

It might be argued that a patient in therapy can choose to leave, which is not always the case in mainstream psychiatry, where patients may be sectioned and compelled to take medication. But one of the most pernicious aspects of negative paternalism is that a patient may *not* be psychologically able to choose to leave the therapeutic relationship because she has become totally dependent on the therapist;

this may result in cases where the therapist presents herself as a benign but all-powerful being, and the patient may elevate her to the status of an indispensable 'guru' and depend upon her 'support' in all aspects of her life. This is not a nurturing paternalism, but rather one where the therapist is indulging her ego needs at her patients' expense. In such cases, there is the risk of long-term dependency developing on the part of the patient. This is arguably more of a risk in private therapy, where patients pay for treatment, than it is in NHS therapy, which is strictly rationed because of limited resources. In the case of private therapy, however, it is entirely possible that the creation of long-term dependency is of benefit to the therapist, who will obviously earn more the longer a patient stays in therapy. The danger arises because there is no externally imposed constraint on the duration of private therapy, and consequently it can be continued ad infinitum if the patient is willing to go on paying for it, irrespective of whether it is necessary. But does this really matter? If someone is willing to pay for a commodity or service that she wants, she has the right to do so, providing that it is not illegal. Why should therapy be any different from, say, hairdressing or holidays? This is a valid argument, up to a point. People rely on a great variety of things to ease the stresses of life; religion, sport, alcohol, food; the list is virtually endless. Why should therapy be an exception? But a therapist does have a duty not to encourage an unnecessary dependency in her patients because the aim of therapy is to develop a patient's emotional autonomy; therefore, whilst it is arguable that if prolonged or even permanent therapy is the best option for a very vulnerable patient who, without such support, would be at risk of suffering far greater distress, this is a different situation from encouraging dependency when a patient could manage without therapy. And there are pernicious arguments that can easily be used by unscrupulous therapists to persuade patients to continue therapy when it is no longer necessary, or when they cannot afford it. A patient may be presented with the argument that her wish to terminate therapy is really a way of avoiding the really painful issues that she now realises she cannot avoid facing up to if she remains in therapy; or she may be told that if she were really serious about her desire to take charge of her life, she would somehow find the money to continue therapy; such arguments may appear entirely plausible coming from an 'expert' upon whom the patient has come to depend, and who claims the specialist knowledge to make professional judgements that the patient is unqualified to make. Therefore, it is ethically necessary for a therapist to say what she is doing and not to claim that she is doing something that she is not doing.

Another possible consequence of dependency, and, indeed, it is arguable, of theoretical perspectives which argue that the basis of therapeutic change is love, is that of sexual exploitation of patients. This is not limited to psychotherapeutic treatment because such abuse can occur in any relationship between a patient and anyone treating her; but the nature of psychotherapy is such that might appear to be easier to justify a sexual relationship within a psychotherapeutic setting than in others. Research suggests that this is a significant issue in psychotherapy. (See, for example, Pope, Schover and Levenson, 1980; Pope, Keith-Spiegel and Tabachnik, 1986; Gartrell et al], 1986; Langs, 1985; Holyroyd and Brodsky, 1977; Kardener, Fuller and Mensch, 1973; Hall and Hare-Mustin, 1983; and Furrow, 1980). In an editorial of 6.4.94, *The Independent* commented on a survey carried out by British Psychological Society that reported that out of 1,000 NHS psychologists, 40 had sexually abused their patients; one in four had a patient who had had an affair with a previous therapist.

Sexual relationships between patient and therapist most commonly involve female patients and male therapists and they pose problems within a therapeutic relationship because sex is generally a complicated matter for human beings, involving a great deal more than the simple gratification of a physical need. The attitude that sexual relationships between therapist and patient are unethical rests on the belief that such relationships are inevitably injurious to the patient, and that they are therefore exploitative. The issue is bound up with wider issues relating to male and female attitudes to sex. It is generally female patients who become involved with male therapists, and this leads to the argument that such a situation must necessarily be exploitative of the woman because women are generally not seen as desiring sex simply as an end in itself; men, on the other hand, are often categorised in this way. Consequently, the 'he should be so lucky' view may be taken if the issue of a male patient seduced by a female therapist is considered. Women, on the other hand, are considered to be victims in any sexual relationship with a male therapist; there are echoes here of the Victorian belief that no 'decent' woman could possibly enjoy sex. If women were to cease to be seen as victims of the sexual attentions of men, it might be argued that a sexual relationship in the context of a therapeutic relationship would not necessarily be wrong; that far from being damaging to the patient, and exploiting her, a sexual relationship might, in some cases be therapeutic by putting her in touch with her sexuality; or allowing her to experience a satisfying erotic relationship. This is exactly the claim made by those who defend such behaviour. Levitt (1977), for example, has argued that sexual relationships between therapists and patients facilitates transference, increases self-esteem and breaks down inhibitions. This is a somewhat dubious argument because the transference and counter-transference that occur within therapy may produce feelings which are the product of fantasy. Consequently, it is hard to see how a sexual relationship can be considered to facilitate transference when it is more likely to be a product of it. And as Furrow (1980) has noted:

> ... most erotic breaches of the therapist-patient relationship occur with women who are physically attractive; almost never with the aged, the infirm or the ugly. (p. 34)

We might also ask who is to define a 'satisfying' erotic relationship, and satisfying to whom? It must be assumed that no therapist is going to offer a patient a sexual relationship unless he desires it himself, and therefore it must be assumed that this would primarily be meeting his needs, because the therapist/patient relationship involves a power relationship in which the patient is the less powerful partner. An unequal distribution of power is not restricted to therapeutic situations, of course; in 'real' life, many couples enter into relationships where there is an unequal distribution of power that may prove to be extremely damaging to the unequal partner. But in these situations, the more powerful partner is not claiming professional authority and power to help the less powerful partner. In a therapeutic relationship, irrespective of the underlying ideology that informs the therapist's practice, this is exactly what is claimed by the therapist. And not only is the power relationship within a therapeutic relationship unequal, one partner is at least distressed, and possibly very ill; it must be assumed that this is the patient rather than the therapist, and so it puts the patient at a considerable disadvantage when it comes to making a rational decision as to whether or not to engage in a sexual relationship.

In view of all these factors, therefore, I would argue that to engage in a sexual relationship with a patient must be considered to be an abuse of power by the therapist, even in those cases where the patient appears freely to consent to and desire such a relationship; this applies regardless of whether the relationship involves a male therapist and female patient; a female therapist and male patient or a homosexual relationship, because the essential issue is that of the imbalance of power between therapist and patient, irrespective of attitudes to male and female sexuality.

Exploitation is not limited to sexual abuse; it is arguable that unjustified claims for the theoretical basis of therapeutic intervention and the moral neutrality and objectivity of therapeutic practice are all fundamental forms of exploitation which operate by making false promises and raising unrealistic expectations in vulnerable people in order to justify the therapist's role, and ultimately, her job; this is a similar kind of exploitation to that which results from the unjustifiable claims made for miracle cures that are administered by pills or medicines, which similarly exploit the vulnerable and incredulous. But there are other forms of exploitation, a primary one being financial; this is closely related to the issues raised by the encouragement of dependency, and is specifically only relevant to those who see a therapist privately, for which they must pay; however, this is a growing trend, both amongst NHS patients who cannot receive the therapy they decide would benefit them, and amongst increasing numbers of people who have been led to believe, rightly or wrongly, that therapy will somehow enhance their lives. There will always be a risk of financial exploitation by unscrupulous practitioners in any therapeutic relationship where the professional's income depends upon the duration of treatment. This is not restricted to therapeutic treatment, but once again, given the likelihood of a high degree of dependency on the part of those seeking therapy, it is arguably a greater risk in this form of treatment that in some others.

There is also another concern about therapeutic treatment of mental illness, which in some respects can be considered to be the opposite of concerns relating to the diminution of a patient's autonomy. This is 'victim-blaming', which some would argue may result from the fact that psychotherapy basically locates the problems which confront the mentally ill within themselves; consequently, they are considered to be ultimately responsible for dealing with their problems. Such a perspective has been criticised by those holding very different view of the world and the nature of society. Some Marxists have criticised psychotherapy on the grounds that it diverts the focus of the cause of human misery away from its 'real' cause, considered to be the class divisions of society, onto the individual; in attempting to 'cure' the individual, therefore, psychotherapy is considered to be merely an attempt to enable people to tolerate that which is intolerable. The same argument may be made against drug treatment and ECT, of course, and it is similar to the argument that it is justifiable to lobotomise a woman whose husband's sadistic behaviour is making her life intolerable, on the grounds that if she can do nothing about it, she can at least be rendered less susceptible to it. I do not propose to discuss the claim that it is the class structure of society which is responsible for human misery, but there are indeed dangers in locating a person's problems entirely within herself and ignoring external factors which may cause or at least exacerbate her problems. This is as simplistic an approach to mental illness as any crude medical model, a criticism with which many therapists would probably agree; nevertheless, in its more extreme forms, psychotherapy can be argued to locate the locus of responsibility for achieving an improvement in her condition firmly with the patient. This may be a justified argument in a minority of cases where the patient is not really very ill, but in the majority of cases of extreme distress it is a distortion of the truth that may have terrible consequences for the patient.

Consideration of the above issues leads to the acknowledgement that psychotherapists are bound by the duties of beneficence and nonmaleficence just as much as any other practitioners. Therefore, promoting unnecessary dependency, making unjustifiable claims as to what they are doing and engaging in a sexual relationship or any other activity which primarily meets the therapist's needs are acts which may be considered to be harmful and unlikely to promote the patient's autonomy, which is the primary aim of therapy; they must therefore be considered to break the injunction of Primum non nocere, considered by Ross (1930) to take precedence over all other duties, all things being equal. Equally, however, a simplistic approach to the problems of mental illness which ascribes too great a degree of autonomy to the mentally ill and consequently essentially holds the sufferer responsible for her illness and which may exclude those who love her from involvement in her care, again justified by a spurious claim on the patient's autonomy, can hardly claim to be observing a duty of beneficence towards a patient. Such a victim-blaming approach must surely exacerbate the already devastating experience of mental illness for many sufferers.

Peter Lomas, in *The Case for a Personal Psychotherapy*, (1981) has addressed the issues raised by psychotherapy which relies too heavily on theory to the detriment of the acknowledgement of what he calls the 'ordinary'. He argues that the reliance on therapeutic theory is made possible because:

> We seek someone who knows. No one conducts this search with greater desperation than the man who has lost his way and needs a guide. Such a man is all too ready to impute special qualities to a prospective helper. (Lomas, 1981, p. 27)

Thus the theories upon which therapeutic systems are built enable their practitioners to construct powerful professional edifices around themselves and perpetuate their position of superior knowledge and power because the therapist becomes the 'one who knows'. The consequence of this, Lomas argues, is the idealisation of therapeutic language and a consequent assumption of inequality between therapist and patient. This idealisation of both therapeutic language and therapist results in the therapist's interpretation of 'reality' having greater validity than the patient's. The problem with therapeutic interpretation, however, is that it is dealing essentially with interpretations of subconscious behaviour, rather than verifiable external phenomena such as the shape of the earth, or the ability of MI5 to direct mind-destroying rays through a television set to obliterate the patient's brain. It is theoretically possible to demonstrate that the earth is round, not flat, and that MI5 does not direct brain destroying rays through television sets, and indeed could not do so even if it wished to, because the technology does not exist to enable it to (although the latter is harder to do, because it is easier prove the existence of something than its non-existence. Of course, it might quite plausibly be argued, on the evidence of the quality of many television programmes and the incomprehensible behaviour of significant numbers of people, that in fact MI5 is very successfully doing just this!) But when it comes to interpreting the meaning of subconscious motivation, things become much more difficult, because there is no generally accepted theory of psychological functioning and dysfunctioning that has been proved to account for the workings of the human psyche. Interpretation of the meaning of subconscious motivation must inevitably be regarded as subjective, therefore, and it is not difficult to see how, if a therapist allows her 'system of thought' to mutate into a 'system of belief', the therapeutic technique of interpretation can begin to resemble the imposition of dogma rather than an exploration of her patient's illusions. It is the therapist's lengthy training which is supposed to prevent her from doing this; but it may well be the case that what this training is really doing is to induct her into an ideology which is really no more than another belief system, whatever its claims to scientific objectivity may be.

There is thus a paradox emerging, best described by what Lomas has called the 'conflict between ordinary and special behaviour'. (Lomas, 1981, p. 22) This conflict, I believe, lies at the heart of the debate about psychotherapy because the therapeutic relationship is essentially ambiguous. It must be 'special' in some way, different from an 'ordinary' relationship, or how else can it be justified in a society which has come to depend upon and demand specialist expertise? In a predominantly secular society its difference must be located in the specialist theories which underpin its ideologies. But these specialist theories appear to be irrelevant to the outcome of therapy, so how can the claim that the therapeutic relationship makes to be 'special', different from 'ordinary' ways of helping distressed people, be justified if there is no evidence that any particular form of therapy is any more effective than another, and if the qualities that patients value in a therapeutic relationship are those 'ordinary' qualities which one might expect to be provided by those who love or care deeply for them but who may not be in the best position to provide all the help that the seriously mentally ill require?

Lomas has illustrated this conflict between 'ordinary and special' behaviour with an example from his own experience.

> ... I was seeing a very sick young woman who suffered from anorexia nervosa. ...she was preoccupied with suicide. I felt that she taunted me with the threat of suicide and played on my anxiety. I came to an 'agreement' with her that she was entirely responsible for her life and an 'agreement' with myself that, in so far as I could, I would not worry about the possibility of suicide.
>
> At the end of one particular session she said good-bye with a peculiar emphasis. Her tone of voice had an air of finality about it. I did nothing except to respond with my usual 'good-bye'. She then went home and killed herself.
>
> It is of course easy to be wise after the event and no event promotes such a tendency to have regrets than suicide. Perhaps it was not possible for me to have helped this woman by any measures, but I now believe that anything I might have done or said would have been preferable to the action I took. It would have been better to hug her, or hit her ... And I think my response was wrong because it was so totally lacking in spontaneity. Not only did I behave with professional formality but I acted rigidly in accordance with a planned programme of my own making. (ibid., p. 22)

The lack of spontaneity on the behalf of therapists can be argued to be a consequence of the limitations of the concept of transference, which treats the patient's reactions to the therapist as unconsciously influenced by earlier experiences; this effectively denies the validity of the patient's 'ordinary' experience. The concept of transference also enables the therapist to retreat from acknowledging a shared humanity with her patient, enabling her to regard herself instead as a symbol upon which the patient relives experiences and responses which legitimately belong to another time, place and person. The therapist is therefore able to deny the relevance of 'ordinary' experience and that there is a non-transference relationship in the therapeutic situation which might need to be investigated; she can thus retreat from engagement with issues her patient may consider to be important. In so doing, not only may the therapist define the agenda to be addressed in the therapeutic arena, her perception of 'reality' may triumph regardless. Thus elegant theories and charismatic practitioners may command the attention and distort our perception just as much as the promise of chemical 'magic bullets' or ECT may do. The results of a therapeutic practice which relies on a simplistic application of method or ideology at the expense of taking seriously the patient's perception of her experiences can be very destructive; and therapy wrongly or unscrupulously used is just as harmful as the uninformed and insensitive use of drugs and ECT.

It was disturbing and unsettling. Like brain washing. Confusion.

It took me 65 sessions to feel sure that I could not continue with the Kleinian analyst even thought I felt unhappy about it from the first session. Like some previous therapists, *he* was convinced and wanted to convince me that I needed his help. (Emphasis mine)

Analytical psychotherapy was done in such a way as to make me feel that my judgement was impaired in areas where it wasn't, i.e. insistence that transference had taken place. (Rogers, Pilgrim and Lacey, 1993, pp. 152, 153)

There is considerable evidence that psychotherapy may cause deterioration in a patient's condition. (Mays and Frank, 1985). Symptoms, far from improving, may become worse or new symptoms may appear. Thus depression may worsen, self-esteem may plummet, the patient may begin to act out her impulses. In extreme cases, according to Robitscher (1980), therapy may precipitate madness; in some cases of schizophrenia, therapy may precipitate a psychotic breakdown. Lambert, Bergin and Collins (1977) conducted a survey of therapeutic outcomes in various types of therapies and concluded that anxiety, depression, psychosomatic and psychotic reactions could all result from treatment; Bergin (1971) coined the term 'deterioration effect' for this, and it is estimated that approximately 10% of patients receiving therapy experience this, although it has not proved possible to determine the extent to which therapy can be claimed to be responsible for causing deterioration in patients' conditions. However, various researchers have concluded that although patient variables such as the degree of disturbance, desire to change and ego-strength may defeat any hopes of treatment succeeding, there is also a range of therapist variables which are likely to have a detrimental rather than a beneficial influence on therapeutic outcome. These are: misjudgement of the appropriateness of therapy or persistence with inappropriate methods; using therapeutic techniques which make the patient's condition worse; and personal characteristics or countertransference attitudes of the therapist which have a detrimental effect on the patient. (See, for example, Dahlberg, 1970; Davidson, 1977; Langs, 1985; Redlich and Mollica, 1976; Stone, 1984)

123

Nonetheless, there is also a substantial amount of evidence which suggests that for a significant number of people, psychotherapy is helpful, and that patients who undergo therapy, of whatever sort, do better than those who do not (Luborsky, Singer and Luborsky, 1975; Shapiro and Shapiro, 1982; Sloane et al, 1975; Smith, Glass and Miller, 1980). A survey carried out for MIND in 1990 reported that out of a sample of 274 people questioned who had received some form of psychotherapy, 74.1% were either 'satisfied' or 'very satisfied'; this compared with 68.8% who found anti-depressants 'helpful' or 'very helpful'; 56.8% who reported that anti-psychotic medication was 'helpful' or 'very helpful' and 42.8% who reported ECT as being 'helpful' or 'very helpful'. (Rogers, Pilgrim and Lacey, 1993, pp. 151.) There is no information supplied about the nature of the conditions for which the respondents were being treated, nor about age, sex, social group etc. And it might be argued that there is a difference between 'satisfied/unsatisfied' and 'helpful/unhelpful'). Comments included:

Understanding, validation and acceptance of experience from my perspective. Opportunity to talk over stresses in social and family life and traumatic experiences in psychiatric system. Complete confidentiality - seen as an individual, not a class of symptoms. Focus of discussion - my experiences from a personal point of view rather than my behaviour from others' points of view. No value judgements made, unlike my experiences with nurses and psychiatrists.

There is more of a personal approach and you get to know your counsellor more so than you would your psychiatrist, and there is more time to discuss your problems.

I felt much more responsible for what happens, in non-medical settings. This enabled me to find ways of dealing with my problems.

An explanation that I could understand for psychotic episodes. Continuity of care. A feeling that the healthy side of me was being encouraged and supported. Making it safe for me to be a bit mad sometimes without recourse to medication. Restored my faith in myself after negative psychiatric diagnoses. (ibid., pp. 154-155)

If traditional theoretical models of therapy are of doubtful value but people value and may benefit from some form of 'talking therapy', what model should inform therapeutic practice? Lomas argues for a personal psychotherapy, a therapeutic approach that, amongst other things, appreciates the value of the 'ordinary':

The failure to appreciate the worth of an ordinary human being stems, I think, from the inclination to lose our sense of balance when presented with someone or something which *commands* our attention. We are drawn, like moths to a candle, towards those who are reputed to possess superior qualities, and we will all too readily listen to a voice that is strident rather then wise. ... And so ... we idealise the powerful, those whom we have cause to fear or from whom, in our vulnerability, we need help. But to the extent that we focus upon the obvious and disturbing we neglect the ordinary; we are unable to see the significance of that which presents itself quietly, with humility or sophistication; we are blinded by the bright light and cannot perceive those things which are revealed in a gentler illumination. ... In sum I would say that ordinariness is the absence of idealisation; it is a state of mind where everything is given its proper due and appropriate meaning in relation to the whole. (Lomas, 1981, pp. 28, 35)

The comments from satisfied users quoted above suggest that the valued aspects of the 'talking' therapies relate to 'ordinary' qualities such as the sense of being seen, and cared about, as individuals, and about being listened to. These qualities are not dependent upon specialist theories and knowledge and professional training; they are all attributes that loved ones and good friends possess. But not everyone is fortunate enough to have loved ones and friends willing and able to offer this type of support; and even in cases where they do, this may not necessarily be the best option for providing help for someone who is seriously ill. Those closely involved with a mentally ill person may not have the objectivity required to distance themselves from entanglement with her problems; they may be too involved with other people in her life who are involved in or affected by her problems; and in cases of very serious disturbance they may not have the skills required to provide the type of help necessary. A personal psychotherapy such as Lomas describes may be what is needed: Hobson (1985) has stated that:

... the centre, the basis of my approach to psychotherapy [is] a developing relationship. What I say and do in therapy is aimed at promoting understanding: a 'conversation', a meeting between two experiencing subjects... psychotherapy is a matter of promoting a personal dialogue. (p. xiii)

Even if a model of a 'personal psychotherapy' is adopted, it is not possible to remove the imbalance of power in the therapeutic relationship; simply by virtue of being ill or extremely distressed, one member of the pair will be less empowered than the other, and one would expect this to be the patient rather than the therapist. But in such approaches to therapy as those of Lomas and Hobson the source of the imbalance of power is external to the therapeutic relationship rather than a constituent feature of the therapeutic process. In a world where there is no longer a formal moral framework to guide actions and increasingly the only values are those of the market and the pursuit of individual gratification, there are few

125

forms of support or comfort on offer to the distressed; a personal psychotherapy may be the best alternative that we can offer the vulnerable. There is therefore a case to be made for therapeutic treatment based on Lomas' concept of a *personal psychotherapy*, rather than informed by doctrinaire theories and ideologies. This will not be easy to achieve; a few gifted, caring practitioners do succeed, but because of the immense demands that are made on therapists confronted by the often unrelenting emotional demands from vulnerable, dependent patients, it is entirely understandable why therapists may take refuge in sterile theories. Therefore, on the pragmatic assumption that not all therapists will achieve the saint-like qualities demanded of them, there must be an acknowledgement of the potential for the abuse of power in the therapeutic relationship, all the more insidious because it may be more effectively hidden than in the physical therapies. Consequently, I think it is naive to assume that because therapy is a 'talking cure' it is necessarily more humane than physical treatments; if there were any doubt about this, it is only necessary to read Masson (1989) for an example of some of the gross abuse that has been inflicted on vulnerable people in the name of therapy,

Mental illness (indeed, all illness) disrupts an individual's 'personal narrative' - her story - and if the resulting chaos that ensues can be made more meaningful by being put into the perspective of a coherent narrative, then the patient may be greatly helped; such an approach will at the very least accord a degree of respect for the patient that results from being listened to and taken seriously. Psychotherapy can therefore offer much-needed support to the mentally ill; it may enable people to explore the root causes of their problems rather than merely alleviating the symptoms by taking drugs; it may help them to develop greater autonomy and therefore to gain more control over their lives; in short, used responsibly, it may offer hope to many ill people. Neither need psychotherapy and physical therapy be mutually exclusive forms of treatment; there are pros and cons to be considered when contemplating either form of treatment for mental illness. None of the issues raised by the practice of psychotherapy as a form of treatment for mental illness is exclusive to therapeutic treatment; they are all raised by other forms of treatment. Neither therapeutic treatment nor the physical therapies has a monopoly on the potential for abuse; the important issue is that the potential for abuse inherent in psychotherapy should be acknowledged, but because the fundamental aspect of therapy is often identified as human contact, which implies a negotiated, shared experience of exploration, a seeking after truth, I think these issues are too often ignored or denied. It is easy to regard drugs and ECT as forms of 'chemical straitjackets', imposed upon people in order to subdue and control them, and completely ignore the fact that human psychological intervention and influence may have the potential for abuse as devastating as any dangerous drug. And it must not be forgotten that to offer maximum support and help, therapeutic intervention for the mentally ill must be provided within a comprehensive system of care:

Just that two hours of his time, and then followed hell.

I wandered around the streets crying after every session. (Rogers, Pilgrim and Lacey, 1993, pp. 152-4)

It is as pointless and unethical offering an hour of therapy a week and leaving people to cope alone with their problems the rest of the time as it is to prescribe psychotropic medication and ignore all the other factors which may exacerbate their condition.

The rights and needs of patients undergoing therapy must also be seen in the wider social context of everyone's rights, just as is the case with other forms of therapy. Thus although confidentiality is a prime requirement of the therapeutic relationship, it cannot be justified to put the patient's right to confidentiality above the right of others not to be harmed. In cases where there is serious concern that a patient undergoing psychotherapy might harm someone, that must be considered to be sufficient reason for taking action, even if it results in the patient's right to confidentiality being over-ridden. (See, for example, Tarasoff, 1974)

Psychotherapy raises the same ethical issues as other forms of treatment for mental illness, and like them, it has strengths and weaknesses; it may do great harm, it may offer great help, it may not make much difference. In considering whether it is an effective and appropriate treatment for mental illness, the same conclusions must be drawn as were reached in the consideration of physical treatments: it depends. The only certain conclusion that can be drawn about psychotherapeutic treatment is that the issues it raises must be acknowledged and considered.

Consideration of the ethical issues raised by psychotherapy leads to the conclusion that there are ethical constraints which must be imposed upon it in order that it may be used ethically and in the most beneficial way to promote the greatest degree of autonomy possible for any individual patient. To summarise, I suggest therefore that:

- There must be greater honesty about the limitations of therapy; it cannot be considered to be all-explaining, always right and always helpful, any more than any other form of treatment. Neither can it be held to be either objective or loving in the full sense of these terms.
- Therapists must therefore acknowledge their own values and how they influence and bias their therapeutic practice.
- Psychotherapeutic treatment should not be divorced from the wider context in which mental illness occurs - i.e. the family and society in general and therefore it must operate within a general set of rights.
- Psychotherapy should form part of a coherent plan for treatment and support.

- The potential for abuse of psychotherapeutic treatment must be recognised and acknowledged; consequently, therapists should be held professionally and legally accountable. This requires that there should be a system of registration of therapists which would enable controls to be exerted over who may operate as a therapist. Any registration system should be enforced by a body which has the powers to impose recognised training requirements and sanctions, including that of de-registration in cases of serious abuse by therapists.

It is only by acknowledging the limitations and risks inherent in therapy that its potential for abuse may more effectively be guarded against and its potential to do good may be realised.

8 Community care

The implementation of the policy of community care for the mentally ill, which has been government policy since the 1962 Hospital Plan was launched, was supposed to herald a new, more humane era in the treatment of the mentally ill. The overall plan for mental health care included short-term treatment in district general hospitals and outpatients departments, (a provision similar to that offered for any other illnesses), and also the provision by local government of a network of hostels, day care centres, sheltered workshops and social work support for the chronically mentally ill. However, the rationale behind this new approach was influenced by a variety of factors, and not motivated purely by the desire to improve life for the mentally ill; these included the acknowledgement of the appalling conditions in some 'asylums'; the work of Goffman and others, which argued for the deleterious effects of institutionalisation on the individual; the advent of anti-psychotic drugs, which for a while appeared, according to the psychiatric profession, to offer 'cures' for mental illness and certainly enabled more people to cope with life outside an institution, and, not least, cost. It combined idealism and the desire to cut costs:

> By bringing the [mentally ill] back into the community, by enlisting the goodwill and the desire to serve, the ability to understand which is found in every neighbourhood, we shall meet the challenge which such ... persons present ... and at the same time ease the financial burden of their confinement in fixed institutions. (Alper, 1973, pp. vii-viii)

There were thus some unlikely bedfellows united in arguing for a policy of community care to be implemented and this has been an underlying cause of some of the chaos that currently surrounds its implementation. It must also be acknowledged that Alper's vision of communities seems to be based on a Utopian fantasy rather than reality. The chaos has been exacerbated by the confusion surrounding the definition of 'community care'. The term appears along with the terms 'de-hospitalisation', 'de-institutionalisation' and 'normalisation' throughout the literature on contemporary mental health care; these terms are frequently used interchangeably, yet they are rarely defined. Chameleon-like, they take on whatever meaning a particular author chooses. Bachrach, considering the term 'de-institutionalisation', gives a sample of meanings from professional and popular literature which includes:

moving mental patients from enormous, remote hospitals into small community residences

a euphemism for official cruelty

a synonym for "homeless"

[a term that should be replaced by] "transinstitutionalisation" to indicate that "the chronically mentally ill patient had his locus of living and care transferred from a single lousy institution to multiple wretched ones".

both a process and a system for helping the seriously emotionally disturbed person achieve his or her right to as normal a life as possible.

"a policy fashion" that, by condemning traditional care for the mentally disabled "romanticises the benefits of community-based care". (Bachrach, 1989, p. 163)

A lack of defined meanings for these terms is perhaps unsurprising, given the different aims of those arguing for a policy of 'community care'. Barham has observed that:

The concept of community care did not seem to require much specification simply because the character of the ex-mental patient in the community remained to a large degree unspecified. The distinctive character of the mental patient of a previous era could, it was believed, now be erased from the script of social life and replaced by a less remarkable or distinguishable persona. Community-care facilities at this time were envisaged as transitional stepping-stones between a brief period of hospitalisation and full reintegration into the community. (Barham, 1992, p. 12)

But the definition of community care has significant implications for its implementation. At the heart of the issue lies the concept of community, defined by the Shorter Oxford English Dictionary as: *the quality of appertaining to all in common; common character [and] identity.* This definition implies a set of shared characteristics and interests; these may be very broadly defined and consequently encompass very large numbers, as in the idea of the human community. By narrowing the boundaries and defining the shared characteristics much more closely, it can exclude the majority of people, as, for example, the community comprised of members of the Viola da Gamba Society.

Thus when talking about community care, the nature of the community that is to provide the setting for care needs to be carefully considered; there is a great difference between community care as a more intimate form of institutional care and as an attempt to achieve integration into the wider community of humanity. The latter definition implies that a policy of community care for the mentally ill will encompass the acknowledgement of a shared common character with the rest of the community, the basic characteristic here being that of a common humanity. Community care, therefore, does not vary only according to geography and size of institutions. Considering treatment facilities for the mentally ill, Ramon has defined the following terms:

> De-hospitalisation implies either the eventual closure of psychiatric hospitals or reducing considerably the very central place currently occupied by these hospitals in the current British psychiatric system;

> De-institutionalisation means that the new settings and structures of the psychiatric system are constructed in such a way as to prevent the continuation of personal and social marginalisation of people who suffer from mental distress;

> Normalisation is concerned with actively ensuring that these people will have opportunities for ordinary living. (Ramon, 1991, p. xiv)

'Community care' can therefore refer to any or all of these, depending upon how 'community' is defined. However, I would suggest that the fundamental ethical issue which must be addressed here relates to the issue of what it is to be human; specifically, we must address the issue raised by Barham of the specification of the character of the 'ex-mental patient' discharged into the care of the community. Is this specification to be that of another human being, albeit with problems and perhaps certain disabilities which may entail her needing help and support, or is it to remain that of a marginalised, perhaps less than fully human individual?

Bott (1976) has argued that the institutionalisation of the chronically mentally ill is fundamentally a social process which reflects the nature of the society which produces the asylum, rather than simply the properties of mental hospitals per se. The social process that Bott identifies as responsible for this situation is the marginalisation of the mentally ill, which causes them to be defined as 'other', and results in their devaluation. She argues that the claim that merely closing mental hospitals will result in de-institutionalisation is unlikely to be realised unless the problems of the chronically mentally ill are addressed in wider social terms.

Bott's argument extends the concept of 'institutionalisation' from suffering the pernicious effects of being incarcerated in a closed society, (which is a well-documented phenomenon) to being excluded from full membership of the human community. If we retain an attitude that perceives the mentally ill as being so different from 'normal' people that they become less than human, the concept of community care in the wider sense of 'community' - that of a shared humanity becomes meaningless; or at best the attempt to introduce 'community care' means that, as there is in fact no community in which the mentally ill can be cared for, because their perceived difference excludes them from the human community, they will in all likelihood suffer a degree of degradation equal to what was experienced in the worst of the asylums. It would appear that all too often this is exactly what the mentally ill are experiencing.

Scull has remarked that:

> This transfer of care [to the community] was supposed to mark a glorious Paradise Regained for the denizens of the backwards, and to preserve future generations of "mental patients" from the damaging effects of institutionalisation. Instead, as we are now all too acutely aware, the outcome has been "the wholesale neglect of the mentally ill, especially the chronic patient and the deinstitutionalised". (Scull, 1991, p. 307)

Scull is writing in an American context, but the situation is no better in the UK; community care certainly does not appear to be achieving a 'glorious Paradise Regained' for the mentally ill; indeed, if the current spate of horror stories given significant prominence in the press is anything to judge by, in some parts of Britain, the overall system of care for the mentally ill bears a far greater resemblance to hell than it does to paradise. Provision for the care of the mentally ill in some areas of Britain is in a state of crisis; the Fifth Biennial Report of the Mental Health Act Commission for 1991-93 has reported a 'crisis in inner-city mental health services':

> Implementation of Section 117 Aftercare and the Care Programme Approach [of the MHA (1983)] is barely evident in many inner city acute units. The high morbidity levels in the inner city populations, lack of alternatives to admission, problems of homelessness, and poor community service, are contributing factors to the crisis in inner-city mental health services. (Mental Health Act Commission, 1993)

The report is a damning indictment of the lack of provision for mental health care. The crisis in the acute wards of the district general hospitals in turn feeds the crisis in community care. Professor Elaine Murphy, vice-chairman of the Mental Health Act Commission and Professor of Psychiatry at Guy's Hospital, London, was quoted in the national press as dreading being the on-call consultant at weekends when conditions in the hospital could resemble 'Bedlam', and staff had to search for beds and decide who was the least disturbed patient to move to another institution or discharge. These prematurely discharged patients then make their way into the 'care' of the 'community', irrespective of whether they are really ready for this move or whether plans for their care in the community have been sorted out.

> If you have someone who is suicidal waiting to come in, and you have someone who is just no longer suicidal who can go on leave, then the latter goes out and the other one comes in. It can mean patients are discharged before the plans are in place. (Dr David Roy, Consultant in charge of the psychiatric unit at South Western Hospital in Lambeth, London, quoted in *The Independent*, 5 January 1994)

The First Report of the Health Committee, Session 1993-94, *Better Off in the Community? The Care of People Who Are Seriously Mentally Ill*, (House of Commons, 1994), set up to review the progress that has been made to date in the transition from institutional to community care for the mentally ill concluded that:

> Most of the evidence acknowledges that reprovision is variable and patchy; some of the functions have been reprovided well, but there are gaps in many areas.

Concern was expressed at:

> ... the intensity of the pressures faced by providers of acute care for mentally ill people in some inner cities. It is wrong that vulnerable and, in some cases, potentially violent individuals may be discharged abruptly, inappropriately and without adequate support into the community. (p. xviii)

The report concludes that provision for medium term care is less than adequate, day care may be inadequate in some areas, emergency and crisis care is generally inadequate, particularly outside of office hours, and that much remains to be done to prevent mentally disordered offenders entering the criminal justice system when they should be receiving care from the health and social services. The report wholeheartedly endorses the concept of community care, but catalogues a range of unsatisfactory and patchy provision for the care of the mentally ill in the community.

A report published by the Mental Health Foundation in 1994 concluded that provision for the care of the seriously mentally ill was underfunded, fragmented, uncoordinated and incoherent. According to the authors of this report, the system of provision is failing the mentally ill because it lacks a comprehensive strategy, lacks understanding of severe mental illness, and responsibility is spread across different agencies. This report is a damning indictment of provision for the severely mentally ill; government departments are accused of self-interest and failure to work together; care professionals are accused of failure to co-ordinate services, and failure to hold anyone responsible when disasters occur. It estimates that there is a spending shortfall of £540 million a year in resources needed for the provision of an adequate system of community care.

The *Mental Health Task Force London Project* (Department of Health, 1994), set up by the government to examine the services provided in London for the severely mentally ill and to assist local agencies to develop action plans to address the most pressing problems, found:

> The team confirms a serious problem of emergency access to appropriate care for severely mentally ill people in several ... London boroughs. As a result, psychiatric wards are overfull and staff are having to discharge prematurely patients who are still very vulnerable to make way for others. Some patients with severe and chronic mental disabilities are being discharged without adequate supervision or the provision necessary to meet their housing, social and health needs. This could increase risk not only to the safety of the individuals concerned, and to the safety of staff in non-specialist accommodation or other services. (p. 10)

The consequences of the chaos surrounding community care are sometimes tragic. On February 24, 1994, the *Report of the Enquiry into the Care and Treatment of Christopher Clunis* (1994) was published. The report catalogued a damning catalogue of failures on the part of the mental health services which arguably contributed to the murder of Jonathan Zito by Christopher Clunis, a schizophrenic who was in the 'care' of the community, on 17 December, 1992, at Finsbury Park underground station. Sadly, this tragic case is not an isolated one; a confidential inquiry by the Royal College of Psychiatrists was set up in 1991, following the killing of an eleven year old girl in a Doncaster shopping precinct by a woman psychiatric patient who had been released from hospital two days earlier, 'in the wake of widespread concern about the care of mentally ill people and their potential for violence' (Steering Committee of the Confidential Inquiry into Homicides and Suicides, 1994, p.5). The report considers thirty two cases of homicide involving former psychiatric patients who had been in contact with the psychiatric services in the twelve months prior to their committing homicide. It found that:

> ... each death was, in the view of those looking after the patient, unexpected and unpredictable. Furthermore, it was generally felt by them that supervision of the patient had been appropriate, that the staffing levels had been adequate and that there had been no indication that greater control was called for.
>
> Yet in parallel with this very genuine response, as indicated in the answers to our questionnaire, there was clear evidence that in almost 60% of cases the

homicides followed a spell when the patient had failed to cooperate in the treatment proposed for them.

There is thus raised, but not answered, the question of whether a level of supervision beyond what was provided might have served to control the disturbed mental state of the homicidal patient. (p. 20)

(It should be noted that this is only a preliminary report, and therefore relies on limited data; the inquiry was set up to review cases of homicide involving mentally ill people and also cases of suicide. This preliminary report only concerns itself with homicide; an item in *The Independent* of 14 August, 1994, claims also that 107 patients have committed suicide; the newspaper reporter chose not to highlight this information, focusing instead on the homicides.)

Faced with report after report which details chaos and confusion in the provision of community care, and tragic cases where members of the public have been murdered by mentally ill people in community care, we are faced with the question of whether it is the policy or its implementation which is flawed.

The implementation of the policy of community care certainly appears to bear a great deal of the responsibility for the appalling situation that currently exists, but there are those who argue that the concept itself is fundamentally flawed, for it is undeniably the case that the mentally ill do have special needs, and it is these needs which lead some to consider the policy to be ill-advised. Jones, for example, has criticised it on the grounds that it ignores the very real disabilities that mental illness can produce and consequently does not acknowledge the specialist support that may be needed:

... an attitude which has its origin in a desire to improve conditions is very easily twisted into an excuse for ignoring real needs; (Jones, 1988, p. 130)

And from time to time a tragedy such as that of Jonathan Zito certainly leads to the questioning of the advisability of community care. Christopher Clunis, a mentally ill man in community care, stabbed Jonathan Zito three times in the face; one stab punctured his eye and entered his brain and killed him. This case has all the ingredients which strike terror into the hearts of 'sane' people at the thought of the mentally ill being amongst them in the community.

Jonathan Zito and his wife, Jayne, were the perfect young couple, deeply in love, newly married; they had just met Jonathan's parents at Gatwick Airport. The family were planning to spend Christmas together; Jonathan and his brother went home by train as there was not enough room in the car for everyone. They were ordinary people, doing ordinary things. They were waiting at Finsbury Park station when Christopher Clunis, who had a history of severe mental illness, wandered onto the platform. Before his fatal stabbing of Jonathan Zito, Clunis had been involved in three incidents with a knife; he had had a considerable amount of involvement with the various mental health services, but was apparently considered to be a suitable case for treatment in the community; there was also evidence of lack of communication between the various agencies responsible for his care. When he entered the station that day his behaviour was sufficiently erratic to worry several people. For no apparent reason, Clunis attacked Jonathan Zito with a knife, and killed him.

If Jonathan Zito had been killed in a traffic accident, it would have been tragic for his family but what makes this tragedy resonate with such horror is the images it evokes; images of a crazed killer, a madman, from whom nobody could be safe by virtue of his madness, wandering the streets, those responsible for his care apparently having lost trace of him, and an ordinary young man, peacefully going about his life. The random juxtaposition of these two lives which led to the injustice of the tragic waste of Jonathan Zito's life provoke the feelings of helplessness that are apt to surface when we are confronted by our fundamental inability to be totally in control of life's events.

Jayne Zito has said:

> I want there to be a full public enquiry into why Jonathan Zito has died. Somebody has to tell me why Christopher Clunis was on the platform that day and murdered my husband. ... Why wouldn't any of the authorities who had looked after [Clunis] before take responsibility for him? (*The Independent*, 19 July 1993)

These tragic cases are inevitably the ones that make headline news; if one adds to them the very real problems highlighted by the Mental Health Act Commissioners' report and from time to time by the media, then it is not difficult to see why there is grave concern that community care cannot work. And many would ask how it can be argued that the mentally ill should be considered to be part of a shared humanity along with 'normal' people, and a policy of community care be argued for when tragedies such as that of Jonathan Zito occur when the mentally ill are treated as normal and 'released' into the care of the community.

However, the term 'mental illness ' does not refer to a single condition, any more than does a term such as 'fever', for example, but covers a considerable number of conditions. I have not been concerned in this book with the classification of different forms of mental illness, because in our present state of knowledge, this appears to be a somewhat limited approach to the problem. However, this is not to deny that mental illness finds expression in a variety of forms, and consequently, different forms of mental illness may require different treatment options. Neither is mental illness a static condition; like any illness, there are degrees of severity, which may vary over time; and different people respond differently to mental illness, just as they may do to physical illness. But none of this invalidates a policy of community care; the fact that it is possible to misuse the concept is not a weakness in the concept, but in those who choose to define it to meet their own ends. Arguing that community care is the ethical and humane basis around which

136

to base the treatment of the mentally ill does not deny difference; it acknowledges the right of the mentally ill to live an 'ordinary' life, but accepts that in order for them to do so will require additional support.

Murphy (1991) has detailed ten criteria that must be met by community care provision:

There must be a mechanism for *identifying persons in need* and for reaching out to those willing to participate; it may also at times be necessary to reach out to those who do not wish to participate but are at risk of harm to themselves or others.

The system must offer service-users assistance in applying for and obtaining financial entitlements in the form of income support and disability allowances

It must offer 24-hour crisis assistance so that individuals are not left untreated or unsupported during an acute episode of illness, no matter what time of the day or night a crisis arises

It must provide opportunities for social rehabilitation

Services must be provided indefinitely and be available for an individual's lifetime if necessary

Services must provide adequate medical and psychiatric treatment on a continuing basis

Services must provide back-up support for family friends and members of the local community in order to minimise the burden of care which fails on other people's shoulders

The system must engage voluntary groups, community organisations and other members of the local community to maximise involvement in normal community activities

The system must operate so as to protect patients' rights and ensure their civil liberties are not denied them

Finally, the system must provide for the co-ordination, integration and binding together of services so that they function as one *'seamless service'*, providing all the elements which one individual requires... (Murphy, 1991, pp. 149-150)

There are many who suffer from some form of handicapping condition which results in their having special needs which must be catered for if they are to live as normal a life as possible. It would not be seriously argued nowadays that the blind or deaf, for example, should be incarcerated in specialist asylums because of their special needs; why then should the majority of the mentally ill be treated separately from mainstream society simply by virtue of their special needs?

Mental illness may cause behaviour that poses great problems, and such behaviour may fall outside the limits of that which is considered 'normal', no matter how generous the category. It is very rarely the case, however, that any danger is posed to others by a mentally ill person's strange behaviour. Nonetheless, this issue cannot and must be not be ignored when faced with the question of how one can justify a policy of community care based on a philosophy of normalisation, if some mentally ill people such as Christopher Clunis do pose such a risk to society in general.

In some cases, exemplified by that of Christopher Clunis, it may be that an individual poses a great enough risk to society to require very specialist treatment and possibly custodial care; I have considered the issues this raises in Chapter 4, where I considered the question of compulsory hospitalisation. It is also possible that Clunis might not have become so ill that he became dangerous to society if he had received proper care in the community; we shall never know. But what is known is that the so-called 'community care' received by Clunis was a travesty of care.

> As will have be (sic) clear from our comments throughout the narrative we are of the view on the evidence we have heard, that Christopher Clunis' care and treatment was a catalogue of failure and missed opportunity. ... the problem was cumulative; it was one failure or missed opportunity on top of another. As a result of these numerous failures and omissions by a number of people and agencies, in our view Christopher Clunis was not provided with the good and effective care that he should have received from the time that he first attended hospital in London in July 1987 until the time he stabbed Jonathan Zito in December 1992. We consider that a lack of resources also played a part in that failure and missed opportunity. While we have found that some individuals, some services and some agencies carried out their respective roles well and to Christopher Clunis' advantage, we feel that such care was all too rare. Hence he received care and treatment that was not effective in keeping him well or the public safe. (Clunis Report, 1994, p. 105)

The catalogue of failures includes failure in communication and liaison between professionals; failure to contact and involve Clunis' family; failure to obtain and verify an accurate history; failure to consider and assess Clunis' past history of violence and to make any assessment of his propensity for violence in the future; and failure to plan, provide or monitor Section 117 of the MHA 1983. It also catalogues a considerable list of shortage of vital resources and a repeated tendency:

> ... to postpone decisions or action when difficulty was encountered or perhaps because the patient was threatening, and intimidating, and possibly because he was big and black. (ibid., p. 107)

The policy of community care will never have a realistic chance of succeeding while such chaos exists within the services allegedly providing it.

In the wake of a number of tragedies like that of Christopher Clunis, the government devised a ten point plan to improve the supervision, control and care of severely mentally ill patients who have been discharged from hospital into community care. (NHS Executive / Dept. of Health, 1994). The plan is an amalgamation of existing measures and new proposals, (see Dept. of Health, 1990 and 1994) but *without any extra funding to implement it*. Supervised discharge orders will only be applied to those patients who have been detained under the 1983 MHA; these patients, however, constituted only 1% - 2% of all mentally ill people admitted to NHS hospitals in the period 1989-1990. Other proposals include greater restrictions on the discharge of patients from hospital into community care and closer supervision and tracking of patients once they have been discharged into the community. It is also proposed to set up an 'at risk' register of seriously mentally ill people, modelled on the children's protection register; a patient could be included on the list irrespective of whether or not she had received treatment in hospital for her illness.

It is difficult to see how any of these proposals can realistically be expected to improve care for the mentally ill when no extra funds are being made available to implement them; nor, indeed, how they will help the vast majority of mentally ill people who have not been detained under the 1983 Act. The idea of an 'at risk' list, with no resources to implement any action being taken seems a bizarre approach to helping such people; lack of resources is one of the failures found to have contributed to the chaos surrounding the 'care' of Christopher Clunis in the community. Nor is it clear how these proposals are expected to improve the lack of communication between agencies and professionals that appears to be so often characteristic of community care. Communication problems are hardly surprising given, as Huxley et al (1990) have noted, the confusion and controversy which surrounds the Community Mental Health movement in the UK.

> There are now in existence in the UK, mental health advice centres, mental health resource centres, community centres, day centres, community mental health teams, in addition to those which prefer to avoid any explicit reference to mental health in their title (an attempt to avoid the stigmatising of clients). (Huxley et al, 1990, p. 3)

In a review of the literature on community health care provision, Huxley found a depressing picture of limited care options, with a referral network so fragmented and uncoordinated that the mentally ill find it difficult to find their way around the system, and once in it are *likely to be lost track of by the different agencies which comprise the community care system.* The care options that exist are delivered in a biased manner to minority groups, ignore the needs of certain groups such as women, and often do not reach those most in need of help, such as the poor or the most seriously ill. Non-psychiatric needs are often ignored, to the detriment of the overall outcome for patients. He concludes that we do not know at present what constitutes efficient and effective services. (ibid., pp 7-10) It is little wonder, therefore, that community care is in a state of crisis, and that the reality of community care for so many of the mentally ill is just a variation on the theme of degradation.

The overwhelming majority of those who bear the brunt of the inadequacies of community care are undoubtedly the mentally ill themselves, but it is the tragic cases like that of Christopher Clunis which make the headlines, reinforcing the stereotype of the mentally ill as crazed madmen who pose a threat to all around them. The consequences of this can be seen in such things as the reluctance to allow sheltered or supported housing schemes in residential areas and the calls for an end to the policy of community care and the closure of mental hospitals. But if the social place of the mentally ill is to be removed from the realm of otherness which is created by their isolation in asylums, to the realm of membership of a shared humanity in the community, that community has to be better informed about mental illness. It is not justifiable to criticise those who reject the presence of the mentally ill in 'normal' society if they only have a stereotype of mental illness upon which to base their conclusions. Ramon has made the point that:

> The move to psychiatric community care is primarily about a shift in the social place of those who suffer from severe mental distress, the so-called 'psychotic', 'schizophrenic', or 'chronically ill'. An element of fear of potential violence as well as of the apparent lack of logic in the way such people behave conditions social and professional reactions. (Ramon, 1991, p. 10)

In order to remove the 'crazed madman' stereotype of mental illness, which is very rarely applicable, attitudes to mental illness and the mentally ill must be changed, for humane treatment of the mentally ill in the widest sense of the term requires more than merely adequate medical care, social care, and support systems with adequate numbers of staff, suitable buildings and sufficient money. It requires an added dimension, that of love, or at the very least, compassion. This is a Utopian ideal indeed! No amount of political will can force us to love our neighbours as ourselves, particularly if we are not even prepared to acknowledge some groups as neighbours. Therefore, given that we cannot realistically expect the

140

'normal' world to love the mentally ill, and short of direct divine intervention bringing about this utopian state, our best hope would appear to be to adopt the more pragmatic approach of attempting to change attitudes towards the mentally ill by trying to get the 'normal' world to acknowledge that mental illness is not a remote state of 'otherness', divorced from the lives of 'normal' people, but is instead an alarmingly common occurrence in the population, and that consequently it is quite possible that one day the bell may well be tolling for any one of 'us', as well as for 'them'. Education is therefore vital, for apart from the 'mental health as prerequisite for self fulfilment' school, mental illness is still a largely taboo subject.

> Education is the main weapon we can employ to ensure that the mentally ill are granted their rights at all times: education of the sufferers, their families, the professionals, but most of all the community at large. People have to be made to view mental illness as an illness, something that can be treated and in many cases cured. Even those who do not achieve a complete cure can lead a much better life if they're allowed to function to the utmost of their ability...
>
> Ignorance and misinformation underlie the alienation of the mentally ill from the mainstream of the community. There is a marked lack of understanding of mental illness by the population at large, including employers, industry, the media and government. Stereotypic and often prejudicial views do not match the reality of mental illness... Such lack of understanding needs to be addressed by appropriate educational and information programs. (HR & EOC, p. 199)

The effectiveness of education in changing attitudes to mental illness is open to debate. Donovan has considered research on this question and concluded that although:

> ... the experiences outlined above seem pretty clearly to indicate that anxiety is often the anxiety of 'not knowing', and that education in the form of straightforward information and reassurance might dispel it and allow more positive attitudes to emerge. (Donovan, J., in Brackx, 1989, p. 41)

this is not invariably the case; her own experience however has convinced her that it is possible to create an environment where attitudes to mental health can be explored positively:

> In groups specifically designed to explore attitudes towards mental illness and mentally ill people, I try to create an environment within which underlying contradictions between feelings and beliefs can be safely explored. ... Sometimes we can learn by confronting deeply-held fears directly, but a far

more effective and natural way of learning is to acknowledge the reality that contradicts the fear. In plain words, we need to get to know and learn from the people who have first-hand experience of mental illness. (ibid., p. 43)

It is interesting to compare the situation regarding education of the general public in the case of AIDS with that of mental illness. There have been widespread efforts to educate people about AIDS - the nature of the illness, its consequences and how to avoid it; vast sums of money are being spent on research aimed at finding a cure for it. Perhaps more interestingly, however, is the way in which many 'media' people are promoting AIDS awareness and one might even think, somewhat cynically, vying with each other to proclaim their 'AIDS friendly' credentials; there was a period in which it seemed to be impossible to open a newspaper or watch television news without seeing the Princess of Wales tenderly and very publicly holding the hand of an AIDS sufferer. All of this is very necessary, given the stigma associated with AIDS and the appalling discrimination sufferers may be subject to on top of the misery caused by such a horrible illness. It is interesting to speculate, however, why nothing similar has occurred to raise the profile of the misery of mental illness, and to attempt to dispel the ignorance and stigma that surround it. Nobody is setting up buddy schemes for the mentally ill; nor do participants at award ceremonies for the film and television industries wear the equivalent of red AIDS awareness ribbons to denote their concern for the mentally ill; and few people seem interested in telling the stories of the mentally ill, or encouraging them to tell their own stories, in the hope of spreading greater understanding.

But if education is to be effective, it must be acknowledged that:

The general public are threatened by mental illness, both by the frightening nature of the illness and by the unfortunate and often sensational way it is reported in the media. (ibid., p. 200)

and that there is a real, and occasionally justifiable, fear of tragedies like the Clunis affair occurring. Ignoring these concerns is both arrogant and counter-productive in terms of obtaining a place for the mentally ill in the community. And in acknowledging these fears, the question of how to prevent similar tragedies occurring must be addressed. The ethical issues here relate to the questions of whose rights are considered paramount when a conflict of interests occurs between the mentally ill and wider society; I have discussed the issues relating to the question of compulsory hospitalisation in Chapter 4. But there must also be consideration of what measures are justified in order to maintain people whose behaviour is seriously threatening or disturbing in a community setting, in order that they obtain the most benefit from community care and that the rights of the other members of society are protected.

Once again we are confronted by the issue of autonomy. Autonomy as an ideal, however, must be approached with caution, for an over-reliance on the perspective which Alistair Campbell has described as:

> ... a presumption in favour of individual self-determination or autonomy, and an implied or explicit criticism of the beneficent approach to the health care relationship as being second best ... (Campbell, A., in Fulford, Gillet and Soskice, 1994, p. 184)

may, well-meaning though it may be, also result in tragedies such as those which I have documented above. Campbell argues that:

> ... the fundamental character of human life is one of dependency, and that therefore a medical ethics which seeks to overemphasise the independence of the individual is in danger of being a dehumanising and inadequate account of the therapeutic relationship. (ibid., p. 184)

His argument is that autonomy and dependency are not the 'polar opposites' they are frequently portrayed as being. In considering why autonomy holds 'a supreme position in moral theory', he cites two different justifications that have been offered; Kant's assertion that only an autonomous agent can be considered to act in a moral capacity and Mill's argument that only a society which gives priority to individual liberty can be said to safeguard the common good.

> Both types of justification depend upon our accepting the prior assumption that morality begins with the individual and his or her personal liberty, and both theories (despite their massive differences in approach), attempt to build a communal morality out of each individual's respect for this freedom. But suppose we were to begin the discussion of the pre-eminence of moral values at a different place - at our interdependence rather than our capacity (or lack of it) for independent choice and action? With such a starting point the predominant obligation would be a respect for the dependency which specific others have upon us, and an attention to the duties which fall upon us as a result of this dependency. Equally we would pay attention to and respect our own dependency upon significant others and seek the support which we knew we required for our own security and fulfilment. With such a starting point, *the society most productive of human good would be the one in which the needs of the vulnerable were given preference over the freedom of the strong to exercise maximum liberty of action.* (ibid., p.190, emphasis mine)

Campbell's approach is a far cry from the aggressive individualism that stresses autonomy at almost any cost so lauded in contemporary Western society. The ultimate form that this takes is the metamorphosis of the individual into the consumer; we might nowadays paraphrase Descartes to read 'I consume, therefore I am'. Consumerism is not limited merely to material goods, but encompasses an ever increasing number of services, from public transport to medical care, from education to energy supplies. Consumers' rights are increasingly the focus of attention and concern, with ever more insistent demands for their protection. But one could be forgiven for thinking that for those who do not have the wherewithal to make their voices heard as consumers, because they do not possess sufficient purchasing power, there appears to be an ever decreasing level of protection for their *human rights*.

The transformation of the individual into the consumer has been accompanied by the rise of the professional 'expert' and an associated paternalism based on this expertise. We thus have a somewhat paradoxical situation, in that a society that aggressively argues for autonomy as a, or even the, primary moral good has at the same time created and even encouraged an unprecedented dependency upon experts. Autonomy is thus expressed through one's right and ability to purchase whatever expertise or service one has autonomously decided that one requires! If the consequences for the marginalised and disadvantaged were not so appalling, it would be a truly laughable situation. But although this ridiculous situation may be all very well for those who can exercise choice in what they purchase, for it is perfectly possible to find an 'expert' to meet one's every need if one can afford to pay for her expertise, if one cannot, one tends to be left to fend for oneself. Human rights are thus at risk of being available only to those who can afford to 'consume' them.

The obsession with individualism and personal autonomy as a primary moral good and the increasing transformation of the exercise of autonomy as consumer 'purchasing power' have serious implications for the mentally ill. Those who are relatively privileged can indulge their individualism and exercise their autonomy through consumption, including the consumption of expertise; increasingly nowadays the consumption of expertise includes the psycho-babble of what I would call the 'fulfilment brigade'. We are led to believe that we have a right to self-fulfilment, a right to discover and achieve our full potential, a right to happiness - a right to almost anything that is deemed a legitimate component of the goal of individualism and the exercise of our autonomy. In the process, we have legitimated mental health concerns that deal with narcissistic individualism. 'Celebrities' now regale their captive audiences almost daily with tales of their experiences of childhood incest, or drug abuse; mental health as entertainment is now established. Counselling and a huge variety of therapies are a growth industry. Paradoxically, the privileged can now exercise their autonomy to buy any form of dependency they deem necessary to the promotion of their individual self-fulfilment!

And yet it is hard to avoid the conclusion that mental health has been put on the consumer agenda by a society whose members are stepping over the homeless schizophrenics lying in the gutters of its city streets, enjoying the 'benefits' of exercising their 'autonomy' through the efforts of the community care programme for the mentally ill. The genuinely mentally ill are rarely the holders of any significant degree of purchasing power; therefore, their needs and rights are not likely to feature very high on the list of priorities in a consumer driven society. And this is where the well-meaning attempts of those who do care about the rights of the mentally ill often go astray; seeing the right to any degree of personal autonomy for the mentally ill so often disregarded, some advocates for the mentally ill have gone to the other extreme and refused to acknowledge the dependency that mental illness, in some stages of its manifestation, inevitably imposes. The doctrine of the primacy of autonomy can have equally pernicious consequences for the mentally ill if employed by well-meaning, but unrealistic, professionals as it does as the rationale of a selfish, individualistic, consumer culture.

This question raises the issue of compulsory treatment orders which would enable the medical profession to administer medication compulsorily to patients in their care who were living in the community if such patients refused to take medication voluntarily, and as a result their condition declined. If someone is discharged from hospital into community care because medication has improved her condition sufficiently for this to be a viable option, is it justifiable to insist that she continue to take that medication after discharge, and to enforce compliance if it is not taken voluntarily?

In 1987, the Royal College of Psychiatrists proposed the introduction of a Community Treatment Order which would enable medication to be administered compulsorily to patients in community care; this was rejected because it was considered that the proposed powers were too sweeping and gave too much power to doctors. In 1993, proposals were made by the college for Community Supervision Orders, which would have forced a patient's return to hospital for treatment if she refused to comply with treatment whilst in the community. These were rejected by the Commons' Health Select Committee after protests that it would infringe patients' civil liberties; instead, the key element of the government's ten point plan is the introduction of supervised discharge orders. (Dept. of Health, 1993). Such orders do not enforce the taking of medication while a patient is in community care; nor would she automatically be returned to hospital for treatment; they do, however, impose conditions upon a patient discharged into community care, including a negotiated treatment plan agreed between patient and carers, and a requirement to attend for treatment. Under a supervised discharge order, a named mental health worker would be responsible for the patient's care and for taking action if treatment were not complied with. If a patient refuses to comply with treatment, an urgent review of her case will be held, at which those responsible for her care will decide if a return to hospital for treatment is necessary; once in hospital, she may be forced to take prescribed medication. Patients will, however, have the right to appeal against the conditions imposed on their discharge into the community.

Is it ethically justifiable to impose treatment (and realistically, such treatment will invariably be medication) on someone who is free to live in the community, and therefore, presumably, able to claim the same rights as the rest of the population, which includes the right to decline medical treatment if so wished? Certainly the image conjured up by the idea of compulsory treatment in the community can be horrific, with images of the police being used to constrain unwilling patients while a community psychiatric nurse administers powerful mood-altering medication, and of course this is a situation that every effort should be made to prevent happening. But is compulsory treatment in the community any more horrific than compulsory treatment being administered in hospital? Is there something about a patient being physically in the community - or perhaps more accurately, out of the hospital - that makes compulsory treatment in that setting worse or less justifiable than if she were in hospital?

A voluntary patient being treated in hospital cannot be compelled to accept treatment, except in a case of 'urgent necessity'. A patient detained under section 58 of the 1983 MHA may have medication administered compulsorily without her consent, but after three months' administration, she must either give her consent for the treatment to continue or, if she is unable to give informed consent or refuses her consent irrationally, an independent doctor must certify in writing that the patient is not capable of understanding the necessity for medication or:

> ... has not given consent, but that, having regard to the likelihood of its alleviating or preventing deterioration of his condition, the treatment should be given. (Bluglass, 1984, p. 81)

The issues here are often confused. The argument against compulsory administration of medication to mentally ill people in the care of the community would appear to be that if they are well enough to be in the community rather than in hospital, they are well enough to give or withhold consent to taking medication, and to make it compulsory is denying them the exercise of their autonomy which is the aim of community care. However, it seems to me that this approach misses the point of community care, which is surely to enable the majority of the mentally ill to live as normal a life as possible in the community. For some, this may require medication to be taken in order to prevent their condition deteriorating to the extent that they cannot live in the community. In such cases, it hardly seems rational to allow someone to deteriorate in a community care situation so that she then has to be compulsorily detained in hospital in order to receive the medication necessary to alleviate her condition, at which point she can then return to community care and the whole cycle can begin again! If the alternative is the compulsory administration of medication within a community setting, this surely makes more sense. This is not an argument for the wholesale, callous administration of drugs to protesting mentally ill people in 'community care', as a cheaper option than providing real care in the community. That would be as barbaric as the old asylums. If it is accepted, as I would argue that it should be, that some people will be able to benefit from a decent system of community care provided that their behaviour is stabilised by medication, it must be administered as part of a comprehensive system of care and treatment for the mentally ill that is flexible enough to cope with different situations. This will not be achieved by adopting a simplistic definition of autonomy.

However reasonable it is to argue for compulsory treatment in the community if it is necessary to maintain the patient's mental state of health sufficiently for her to benefit from community care, the method of its implementation may still lead to problems, as experience in Australia demonstrates. Compulsory Treatment Orders are provided for in certain states of Australia: in the states of Victoria and NSW, legislation specifically provides for compulsory treatment orders. In South Australia, the Guardianship Board has the power to compel anyone suffering from mental illness to accept treatment in the community if she is considered to be incapable of managing her own affairs; in Western Australia there is provision for compulsory treatment after discharge from hospital, and legislation in the Australian Capital Territory allows for compulsory treatment orders in some circumstances. There is no provision for compulsory treatment orders in the other Australian states. Compulsory treatment orders in Australia can only be issued in cases where the criteria for compulsory hospitalisation are met, and if it is felt that there is no viable alternative course of action.

Conflicting evidence was received regarding the costs and benefits of CTOs by the *Report of the National Inquiry into the Human Rights of People with Mental Illness* produced by the Federal Human Rights Commissioner of the Australian Human Rights and Equal Opportunity Commission (1993).

> We feel that, in Victoria, the Community Treatment Order has become almost too easy an option for psychiatrists in their treatment of patients ... We also feel that, on occasion, they are used as a cajoling device to manipulate patients. For example: 'if you go on your CTO, we will discharge you sooner rather than later', notwithstanding that the criteria for involuntary detention may no longer apply. ... We feel that the original reason for Community Treatment Orders - that is, the provision of appropriate treatment, supports and resources in the community to facilitate recovery in a non-institutionalised setting - has been lost ... In many respects, Community Treatment Orders, in our experience, seem to be no more than rubber stamps for the fortnightly administration of Modecate [and similar drugs]. This is, of course, due ... to the severe lack of resources spent in this area. (HR & EOC, 1993, p. 312)

Other criticisms of the operation of Community Treatment Orders were also submitted to the Enquiry. These included:

... requiring attendance at inconvenient places, interfering significantly with the rights of consumers and changing the relationship between consumers and police and consumers and community mental health workers. Other problems concerned lack of choice in a treating doctor and lack of consultation and information. ... Service providers such as nurses and police also dislike the enforcement role CTOs place them in. (ibid., p. 312)

These inadequacies in the administration of Community Treatment Orders would inevitably occur were they to be introduced in the UK because for CTOs to work as they are intended to would require a system of community mental health care very greatly superior to the chaos that currently exists - and this would be extremely expensive to provide.

The South Devon Inquiry Report into the death of Georgina Robinson was published in 1995. (Blom-Cooper et al, 1995). Georgina Robinson was an occupational therapist at the Edith Morgan Centre Psychiatric Unit attached to Torbay District General Hospital; she was murdered by a patient at the centre, Andrew Robinson (no relation), who had a history of violence. He was illegally allowed out of the centre on leave; while released, he bought the knife with which he stabbed Georgina Robinson. Her attack was described as 'predictable and preventable'. It is important to note that Andrew Robinson was not living alone in the anonymous 'community' which is often the case where such tragedies occur, but was a detained as a patient under section 3 of the MHA, 1983, at an acute psychiatric unit. The report nonetheless identifies a series of failures in the community care system from the time when Andrew Robinson was discharged from a restriction order after being released from Broadmoor maximum security hospital, where he had been sent in 1978 after trying to shoot a female student with whom he had become obsessed. The responsibility for key failures in the management of Andrew Robinson's treatment is placed on management and staff. In an article in *The Independent* of 18 January, 1995, Professor Elaine Murphy, a psychiatrist, recently retired vice-chairwoman of the Mental Health Act Commission and joint author of the South Devon report, argues that it is time to jettison the 1983 Act. She argues that the report on Georgina Robinson's death is merely the latest example of the inadequate state of current mental health provision, even though the provision made by the South Devon Healthcare Trust is considerably better overall than much of the provision made throughout the UK.

The problem is not the policy but its implementation, which is struggling woefully. ... Patients want practical help and support, for example, with housing, finance and employment, something to do during the day, and social relationships which give meaning to their lives. But at present they are often offered a monthly injection of drugs and little more.

Targeting of services is especially poor; many community psychiatric staff do not work with those with the most serious long-term problems; staffing of the service is dominated by health professionals (doctors, nurses): when what is required is an army of people to provide practical social care and help people who are far less expensive to employ but who, with the right training and support, are able to provide a more flexible type of service. (Murphy, 1995, p. 18)

The authors of the South Devon report concluded that the 1983 Act is now obsolete, and that the proposed supervised discharge order which is aimed at enabling the monitoring of seriously mentally ill people after their discharge from hospital. is no more than 'tinkering' with the Act and will not improve the way that community care works.

Murphy argues that the 1983 Act works against effective community care for the mentally ill because its philosophy is based on the premiss that compulsory care requires detention in hospital, and medical treatment is removed from the social context of care. What is needed is a new Mental Health Act based on a more comprehensive concept of care which would allow for compulsory medication if necessary, administered at a licensed place such as a doctor's surgery, *but only within the context of an overall, comprehensive plan of treatment.*

The principles on which a new Mental Health Act should be constructed should provide a more therapeutic framework for care, continue to control the unwarranted interventions of doctors, and yet provide more safety and security for patients, their families and the general public. Adopting these principles, one could devise a power for the compulsory care of seriously mentally disordered people.

This broader concept of a comprehensive care plan order, in which specific medical treatment could be given compulsorily only in the context of a wider plan of supervision and care, would protect patients' welfare, particularly while they were receiving medication against their wishes. (ibid.)

There are those who would argue that the compulsory administration of medication can never be justified, a stance which I have argued is too simplistic. However, the routine administration of a monthly injection and no other support or care is an equally simplistic, and very cruel, stance to take to the issue of community care.

The problems surrounding all aspects of community care are immense, but it is not the fundamental principle that is flawed, but rather its implementation and, in relationship to certain issues, woolly thinking which employs a simplistic notion of autonomy and a reluctance at times to face difficult issues and accept that in some cases there are no fully satisfactory answers because the nature of the problem is so severe that this is impossible. The case for a community care policy for the mentally ill rests on the acknowledgement of a common humanity between the mentally ill and 'normal' members of society, and consequently the acknowledgement that they share similar fundamental human needs and rights; and it is based on need not consumerism. It does not deny difference; it does mean that acknowledging the difference which mental illness can impose upon a sufferer renders a simplistic notion of autonomy and its pursuance at any cost an inadequate measure by which to ensure the best provision for those suffering from it. This is because a simplistic notion of autonomy ignores the interdependence that human beings have on each other, particularly when they are ill, and because autonomy pursued relentlessly in a consumer society such as ours can result in the gross disadvantage of those who lack the necessary autonomy to pursue their own ends as consumers.

To support and rehabilitate the mentally ill into the community, to grant them the same human rights as everyone else, requires a great deal of effort and money. The cosy idea that 'out there' there lies a caring, cohesive community, willing and able to support its weaker, most vulnerable members is a myth. Community care can be difficult both for the 'community', with its largely unjustified fears and misconceptions about mental illness and the mentally ill themselves.

> To be understood, strengthened and helped in being re-integrated into the community can be a daunting task for a mentally ill person... [We may be feeling] confusion; strange behaviour; awkwardness in human relationships; perceptions which can stimulate particular memories and can create tremendous problems. (HR & EOC, 1993, p. 317)

A policy of community care demands many things - many practical suggestions are contained in *The Report of the Inquiry into the Care and Treatment of Christopher Clunis* and *Human Rights and Mental Illness: The Report of the National Inquiry into the Human Rights of People with Mental Illness.* (The latter is an Australian report, but its findings are equally applicable to the UK.) In order to implement improvements, however, political will is required to find the necessary funding, for successful community care is far more expensive than institutional care. Extra money alone will not be adequate to improve the situation unless it is employed sensibly to remove the complexity of the current system of care, which appears to have been designed to tax the resources of the most mentally resilient in society; if the professionals are not always able to cope with the chaos in community care, what hope is there for the mentally ill and their carers of coping with the system?

A community care policy also requires an acknowledgement that for some people, community care is not a viable proposition, because the nature of their illnesses poses too great a threat to other members of society or to themselves to allow them to live in the community. Denying this on spurious grounds of granting such people autonomy is a travesty of care. Similarly, if medication is required to enable a mentally ill person to live in the community, there should be measures available to ensure that it is taken; ideally, this would be achieved by means of close contact and active support of the mentally ill thus encouraging patients who need to take medication to do so, rather than crisis management where the spectre of burly policemen subduing a resistant patient raises its head, to the detriment of all concerned.

Thus to provide a better system of care for the mentally ill requires a lot of practical changes to be made to the current system. Above all, in making the extremely difficult decisions that arise when the care of the mentally ill is under consideration, and in endeavouring to construct systems to help mentally ill people that are humane and considerate of them as people, we must acknowledge that:

> It is because money cannot buy the human gestures which confer respect, nor rights guarantee them as entitlements, that any decent society requires a public discourse about the needs of the human person. It is because fraternity, love, belonging, dignity and respect cannot be specified as rights that we ought to specify them as needs, and seek, with the blunt institutional procedures at our disposal, to make their satisfaction a routine human practice. (Ignatieff, 1990, pp. 13-14)

Failure to achieve a successful community care programme will result in the status of the mentally ill - defined as 'other' by virtue of the nature of their perceived difference excluding them from the status of fully human - being very unlikely to improve. Any definition of 'success' for community care will be measured by the extent to which the mentally ill are able to be helped to integrate into the human community; this requires that the needs of the mentally ill, their families and the wider community must all be considered, because all of these elements are intertwined. Thus I would argue that those mental health professionals who consider the needs of their 'clients' in isolation, on the grounds of confidentiality or the irrelevance of others' needs and rights are not only being unethical, they are possibly ignoring valuable additional resources that could be employed to help the mentally ill and are employing a strategy that may turn out to be counter-productive; community care will only have a chance to be effective if there is a community in which the mentally will be received and cared for. This is unlikely to happen if the fears and concerns of members of society are ignored; it must be acknowledged that mental illness can impinge upon the lives of others in a way characteristic of no other illness, in that it can result in behaviour that is distressing and even frightening. The complexities raised by the issue of autonomy when considering the mentally ill must also be acknowledged, including the painful fact that there will be times when it is impossible to meet the needs and desires of all parties involved with the mentally ill.

Mental illness imposes great burdens on sufferers and all involved with them. To deny that there is a difference between the mentally ill and 'normal' people is ridiculous; but what is needed is the acknowledgement that it is not an absolute difference in kind, but a difference in degree. It is possible that if we were to stop defining terms in absolutes, such as 'sane', 'insane', 'normal', 'abnormal', and see mental health in terms of the continuum that it undoubtedly is, seeing the mentally ill only in terms of their difference from 'normal' humanity would be far less of an issue. This is unlikely to be achieved, however, if the mentally ill continue to be regarded as so different from 'us' that they must lead a separate existence.

This perceived difference may also deny the mentally ill the right to tell their own stories, because if one is to be able to tell one's story, one needs a voice, and to have that story heard and taken seriously, increasingly nowadays one needs a powerful voice. The mentally ill have no powerful media voice to argue their case for them; and given that the mentally ill themselves are often less articulate about their illness than those unfortunate enough to have contracted AIDS, it must be acknowledged that sometimes the mentally ill need other voices to speak on their behalf, or to help them speak for themselves, for situations will inevitably arise where, for any of a variety of reasons, a mentally ill person's voice alone might not be heard.

However, the message being given needs to be thought about; the pressure group SANE ran a poster campaign in 1989 expressing their concern at the closure of mental hospitals. They were justifiably concerned by the terrible conditions experienced by many schizophrenic patients and their families, and their motives were arguably well-intentioned. However, large posters in public places showing a photograph of a distraught young man and bearing captions such as:

He thinks he's Jesus

You think he's a killer

They think he's fine

Followed by: STOP THE MADNESS

surely cannot be argued to be anything but a disaster for the mentally ill, reaffirming, as they must have done, the stereotyped image of the mentally ill as dangerous madmen. This is not giving the mentally ill a voice; on the contrary, it is likely to deny them a voice by virtue of the images of irrational lunacy portrayed confirming the commonly held view that 'they' are different from 'us' and therefore to some extent outside the human community. It is unrealistic to pretend that it will be easy to change popular images of mental illness. It can be a frustrating, perplexing condition at best, and very frightening at worst, both for sufferers and those who witness or are involved with it. But if community care is to be more than merely a way of providing cheap 'care' for the mentally ill, we must address this issue, and give the mentally ill themselves as effective a voice as possible, not rely on sensationalist messages, even when inspired by very real concern for what is going on, as SANE undoubtedly was when it commissioned its poster campaign.

For community care to have a chance of succeeding its aims and philosophy must be more clearly defined; professional care provision must be much better organised and must not adopt an adversarial relationship to family and friends of the mentally ill who often have the intimate knowledge of patients' conditions that is a vital prerequisite for working out effective care plans; medical treatment must be part of an overall care policy, which includes the social needs of patients and there must be the political concern and will to resource the system properly. From the evidence so far, it is the latter prerequisite that appears to be the least likely to be provided; the consequences of this will be that other areas will be less likely to improve, because it is difficult to see how the necessary improvements can be made to an inadequate system without sufficient money. Ultimately, this will depend upon society as a whole accepting a shared humanity with the mentally ill, and caring enough to want to improve their lot.

9 Conclusion

Milton wrote:

> The mind is its own place, and in itself
> Can make a Heav'n of Hell, a Hell of Heav'n
> (Milton, 1972, 1, 254-5)

His observation was extremely perceptive; he might also have observed, however, that when the mind has made its own, uniquely private, hell, the horror is frequently compounded by the actions of one's fellow people. Even a brief glance through the history of the treatment of the mentally ill confirms this: it does not make pleasant reading. Nowadays, the situation is generally considered to be greatly improved. We no longer consider the mentally ill to be possessed by the devil or morally defective and deserving of punishment, and the welfare state (or what is left of it) claims to provide for the basic needs of the mentally ill, albeit not very generously. In other words, we can pride ourselves on our humane treatment of the mentally ill. To some extent this is true, of course, and the improvements that have occurred must be acknowledged. But although we may not express such overtly cruel attitudes to the mentally ill as in earlier ages, and we may not employ such cruel methods of treatment (although some would dispute this), the cases examined in earlier chapters have illustrated that inhumanity towards the mentally ill is far from being a thing of the past.

One of the causes of contemporary inhumanity towards the mentally ill is the attitudes taken towards mental illness by the 'normal' members of society; another is the chaos surrounding care policies for the mentally ill. This chaos is caused by the underfunding of community care, and by ill thought-out good intentions that were the result of justifiable concern about some of the appalling practices meted out to the mentally ill. The situation is further complicated by disputes about drugs versus psychotherapy, an issue which I would argue is largely a red-herring. Treatment for mental illness should not be seen in simplistic either/or terms; what is required is a comprehensive care policy which looks at the sufferer as a whole person, not a case to be treated with x or y method, depending on the orientation of the specialists treating her. Drugs and psychotherapy both raise particular ethical issues which have been considered in earlier chapters; these treatments need not be mutually exclusive and there is a place for both in the treatment of mental illness.

To implement a comprehensive treatment policy for every sufferer from mental illness will require much better liaison between the professionals involved in treatment, sufferers and their families, and this will require considerably more money than is currently being put into community care. It is hard to avoid the conclusion that community care is being implemented 'on the cheap' and such an approach is doomed to failure.

But what constitutes humane treatment of the mentally ill? More money and resources alone are not enough to ensure humane treatment; attitudes towards mental illness and the mentally ill must change. I have argued that well-meaning but simplistic definitions of autonomy contribute little or nothing towards humane treatment. And certainly defining the mentally ill as entirely lacking in autonomy results in inhumane treatment. In essence, to treat the mentally ill humanely requires that we accept that they are people like us, with the same rights as us. Language is not helpful here: terms such as 'the mentally ill' and 'us' immediately set up a condition of opposition and condition us to think of 'them' and 'us'. Yet we cannot ignore that there are significant factors in the conditions called 'mental illness' which do differentiate those suffering from mental illness from those who are not. If this were not the case, there would be no need for the term. Thus humane treatment of the mentally ill requires that we accept a shared humanity and equal rights whilst acknowledging difference. The problems that may and often do result from the nature of mental illness pose serious ethical problems which must be acknowledged, and it must also be acknowledged that there will often be no totally satisfactory answers to some of these problems. How then might the question of how to ensure humane treatment for the mentally ill be addressed?

Much inhumane treatment of the mentally ill manifests itself in a variety of 'little' ways: for example, the embarrassment, shame and ridicule which may surround them. There is also fear - occasionally justified, but emphasised out of all proportion by the media - that the mentally ill are dangerous; and there is neglect. These attitudes influence the way the mentally ill are treated and they are inextricably involved with the question of what it is to be human. Once one has an idea of what it is to be human, the question of what constitutes human needs arises. Ignatieff, in a brilliant and thought provoking article on *The Natural and the Social*, in which he uses *King Lear* to illustrate his argument, considers the nature of human needs and human rights. He argues that the language of right derives from the language of need and that the language of human needs is a basic way of referring to the idea of a natural, shared human identity. This language of human needs is distinguished by its claim that humans are aware of a common identity in their biological needs, upon which rests the possibility of human solidarity:

A society in which strangers would feel common belonging and mutual responsibility to each other depends on trust, and trust reposes in turn on the idea that beneath difference is identity. (Ignatieff, 1990, p. 28)

155

He goes on to make a distinction between human needs and human dues:

> What a man needs he does not earn or deserve. He does not have to justify his entitlement, only the extent of his necessity. His entitlement inheres not in his person but in his humanity. (ibid., p. 35)

It is a common humanity that links all people together and entitles anyone, of any rank, to the bare necessities of life that will ensure physical survival. But:

> ... [w]hat a person is due, on the other hand, is what they deserve. These are additional claims, above the floor of basic need, that people can make by virtue of their merit, station, rank in life. If basic need is what is necessary to man as a natural being, these additional claims are due him as a social being. ... This is a... paradox: that to treat men equally - only as men - is to deny them the respect due to their humanity. (ibid., p. 35)

Ignatieff then makes the point that in today's world, in contrast to Shakespeare's time, we have a more humane view of human nature. Thus contemporary ideas of human dignity relate to the idea of equality based on the idea of a shared, common humanity, not rank or social status. As creatures of reason, our needs are not seen as limited to mere bodily ones: it is acknowledged that humans also have a need for respect, love and understanding. But there is a price to pay for this:

> Yet humane assumptions have unintended consequences. As soon as one enlarges the definition of the human, real human beings begin to be excluded: the Tom O'Bedlams of our time, the mad kings, the insane, the retarded, the deaf and dumb, the crippled and deranged. Those doctors and magistrates who have taken upon themselves the awesome business of deciding who is human - i.e. who is rational - have created a vast array of institutions designed to make Tom O'Bedlam and the mad king human again. ... Enlarging the criterion of the human beyond the body has had the unexpected effect of legitimising the despotism of reason over unreason. ... It is our poor and weak flesh we share, and nothing else. But if this is so, what respect is due to it? What pity is owed to all forms of human suffering? Lear insists that the test of human respect is in life's hardest cases. not in one's neighbour, friend or relation, but the babbling stranger, the foul and incontinent inhabitant of the back wards of state hospitals, the mongol child. If poor unaccommodated man is no more than this, it is no wonder our pity conceals contempt. (ibid., p. 44)

By enlarging our conception of what it is to be human beyond the physical, 'humanity' becomes a social construction.

> Each and every society creates, within what must be called its cognitive closure - or, even better, its closure of meaning - its own world, which is both "natural" (and "supranatural") as well as "human". ... In this world, other societies (other human groupings) have a (generally very poor) limited and defined place, meaning and role. ... The construction of its own world by each and every society is, in essence, the creation of a world of meanings, its social imaginary significations, which organise the (presocial "biologically given") natural world, instaurate a social world proper to each society (with its articulations, rules, purposes etc.), establish the ways in which socialised and humanised individuals are to be fabricated, and institute the motives, values, and hierarchies of social (human) life. (Castoriadis, 1991, p. 38, p. 41)

This has immense consequences for the mentally ill. The way they are 'fabricated' - the ways in which they are constructed as a specific category within the overall category of 'other human groupings' - will largely determine their rights and responsibilities in society, and this in turn will affect their treatment, both in the general sense of how they are regarded as people and in the specific sense of treatment for their illness.

The essential characteristic attributed to the mentally ill which defines the 'specific category' they occupy is that of irrationality, and in a society where to be human is to be rational, this immediately jeopardises their claim to a 'shared human identity' with 'normal' people. This has a number of consequences; to begin with, it limits or denies the autonomy of the mentally ill. for autonomy is a prerequisite in the contemporary western world for inclusion in the category of 'fully human', and autonomy depends upon rationality. This then denies the mentally ill a voice, and to have no voice is effectively to be powerless.

Dehumanising the mentally ill and consequently denying them any autonomy is the basis for the 'voiceless patient' model of treatment discussed in Chapter 3. At its best, this may be implemented by genuinely caring people as an honest, although I would argue nonetheless misguided, way of trying to protect the mentally ill both from undesirable consequences of their own actions and from the actions of others. At its worst, it is a prescription for cruelty.

Denying the mentally ill a voice has considerable advantages for the 'sane'. Those without a voice cannot be heard; if by some chance the mentally ill do make themselves heard, they can be ignored, because what they say is not worthy of attention. This offers a form of protection to the 'sane', enabling them to ignore, for example, the perilously narrow boundary between sanity and madness: the mentally ill reach those parts of the human condition that 'normal' people do not reach - and choose not to acknowledge. Not only would giving the mentally ill a voice force 'normal' people to acknowledge some painful truths about 'madness' and 'sanity', but, as Porter has noted:

> ... what the [mentally ill] say is illuminating because it presents a world through the looking-glass, or indeed holds up the mirror to the logic (and psycho-logic) of sane society. It focuses and puts to the test the nature and limits of the rationality, humanity and 'understanding' of the normal. ... Rather like children playing at being adults, the [mentally ill] highlight the hypocrisies, double standards and sheer callous obliviousness of sane society.
> (Porter, 1987, p. 3)

We can see one of these hypocrisies highlighted by contemporary attitudes towards drugs. There is immense, world-wide concern about the spread of drug-taking amongst 'normal' people, and vast sums of money are spent annually in order to prevent these 'illegal' drugs reaching those who are very willing to take them. The concern about illicit drug taking is justified because of the ultimately grim consequences they may have for those taking them, and also because they may cause changes in behaviour which may have adverse effects on other members of society. Yet despite this justified concern about illicit drug taking, there are many who urge a simplistic acceptance of drug treatment for mental illness and ignore the very real fears that these drugs evoke in terms of their side-effects and what they may be doing to the conception of self of those who take them. At the other extreme, there are others who share the concern about illicit drug-taking because they too acknowledge that drugs may significantly alter the state of mind and behaviour of those who take them; however, they appear unwilling to acknowledge the possibility that if drugs can have such a profound effect on mental state and behaviour, they may have the potential to help some of the mentally ill, because this appears to argue for a reductionist conception of humanity where all those characteristics which are prized as being essentially human might be argued to be reducible to chemistry, a view which they perceive as deeply offensive.

In 1987 the advent of the 'designer drug' Prozac threw these issues into the headlines. Prozac, an antidepressant, was claimed to have fewer side-effects than other antidepressants and to be very effective in treating depression. What caused Prozac to hit the headlines, however, was its apparently amazing effects in transforming people who were not mentally ill, but instead were typical of those who might have been expected to seek psychotherapy in a society where achievement, fulfilment and realising one's full potential appear to be the contemporary equivalents of finding the Holy Grail, those whom Lasch has characterised as:

> Plagued by anxiety, vague discontents, a sense of inner emptiness, the "psychological man" of the twentieth century seeks peace of mind ...

Therapists, not priests, become his principal allies in the struggle for composure; he turns to them in the hope of achieving the modern equivalent of salvation, "mental health". (Lasch, 1991, p. 13)

This is mental health as personal salvation, and the road to personal 'salvation' is long, hard and expensive. At its end, hopefully, insight and self-understanding lead to finding one's true self and the attainment of real autonomy. Prozac appeared to be able to effect this transformation chemically.

I was used to seeing patients' personalities change slowly, through painfully acquired insight and hard practice in the world. But recently I had seen personalities altered almost instantly, by medication. (Kramer, 1993, pp. xiv-xv)

If the claims made for Prozac were to be proven, the ethical implications would be enormous, as the following case illustrates.

... Ms B [was] prescribed Prozac for trichotillomania, a syndrome in which a person cannot resist the impulse to pull out her own hair. Hair-pulling in moderation is a sign of anxiety; but the need to pull hair relentlessly, to the point of disfigurement, is recognised as an illness, related to obsessive-compulsive disorder. Besides hair-pulling, Ms B has a second concern: she is unmarried at age thirty-six, despite her "appropriate, if somewhat strenuous efforts to meet eligible men". On Prozac, Ms B's hair-pulling diminishes, but so does her feeling of urgency about meeting men. Ms B does not isolate herself: on the contrary, she now enjoys time spent with people, such as her parents, with whom she argued in the past. She is more content with life, more reconciled to the possibility of never marrying, and though still interested in men, is no longer driven. (ibid., p. 265)

The idea of transformation leads us to address a new set of ethical issues. Who is Ms B? The change Prozac brings about in her is so profound that there are almost two different persons in the story, one discontented and driven, the other contented and complacent. Whose autonomy are we out to preserve? (ibid., p. 268)

Whose indeed. Where does this leave the treatment of the mentally ill? Where does it leave our notion of autonomy? In turning away from the consideration of these difficult ethical issues while encouraging the 'psychological society' obsessed with the goal of mental health as personal salvation, 'sane' society is being hypocritical. In effect we are saying that issues of self and autonomy are only appropriate considerations for the 'normal', not the 'mad', because the 'mad' cannot be considered to have any autonomy by virtue of being less than fully human.

The appalling consequences of treating the mentally ill as having no autonomy led to some well-meaning professionals to take an entirely opposite view. It was argued that the mentally ill were in possession of autonomy and that this must be respected, whatever the cost. This has led to cases of the mentally ill 'rotting with their rights on'. Jonathan Deveson's case illustrates the horrors and injustice that this approach to the autonomy of the mentally ill may result in. Thus while it is the case that negative attitudes towards mentally ill which classify them as less than human and consequently deny them any autonomy must necessarily result in inhumanity and injustice, it is also the case that good intentions may also result in inhumanity and injustice if they find expression in entrenched dogma which ignores the very real problems posed by the mentally ill. And the mentally ill may still be denied a voice even by 'enlightened' professionals, if their voice is heard to be saying something which does not support the current dogma, as the following case illustrates.

During my research for this book I received a large quantity of information from a man who thought I might be able to help him. He sent four cassette tapes and a pile of correspondence on A4 paper that measured about 8 cm in depth. He had written to his MP, pressure groups, the press - anyone he thought might possibly be able to help him. The gist of his complaint was that he wanted to be allowed to be an in-patient in hospital. He said that he could not cope with community care, had been happy in hospital and wanted to return there. There was a degree of desperation about his letters that made them disturbing and painful to read. Irrespective of the rights and wrongs of his individual case, which I am in no position to comment upon, it nevertheless illustrates the problems the mentally ill may have in being heard and being taken seriously. The official compassionate theoretical stance on the care of the mentally ill considers that community care is the humane policy; most mentally ill people would probably agree. But as a result, this man effectively has no say in his treatment because the option he would prefer has been deemed to be undesirable by those who 'know' that their approach to his treatment is better for him.

So what might be done to try and improve the care and treatment of the mentally ill? It is unlikely to be achieved merely by respecting impersonal, disembodied 'rights':

> The administrative good conscience of our time seems to consist in respecting individuals' rights while demeaning them as persons. In the best of our... psychiatric hospitals, for example, inmates are fed, clothed and housed in adequate fashion; the visits of lawyers and relatives are not stopped; the cuffs and clubs are kept in the guard house. Those needs which can be specified in rights are more or less respected. Yet every waking hour, inmates may still feel the silent contempt of authority in a glance, gesture or procedure. The

strangers at my door have welfare rights, but it is another question altogether whether they have the respect and consideration of the officials who administer those rights. (Ignatieff, 1990, p. 13)

Our only hope of obtaining 'respect and consideration' for the mentally ill is to acknowledge the common, shared humanity between the mentally ill and the 'sane'. This is easy to say, of course, but harder, if not impossible, if we are realistic, to achieve in the 'real' world. There is nothing in the history of Homo sapiens to inspire hope that people will ever adopt such an approach wholeheartedly. Nevertheless, we must at least endeavour to foster acknowledgement of this common humanity. The only, admittedly slim, hope of doing this is by education. And we must certainly, at the very least, try to ensure that this common humanity is acknowledged by the professionals who treat and care for the mentally ill, and by their families and friends. Education might be more likely to succeed in these contexts, and the more ignorance is dispelled, the greater are the chances of understanding growing.

Above all, we must give the mentally ill a voice. How might this be done? The issue of practical and positive ways of giving the mentally ill a voice raises the issue of advocacy. Advocacy for the mentally ill is not a new idea: the Alleged Lunatics' Friends Society, founded in 1845, was concerned with issues relating to mentally ill patients' rights from its foundation until its demise in 1863. (Hervey, 1986) The early years of the nineteen-eighties saw the emergence of consumers' groups in the field of mental health care. organisations such as Good Practices in Mental Health promoted user involvement in mental health care.

'Advocacy' is a word much banded around at present, both inside and outside the mental health world, but what exactly does it mean? Why has this term suddenly caught on - why not 'advice', 'welfare rights', 'litigation', 'counselling', 'enabling' or 'representing'? Perhaps because advocacy has elements of all these and also just a little bit more. (Robson, in Barker & Peck, 1987, p. 18)

Robson identifies three different approaches to advocacy:
(a) one who pleads for another on a voluntary basis
(b) one who is paid to do it
(c) one who supports another, perhaps in presenting their own
case. (ibid.)

Simons defines three forms of advocacy; (he is considering advocacy in the context of those with learning difficulties, which is where the movement first developed in the UK, through such groups as Advocacy Alliance, launched in 1981 by five national voluntary organisations in order to introduce citizen advocacy in long-stay hospitals.) Self advocacy is:

161

... sometimes used to describe the processes of individual development through which adults with learning difficulties acquire the skill and confidence to assert their own views. More often it refers to the activities of groups of people... who have got together to voice their collective concerns. (Simons, 1993, p. 3)

Class advocacy:

... involves public support or campaigning for a group or class of people, usually by established organisations. (ibid.)

Professional advocacy:

... takes a number of different forms. ... paid individuals who offer support and advice to anybody who seeks their help; for example, some Citizen Advice Bureau workers. Many services employ people whose specific role is to offer advice and help service users gain things to which they are entitled; an example here would include welfare rights workers. Finally, there are a few examples of independent professional advocates ... [who] have a quite different relationship to the people they help. ... Because of their employment by services, many face conflicts of interest ... (ibid., pp. 3 & 4)

Advocacy is not a simple issue, therefore, and there is considerable debate within the movement as to how terms such as 'advocacy', 'user involvement', 'consumerism' and 'patients' rights' should be defined and employed; there appears to be little consensus among different groups. It is beyond the scope of this book to go into this issue in any depth; Barker and Peck (1987), considering the theoretical perspectives of advocacy, consider that:

... the user movement is rooted more in experience than in theory and it is this which makes it dynamic. Since it is a growing movement it is also diverse. Various user groups are involved in different sorts of activity and would sympathise with differing theoretical perspectives. (Barker and Peck, 1987, p. 3)

This last statement seems rather optimistic: they go on. however, to make the point that:

What remains clear, however, is that the thinking behind our new 'buzz' words of advocacy, consumerism and so on does not lend itself to consensus. What have been uncovered are ways of thinking about our services which reveal conflicts of interest. This is positive. Workers for too long have believed that they know what is best for the user. Users' interests have been subsumed under workers' interests. (ibid., p. 3)

They conclude from this that:

A new clarity of thinking will enable workers to respond more sensitively to users' needs. It will also clear the way for a power base from which users may declare their views. (ibid., p. 3)

Such certainty also seems rather simplistically optimistic, although it is to be hoped that they are correct in their assumptions, because the views of the users of mental health care provision are long overdue to be heard and taken seriously.

If the mentally ill are to be given a voice, the training of those who treat them and care for them in a professional context will need to be altered and improved. In written accounts, and amongst the people with whom I corresponded and to whom I spoke about their experiences of mental illness, I found a great deal of dissatisfaction with the medical treatment that they had experienced. To some extent this might be explained by the human tendency to voice complaints but remain silent about satisfactory experiences; it might in part be explained by the nature of mental illness - it can be difficult to appreciate efforts made to help one if the nature of one's distress is such that it distorts one's perception of the world and one's experience of it. But such explanations do not address the problem voiced again and again by the recipients of treatment for mental illness, which I can best describe as not being taken seriously.

Included amongst the complaints were not being listened to; having worries about treatment ignored or dismissed; having no notice taken of complaints about undesirable effects of treatment; not having treatment explained; not being allowed to discuss treatment options; not having one's past history considered and having one's problems assessed as a purely medical situation, divorced from the context of the sufferer's life; not having access to decent housing and employment; and being defined simply in terms of illness, rather than as a person with an illness, or who had had an illness.

Being taken seriously depends upon being respected; it implies that if one voices one's feelings, opinions and complaints they will, at the very least, be acknowledged, and possibly acted upon; or if action is not taken, then it implies that at least one can expect to receive a reason as to why this is not possible. Obviously what constitutes a good reason for not acting to satisfy someone's wishes may well be different for the various parties involved in a particular situation and so this is always going to be an area of possible conflict, because being taken seriously does not mean that one's wishes will necessarily be met. However, this is still a different situation from that in which no attention is paid to what one is saying. The significance of these complaints goes far beyond the specific instances which caused distress to particular sufferers from mental illness, for they reaffirm the construction of the popular image of the mentally ill as 'other', denied a voice (or at least a voice which needs to be taken seriously) by virtue of their irrationality. This attitude on the part of the professionals involved in treating the mentally ill is at least in part fostered by the primary model employed in the contemporary treatment of mental illness.

The theoretical framework most generally employed in the treatment of mental illness in the contemporary Western world is the medical model, legitimated by the claims to scientific objectivity and rational enquiry upon which Western biomedicine is built. It is thus a mechanistic model, and

> ... [m]echanism implies the ignoring of the omnipresent individuality of the real and the imposition upon it of an abstract law which determines every case indifferently from the outset. (Collingwood, 1924, quoted in Lederman, 1986, p. xix)

Ignoring the 'omnipresent individuality' of sick people is a short-sighted approach to the treatment of any form of illness; in the case of mental illness, which is surely the most 'individual' of all afflictions, its consequences may be devastating for patients. Taussig has argued that Western biomedicine:

> ... reproduce[s] a political ideology in the guise of a science of (apparently) "real things". This process of reification results in complex ideas being transformed into "real" things, which can then be named, and thus assume an identity of their own. By this process, it is argued, concepts such as schizophrenia can be employed to construct a biological view of severe mental distress which enables other factors to be ignored. Members of the medical profession, legitimated by virtue of their specialist knowledge, are thus able to emphasise a chosen view of reality; or in other words, promote their own ideology. (Taussig, 1980, p. 8)

This is arguably a distorted view, as simplistic in its own way as a purely mechanistic model of medical treatment. Nonetheless, it contains an element of truth. Indeed, the ideological function of the medical model of mental illness and its treatment could be argued to be the distancing of the mentally ill from 'normal' people through the emphasis on undesirable difference which results from the mentally ill being seen only in medical terms of their pathology. (But we cannot simply blame the medical profession for this; we might do well to ask how much of the fuss made about the numbers of mentally ill people increasingly being found living on our city streets results from the discomfort we feel at having these people made visible to us, instead of being where we would perhaps prefer them to be, comfortably hidden from our view - a case of out of their minds, out of our sight. Bott (1976) has commented that one of the problems mental hospitals have always had to face is being in the paradoxical situation of trying to help people on behalf of a society which does not acknowledge or even recognise its wish to get rid of these individuals as well as to help them.)

But a mechanistic medical model is too simple, on its own, to deal with the complexities of mental illness. It seeks, by gathering objective evidence wherever possible, to classify an individual's symptoms in order to analyse them to see into which category her illness fits. The category to which someone's illness is assigned will be very significant in determining treatment, which will focus on treating the illness; in so doing, the person suffering the illness is frequently ignored. Sacks has discussed this:

> Our health, diseases, and reactions cannot be understood in vitro, in themselves; they can only be understood with reference to us, as expressions of our nature, our living, our being-here (da-sein) in the world. Yet modern medicine, increasingly, dismisses our existence, either reducing us to identical replicas reacting to fixed 'stimuli' in equally fixed ways, or seeing our diseases as purely alien and bad, without organic relation to the person who is ill. The therapeutic correlate of such notions, of course, is the idea that one must attack the disease with all the weapons one has, and that one can launch the attack with total impunity, without a thought for the person who is ill. (Sacks, 1982, p. 205)

One of the greatest weaknesses of this approach to illness lies in the significant likelihood that what the patient says may not be taken seriously, indeed, may not even be heard, because the patient and those treating her will in all probability be speaking different languages.

Language is a powerful medium; through it we can construct our world and tell our individual stories; 'ordinary' language, mostly spoken in form, is negotiated in specific situations between those involved at the time, and meaning is therefore dependent upon context to some degree: it is only necessary to read a transcript of a conversation to see the apparently disordered, fluid nature of the language. Specialist language, on the other hand, has predetermined meanings, shared only by those who have been initiated into those meanings, and is independent of context; such language is often shared via the medium of the written text.

> With written discourse, the author's intention and the meaning of the text cease to coincide. This dissociation of the verbal meaning of the text and the mental intention is what is really at stake in the inscription of discourse. Not that we can conceive of a text without an author; the tie between the speaker and the discourse is not abolished, but distended and complicated. The dissociation of the meaning and the intention is still an adventure of the reference of discourse to the speaking subject. But the text's career escapes the finite horizon lived by its author. What the text says now matters more

than what the author meant to say, and every exegesis unfolds its procedures within the circumference of a meaning that has broken its moorings to the psychology of its author. Using Plato's expression .... written discourse cannot be 'rescued' by all the processes by which spoken discourse supports itself in order to be understood - intonation, delivery, mimicry, gestures. (Ricoeur, 1988, pp. 200-201)

Thus the text acquires a power of its own by virtue of its authority; in the medical world where psychiatric training takes place, the mode of transmission of its specialist knowledge is done via the medium of textbooks and learned journals; through lectures; at conferences and through professional organisations. Even when spoken discourse is utilised to transmit knowledge and information, it is frequently couched in the language of the textbook; consequently when patients enter the scene, real, live, disorganised patients, with their 'chaotic' spoken discourse, they are confronted by experts whose training has been conducted in the ordered, classified, and authoritative discourse of the written text. In the majority of cases, they speak an entirely different language from their patients. Patients have a story to tell; doctors have a history to take. Taking a 'good' history requires taking down facts, identifying links between events, classifying symptoms and imposing some sort of order on the information gained in order to reach a diagnosis, which will determine treatment; it may also be offered as an explanatory model for the patient. This is fine as far as it goes; there is no virtue in being the world's most empathic, listening doctor if one fails to gather the 'hard' information that would suggest the possibility that one's patient is suffering from acute appendicitis! The problem is that this approach does not go far enough - even in the case of purely physical illness. it causes problems:

A recent study of the difference between patients' and doctors' interpretations of some common medical terms confirmed that we are frequently talking at cross-purposes with our patients. (Beck, Francis and Southam, 1977, p. 1)

In the case of mental illness, this approach is even more limited.

... any narrative combines, in varying proportions, two dimensions: a chronological dimension and a non-chronological dimension. The first may be called the 'episodic dimension' of the narrative. Within the art of following a story, this dimension is expressed in the expectation of contingencies which affect the story's development; hence it gives rise to questions such as: and so? and then? what happened next? what was the outcome? etc. But the activity of narrating does not consist simply in adding episodes to one another; it also constructs meaningful totalities out of scattered events. This aspect of the art of narrating is reflected, on the side of following a story, in the attempt to 'grasp together' successive events. The art of narrating, as well as the corresponding art of following a story, therefore require that we are able to extract a configuration from a succession. This 'configurational' operation ... constitutes the second dimension of the narrative activity. (Ricoeur, 1988, p. 278)

The question of 'constructing meaningful totalities out of scattered events' is the area where problems will in all likelihood arise between the 'expert' and the patient, by virtue of the limitations of a medical model, because:

Diseases have a character of their own, but they also partake of our character; we have a character of our own, but we also partake of the world's character: character is monadic or microcosmic, worlds within worlds within worlds, worlds which express worlds. The disease-the man-the world go together, and cannot be considered separately as things-in-themselves. (Sacks, 1982, p. 206)

Sacks makes the point - and it is a vital one - that both the discourse of the scientific world, whose terms of reference are 'quantities, locations, durations, classes, functions etc.' (ibid., p. 204) and the discourse of our own personal experiences:

... the terms in which we experience health and disease, and which we naturally use in speaking of them, [which] neither require nor admit definition, [which] are understood at once, but defy explanation; [which] are at once exact, intuitive, obvious, mysterious, irreducible and indefinable ... metaphysical terms. (ibid., p. 203)

are both essential in understanding the world, although both forms of discourse are complete in themselves. Considering the work of Leibniz, he comments:

Leibniz stresses, however, that metaphysics comes first: that although the workings of the world never contravene mechanical considerations, they only make sense, and become fully intelligible, in the light of metaphysical considerations; that the world's mechanics subserve its design. ... If this were clearly understood, no trouble would arise. Folly enters when we try to 'reduce' metaphysical terms and matters to mechanical ones: worlds to systems, particulars to categories, impressions to analyses, and realities to abstractions. (ibid., p. 205)

And folly also enters when we take a patient's history, and ignore her story. The over-reliance on a purely medical model of mental illness and its treatment, I would suggest, is one of the causes of inhumane treatment of the mentally ill, not because it is an inhumane model as such, but simply because the complexities of

167

mental illness are so great that it is largely impossible to be as humane as we should if the human, i.e., the complex person, is left out of the equation - if 'How are you?' is reduced to a series of measurements of isolated attributes of the patient, such as levels of depression, alertness etc.

> The dialogue about how one is can only be couched in human terms, familiar terms, which come easily and naturally to us all; and it can only be held if there is a direct and human confrontation, an 'I-Thou' relation, between the discoursing worlds of physicians and patients. (ibid., p. 204)

How might psychiatrists be trained to develop such an 'I-Thou' relationship with their patients? Some gifted individuals do it naturally, of course. But the nature of psychiatric training is such that it might appear specifically designed to destroy any hope of such sensitivity developing.

The first hurdle the would-be psychiatrist must surmount is that of medical training; six years of fundamentally scientifically oriented study, with arguably the emphasis on sick people as syndromes of symptoms rather than as members of a collective humanity which they share with their doctors:

> The continuous exposure to critical situations reduces one's sensitivity to more trivial experiences, just as bright sunlight reduces one's awareness of delicate shade. A numbness settles in and as the callous attitude develops there is an inevitable drying up of finer feeling. One acquires a cold clinical indifference. (Birtchnell, 1987)

The 'continual exposure to critical situations' is not restricted to clinical situations. As one doctor put it to me:

> They seemed deliberately to have designed the teaching process to humiliate you. If you got the answer to a question wrong, you'd be put down. If you got it right, they'd simply ask you a harder question and so on until you got one wrong. Then they'd humiliate you! After a while, you learn to switch off and ignore it.

It is even arguable that the system of selection for medical training selects people who are most likely not to possess the personality characteristics most likely to be able to develop an 'I-Thou' relationship with patients:

> Concentration on school-leaving attainment in science subjects may lead to negative selection as far as potential interest in psychiatry is concerned. The present restrictive entrance requirements... act to screen out school leavers who have the general interest in literature, philosophy and the arts which

often accompanies what may broadly be called a psychological orientation. (Association of Psychiatrists in Training, 1979, p. 7)

Acknowledging the inadequacies in the system whereby psychiatrists are trained is relatively easy, of course; it is much harder, given the nature of mental illness, to work out how to improve it.

The psychiatrists ... if they were to put themselves in a position to truly understand their patients, would have to get inside of experiences which are extremely painful and disturbing. Even then, they would only be able to truly understand to the extent that they understood similar things in themselves. ... You are obviously aware that a theoretical understanding is by no means the same thing as one which is based on experience. Even those of us who think we understand pretty well how a motor car engine works, find that we meet quite a lot of unexpected problems when it actually comes to trying to repair one. The temptation to give the darned thing a good kick for causing you such trouble can be quite strong at times, and that's nothing to the aggravation even a mildly maladjusted person can sometimes cause you!

How, then, is it possible to train psychiatrists properly if such an excruciatingly painful process is involved? In effect, you would risk driving them insane if you were even to try it, and in practice the drop out rate would probably be one hundred percent.

So wrote one of my correspondents, a man who had been diagnosed as a paranoid schizophrenic and considers himself to have been mad at the time; he is now recovered, and the point he makes is very important. We do not, and could not, insist that those who treat physical illness experience what they are treating before they are allowed to treat patients; neither can we insist that those who wish to practice as psychiatrists must themselves have experienced the misery of mental illness. But we could accept that the limited medical model generally employed in the treatment of mental illness is grossly inadequate, and consequently offer a broader training for psychiatrists; it could also be acknowledged that other approaches to treatment may be appropriate, either as alternatives to or complementing psychiatric approaches.

This criticism might suggest that the treatment of mental illness should no longer be the province of medicine. But given there is evidence that some sufferers from mental illness are helped by the physical treatments of drugs and ECT, and that it is also the case that some physical illnesses produce symptoms which can be mistaken for functional symptoms, it is necessary for a patient presenting with what might be mental illness to have the possibility of a fundamentally physical cause to her problems excluded. It does not seem reasonable, therefore, to remove the treatment of all mental illness from doctors because some aspects of medicine are relevant to the treatment of mental illness. The problem is that the psychological aspects of mental illness - indeed, one could argue that the psychological aspects of being human - are too easily ignored by the classical medical model and many of its exponents. However, rejecting the simplistic mechanism of the pure medical model because it ignores (or in extreme cases, even denies) the subjective individual person who experiences mental illness is not an argument for adopting an equally simplistic model of mental illness which sees it as having no connection with the body. Therefore, if we wish to try and make the treatment of mental illness more humane than it currently is, it would appear to be imperative that the theoretical syllabus for training psychiatrists be amended to include more about people, well and sick, and what best can be done to meet their needs as people and not simply as medical cases. This will require the adoption of a more sophisticated model of care and treatment than a simple mechanistic model; it requires a model which acknowledges and values the subjective experience of the patient and acknowledges the multiplicity of interrelated factors which may be involved in the development of mental illness and indeed, which may influence the outcome of treatment. In essence, what is needed is a more holistic approach to mental illness than that currently used by many psychiatrists.

This will demand a great deal of sensitivity on the part of psychiatrists and great changes in the system of training. Assuming that her training does not instil in her a cold, clinical indifference to her patients as people, the system the would-be psychiatrist finally enters as a junior doctor may well do so:

> [Such a setting] is the [one] which uses only an assembly-line approach to patients and where the official attitude is to scorn sustained individual interaction and to take pride in brief interviews and rapid turnover. (Kubie, 1971 p. 102)

Given the nature of their training and the current situations in community care and psychiatric wards in our hospitals, where too many patients vie for too few beds, and in some areas the services are approaching collapse, one can only wonder that any psychiatrist manages to retain any vestige of humanity towards her patients. I do not doubt that the majority of psychiatrists are concerned to provide humane treatment for their patients; their training at the moment does not seem to facilitate this, however, and one cannot help but feel that humane treatment occurs despite the system, rather than as a result of it.

Another consequence of the adoption of a purely medical model of mental illness and treatment is that those who espouse it are at risk of taking an anti-normalisation stance in their approach to their patients, focusing on their difficulties and perceived deficiencies - in other words, highlighting negative difference - and thus focusing intervention only in medical terms, instead of acknowledging the importance of personal and social support systems in determining the prognosis of someone suffering from mental illness.

The problem of treating mental illness is complicated, I would suggest, by the fact that psychiatrists are often called upon to treat many forms of deviant behaviour which fall into the categories of 'sad' or 'bad', rather than 'mad', because such behaviour often results in, or from, psychological distress. Yet there is no evidence that psychiatrists are any better at dealing with psychological distress than any other group; indeed, in view of their training, it is arguable that in many cases they will be less successful than others who may employ less simplistic models. It is therefore important to attempt to differentiate between mental illness and psychological distress.

Mental illness will, in almost all cases, result in considerable psychological distress for the sufferer, but psychological distress is neither a necessary nor a sufficient condition for mental illness; it is possible to imagine a seriously deranged person with absolutely no awareness of her state being perfectly happy if she is not persecuted by others. This is an unlikely scenario, admittedly, but it is not inconceivable. Equally, it is the case that one can suffer severe psychological distress, as, for example, on the death of a loved one, and not be mentally ill. As another of my correspondents put it in a letter to me: 'During the period from 1981 to 1984 1 was very unhappy but not mad.'

I do not wish to suggest that psychological distress is insignificant or trivial, but I would nevertheless argue that it is less serious, in the sense of its implications and prognosis, than mental illness; (but it must also be acknowledged that extreme unhappiness can 'tip over' into mental illness). Neither am I suggesting that people whose behaviour is more appropriately classified as 'sad' or 'bad' should not receive help; indeed, it is arguable that appropriate help might well prevent extreme distress worsening and becoming mental illness. Nevertheless, this does not mean that psychiatrists are necessarily the appropriate people to deal with such cases.

Other professionals involved in the treatment of mental illness - nurses, occupational therapists, psychologists and social workers - all employ theoretical models of mental illness which inform their approaches to treatment. It is often considered that these are more enlightened than the medical model espoused by the majority of psychiatrists, and to some extent this may be true. But it is important to remember that any model of treatment, if too rigidly adhered to, can lose sight of the person whose treatment is the rationale for its creation.

If patients' stories are to be listened to, if they are to be taken seriously, then those caring for them must be taught how to listen and how to recognise the shared humanity that lies beneath any difference that they may exhibit. I have argued that mental illness does force us to acknowledge difference, and that this cannot and should not be ignored; if there were no significant differences in those we identify as mentally ill, we would not identify them as mentally ill (or possessed by the devil, or whatever.)

However, there is a difference between classifying difference in absolute terms - good/bad; rich/poor; clever/stupid; sane/mad; and classifying it in terms of degree.

In order to treat the mentally ill more humanely, we need to adopt a model that acknowledges the shared humanity between the 'sane' and the 'mad'; we need to acknowledge the stresses and strains that are imposed upon all people in the course of their lives, and how much harder it is for some to cope well with them if they are less fortunate in some significant area (whether that be genetic, social, personality, family membership etc.) than others.

The acknowledgement of difference also means that we must adopt a notion of autonomy in relation to the mentally ill that is far more comprehensive than the rather limited conceptions currently in use. Harris has characterised autonomy as:

> ... critical self-determination in which the agent strives to make decisions which are as little marred by defects in reason, information or control as she can make them. (Harris, 1985, p. 215)

It is all too easy, fired by good intentions, to ignore the qualifying 'as little marred by defects in reason', when trying to give the mentally ill a voice. We need to construct a notion of autonomy that allows for what Campbell has described as 'the basic human need for dependency'.

> It really takes little time to ensure that people take charge of their own lives, if they can. It is having the compassion and commitment to help those who have lost the capacity for self-determination that properly tests our moral seriousness as providers of health care rather than mere contractors of medical intervention. (Campbell, in Fulford, Gillett and Soskice, 1994, p. 192)

But arguably it does cost more money, and also involves more moral dilemmas; it is easier and cheaper to take refuge in our simple notion of autonomy, particularly in a society which appears to be obsessed with individualistic, self-gratifying notions of autonomy. Thus we may argue that we are respecting the rights of the mentally ill to be accorded autonomy when we refuse to acknowledge their dependency, when what we are really doing is reneging on our responsibilities to dependent members of society. We similarly renege on our responsibilities when we argue for community care as a means of encouraging autonomy but fail to provide either community or care. In the process, we keep our consciences clean and leave the mentally ill to rot.

To summarise, therefore, I would suggest that the philosophical approach that should inform efforts to improve the treatment of the mentally ill should be that of normalisation, justified by the acknowledgement of a shared, common humanity between the mentally ill and the 'normal'. Normalisation does not simply seek to improve treatment conditions for the mentally ill; it is a philosophy of treatment which seeks to give them access to the conditions of 'ordinary' living, instead of being categorised and isolated from mainstream life by virtue of their problems.

But the concept of a shared, common, fundamental humanity does not depend upon uniformity nor even conformity of beliefs, ideas and behaviour. Neither does it depend upon simplistic, impoverished notions of autonomy, no matter how well-meaning they may be: we must acknowledge the shared humanity of individuals whilst acknowledging their differences and their problems.

To be effective, normalisation must be implemented through a policy of community care and treatment wherever possible. But it is another of the hypocrisies of the 'sane' that allows the mentally ill to be sent to be cared for in a community that is often ill-equipped to deal with them and more often than not does not even exist. To meet the needs of the mentally ill in the community demands a more flexible, sensitive response than can be achieved by a rights based system only, or, indeed, by simplistic, emotionally informed notions of autonomy. It also demands better procedural processes, and certainly more money to implement them.

Illness is rarely a static state, and consequently the needs of the ill vary over time. Therefore community care must be only one element, albeit the major one, in a comprehensive range of treatment facilities. It must also be acknowledged that for some people community care is not a viable option, or may not be a viable option through all phases of their illness. And it should be acknowledged that some people will occasionally need asylum, in the true sense of the term, even though they may not be a danger to others or themselves, and that this might be most appropriately provided in a residential setting for a time. What is needed is a flexible, responsive system of mental health care provision which acknowledges that illness is not static and neither are people's needs; and that most people do not live in isolation from family, friends and loved ones, and therefore, wherever possible, these people should be involved when trying to reach the best treatment options. All of this, it goes without saying, will require a great deal more money than is currently being spent on the provision of mental health care.

Education will be vital if there is to be any hope of changing people's attitudes to the mentally ill. The mentally ill must also be given a voice with which to tell their stories, and the adoption of advocacy schemes is one way of helping them to do this. Treatment in the narrower sense of medical treatment must also be improved by the better training of psychiatrists and other health care professionals.

I do not accept the argument that mental illness is merely socially constructed or a category applied to those considered to be socially deviant, in order to control them. I would therefore argue that scientific research into the causes and treatment of mental illness should continue, because at the moment we really understand very little about these things. Nevertheless, there seems to me to be a wealth of evidence to suggest that physical factors are involved in at least some forms of mental illness and to stop research would be irresponsible. This seems to me to be no more reductionist than continuing research into the causes and treatment of brain tumours, for example.

Ultimately, the implementation of practical schemes to improve the treatment of the mentally ill is dependent upon will - the will to improve things, and this will can only come from concern; if we have no concern for the mentally ill, how can we have the will to improve their treatment? And if we wish to consider ourselves a civilised society, we must be concerned; we have no option but to improve the treatment of the mentally ill, for the mark of a civilised society can surely be argued to be the compassion with which it treats its most vulnerable members. Otherwise, our society will become the heath:

> The heath is both a real place and a place in the mind. It is what the human world would be like if pity, duty and the customs of honour and due ceased to rule human behaviour. It is the realm of natural man, man beyond society, without clothes, retinue, pride and respect. But natural man has a terrible identity, Lear learns - the identity of life at degree zero, a hair's breadth from death. It is an equality of objection that no man can endure. (Ignatieff, 1990, p. 41)

But if we wish to avoid our society becoming like the heath, it is not enough to pass the responsibility for preventing this to others. It is easy to blame professionals for using the wrong models of illness and treatment; to blame governments for not investing enough money in the provision of care; to adopt simplistic stances on freedom and autonomy rather than accept the painful decisions that frequently have to be made when the treatment of the mentally ill is being considered. If we are to turn the heath into the garden, we must all be responsible for taking part in its cultivation. To achieve this will require both a change in attitudes towards the mentally ill and the willingness to provide the money necessary to implement the structural changes that a policy of community care based on the principle of normalisation requires to have any chance of being successful.

And if we are not moved by compassion to take part in this cultivation, we might do well to reflect that perhaps we should be moved by self interest, for the heath in *King Lear* makes no differentiation between king and fool, and if it finally encroaches on us, who is to say that any of us will escape it?

Appendix

By far the largest group of minor tranquillisers are the benzodiazepines, most famous, or perhaps infamous, amongst which is Valium. All these drugs have a calming effect because they act by depressing the central nervous system; in lower doses this results in sedation; higher doses cause sleep, hence their classification as sedative-hypnotics, along with alcohol and barbiturates. These drugs have been very widely prescribed for the treatment of anxiety; prescriptions for them in the UK peaked in 1971 at around 31 million; by 1987 this had dropped to 25 million. Women are prescribed minor tranquillisers twice as frequently as men. (Office of Health Economics, 1990). It is now acknowledged that minor tranquillisers can cause addiction if taken in therapeutic doses over several months. [See Lacey, 1991, for a layman's guide to psychotropic drugs; the standard specialist reference guide to drugs is the British National Formulary). Withdrawal from minor tranquillisers can cause a very unpleasant reaction including panic, insomnia, tremor, muscle tension, sweating and palpitations; more serious reactions can include epileptic seizures, hallucinations, paranoid delusions and the first rank symptoms of schizophrenia. (Tyrer, 1987; see also Covi et al, 1973; Lader and Petursson, 1983; Rickels at al, 1983; Rickels et al, 1986; Winokur et al, 1980)].

The side-effects of the neuroleptic drugs (major tranquillisers), commonly used to treat schizophrenia and other psychotic states, can be devastating; they include problems with vision; stomach, bladder and sexual function; temperature regulation; photosensitivity; obstructive jaundice; circulatory problems and weight gain. Horrendous though this list is, however, arguably the two worst side-effects are tardive dyskinesia and 'pseudo-Parkinsonism'. 'Tardive dyskinesia' means delayed (tardive) abnormal movement (dyskinesia); it is a disorder of movement that can affect any of the voluntary muscles causing uncontrollable twitching, writhing and spasms. According to Gardos and Cole (1980), figures for the incidence (defined as the number of new cases emerging in a defined population) are not known; they cite research which puts its prevalence (defined as the proportion of patients with tardive dyskinesia at a particular time in a given population) ranging from 0.5% to 40% , a huge range, but as they point out, it is hard to reach conclusions from such research as it is difficult to evaluate because of problems of definition, measurement, reliability of rating scales and the generalisability of results. Nonetheless, despite uncertainty and disagreement about the extent and severity of the problem, no-one in the medical profession appears to deny that tardive dyskinesia is a serious problem, and one which is complicated by the fact that withdrawal of anti-psychotic medication does not necessarily result in withdrawal of symptoms; in some cases this even makes matters worse:

> Withdrawal of anti-psychotic drugs and occasionally of anti-depressants may result in an increase in the severity of tardive dyskinesia or in the appearance of new dyskinetic movements. The prevalence of withdrawal-emergent dyskinesia has been estimated to be 5% - 40%. (Gardos and Cole, 1980, p. 778)

It is not possible to predict which patients will suffer problems from the withdrawal of medication.

'Pseudo-Parkinsonism' can cause a shuffling walk, rigid facial expression, apathy and extreme restlessness; these symptoms mimic the symptoms of Parkinson's Disease and may be treated with the same anticholinergic drugs that are used to treat Parkinson's Disease, but these also have unwanted side-effects, and they increase the risk of tardive dyskinesia. (Re the routine use of anticholinergic medication with anti-psychotic drugs, see Lacey, 1991, pp. 165-166; Johnstone at al, 1983; and Loga, 1975.)

The powerful effects of the major tranquilliser Haloperidol have been documented by Belmaker and Wald (1977), two psychiatrists who each took 5 mg of the drug; this is only one tenth of the lowest dose recommended by the British National Formulary for patients. They experienced slowness in thinking and moving and profound feelings of restlessness. They were unable perform even simple tasks of their own volition, and had to be told what to do. Far from feeling tranquil, they both experienced severe anxiety. It was 36 hours before either was able to return to work. If this is the effect of only 5 mg of Haloperidol it is not difficult to see why so many patients resent or reject taking the usually very much larger doses of major tranquillisers prescribed for them.

A new anti-psychotic drug, Clozapine, has recently become available for the treatment of schizophrenia. It is claimed that this drug has few of the unpleasant side-effects of other anti-psychotic medication, and is effective in treating some patients for whom other medication has proved ineffective. However, Clozapine does have some extremely serious side-effects, not least of which is agranulocytosis, a serious blood disorder which damages bone marrow and may be fatal. Regular blood tests are essential for patients taking Clozapine to monitor any adverse effects of the drug. (See The Lancet, 1989; Kerwin, 1993; BMJ, 1993)

Anti-depressants come in two main types; the monoamine oxidase inhibitors (MAOIs), less frequently used nowadays because they can interact dangerously with certain common foods such as cheese and chocolate, and the tricyclic anti-depressants which are chemically very similar to the major tranquillisers. The side-effects of tricyclic anti-depressants include difficulty in concentrating, blurred vision, dry mouth and confusion. They are extremely dangerous if an overdose is taken.

The side-effects of anti-depressants may start immediately, but the benefits take from between four to six weeks to be felt, with the result that some patients stop taking the drugs before they have a chance to work. Like other psychotropic drugs, their efficacy is difficult to assess, and varies greatly: There is a safer form of anti-depressants now available, known as SSRIs - selective serotonin re-uptake inhibitors - but these are much less commonly prescribed than the more toxic tricyclic anti-depressants. (It has been claimed by some psychiatrists that this is because they are considerably more expensive.) The most famous (or infamous) of the SSRIs is Fluoxetine - trade name Prozac; this is the designer drug (so-called because it was specifically designed to affect particular chemical transmissions in the brain) that has caused considerable controversy because of the extraordinary claims that have been made for it. Put briefly, Prozac is claimed to have the power to transform people - people who are not considered to be suffering from mental illness, but simply from what might be called aspects of the human condition: shyness, introversion; insensitivity; lack of confidence, so as well as treating depression far more effectively than other drugs, Prozac was claimed to be able to change personality for the better, and with negligible side-effects. However, there has been a backlash against the euphoria generated by Prozac; claims are now being made that it has been responsible for a number of suicides and adverse personality changes; there are Prozac Survivors Support Groups springing up in America and a number of lawsuits in progress.

The possible side-effects of Lithium, which is used to treat manic-depression, include kidney damage, thyroid damage, blurred vision, hand tremors and muscular twitching as well as host of less serious but unpleasant effects such as dry mouth, increased thirst and urination and aggravated acne. Lithium is one of the most toxic substances used in medicine; regular blood tests are essential for those taking Lithium in order to establish the correct dose.

The list of side-effects of these drugs is alarming, but it must be seen in context. No drugs are free of side-effects, even the common ones sold without prescription in newsagents and supermarkets, and there will always be a small number of individuals who have an extreme and atypical reaction to a specific drug. This is not to deny the power and potential danger of these treatments, however, nor the need for them to be used subtly and sensitively, with an awareness of the trade-off between costs and benefits, and an acknowledgement of whose costs and whose benefits are involved.

Bibliography

Abbott, R. J., and L. A. Loizou (1986), 'Neuroleptic Syndrome', *British Journal of Psychiatry*, Vol. 148, pp. 47-51.

Abraham, F., and B. Webb (1989), *Mental Health and Self Help Support*, Community Organisations, Voluntary Action and Social Welfare Occasional Paper No. 5, Tavistock Publications, London.

Ackner, B., A. Harris, and A. J. Oldham (1957), 'Insulin Treatment of Schizophrenia - A Controlled Study', *Lancet*, Vol. 2, pp. 607-11.

Adams, M. M., and R. M. Adams (eds) (1992), *The Problem of Evil*, OUP, Oxford.

Alexander, F. (1957), *Psychoanalysis and Psychotherapy*, Allen and Unwin, London.

Allderidge, P. (1979), 'Hospitals, Madhouses and Asylums: Cycles in the Care of the Insane', *British Journal of Psychiatry*, Vol. 134, pp. 321-34.

Alper, B. (1973), 'Foreword', in Bakal, Y. (ed.), *Closing Correctional Institutions*, Lexington Books, Lexington, Mass.

American Psychiatric Association (1978), *Task Force Report 14: Electroconvulsive Therapy*, Washington DC.

Anonymous (1965), 'The Experience of Electroconvulsive Therapy by a Practising Psychiatrist', *British Journal of Psychiatry*, Vol. 111, pp. 365-7.

Appelbaum, P., and T. G. Gutheil (1980), 'Drug Refusal: A Study of Psychiatric Inpatients', *American Journal of Psychiatry*, Vol. 137, No. 3, pp. 340-45.

Appelbaum, P. S. (1988), 'The Right to Refuse Treatment With Antipsychotic Medications: Retrospect and Prospect', *American Journal of Psychiatry*, Vol. 145, pp. 413-9.

Aristotle (1986), *Ethics*, trans. J. A. K. Thomson, Penguin, Harmondsworth.

Arlidge, J., and C. Hall (1992), 'Crisis Talks Over "Irresponsible" Aids Virus Carrier', *The Independent*, 24 June, p. 1.

Association of Psychiatrists in Training (1979), *Who Puts Medical Students Off Psychiatry?*, Smith, Kline and French Laboratories, London.

Bachrach, L. (1989), 'Deinstitutionalisation: A Semantic Analysis', *Journal of Social Issues*, Vol. 45, No. 3, pp. 161-71.

Bakal, Y. (ed.) (1973), *Closing Correctional Institutions*, Lexington Books, Lexington.

Barham, P. (1992), *Closing the Asylum: The Mental Patient in Modem Society*, Penguin, Harmondsworth.

Barker, I., and E. Peck (eds) (1987), *Power in Strange Places: Good Practices in Mental Health*, London.

Barker, P. J., and S. Baldwin (eds) (1991), *Ethical Issues in Mental Health*, Chapman and Hall, London.

Barraclough, B. (1974), 'A Hundred Cases of Suicide', *British Journal of Psychiatry*, Vol. 125, pp. 355-73.

Baruch, G., and A. Treacher (1978), *Psychiatry Observed*, Routledge Kegan Paul, London.

Bavidge, M. (1989), *Mad or Bad?*, The Bristol Press, Bristol.

Bean, P. (1980), *Compulsory Admissions to Mental Hospitals*, John Wiley, Chichester.

Bean, P. (ed.) (1983), *Mental Illness: Changes and Trends*, John Wiley, Chichester.

Bean, P. (1988), *Mental Disorder and Legal Control*, CUP, Cambridge.

Beauchamp, T. L., and J. F. Childress (1983), *Principles of Biomedical Ethics*, second edition, OUP, Oxford.

Bebbington, P. E. (1977), 'Psychiatry: Science, Meaning and Purpose', *British Journal of Psychiatry*, Vol. 130, pp. 222-8.

Beck, E. R., J. L. Francis, and R. L. Southam (1977), *Tutorials in Differential Diagnosis*, Pitman Medical, Tonbridge Wells.

Belmaker, R. H., and D. Ward (1977), 'Haloperidol in Normals', *British Journal of Psychiatry*, Vol. 131, p. 222.

Bentall, R. (1992), 'A Proposal to Classify Happiness as a Psychiatric Disorder', *Journal of Medical Ethics*, Vol. 18, pp. 94-8.

Bentall, R., H. Jackson, and D. Pilgrim (1988), 'Abandoning the Concept of "Schizophrenia": Some Implications of Validity Arguments for Psychological Research into Psychotic Phenomena', *British Journal of Clinical Psychology*, Vol. 27, pp. 303-24.

Bentall, R. P. (ed.) (1992), *Reconstructing Schizophrenia*, Routledge, London.

Bergin, A. E. (1971), 'The Evaluation of Psychotherapy Outcomes', in Bergin, A.E. and S. Garfield (eds), *Handbook of Psychotherapy and Behavior Change*, Wiley, New York.

Bergsma, J., and D. C. Thomasma (1982), *Health Care: Its Psychosocial Dimensions*, Duquesne University Press, Pittsburgh.

Birtchnell, J. (1987), 'A Psychiatrist Speaks Out', *British Journal of Clinical and Social Psychiatry*, Vol. 5. No. 2, pp. 223-5.

Bloch, S., and P. Chodoff (eds) (1984), *Psychiatric Ethics*, OUP, Oxford.

Bloch, S. (ed.) (1986), *An Introduction to the Psychotherapies*, second edition, Oxford Medical Publications, Oxford.

Blom-Cooper, L., H. Hally, and E. Murphy (1995), *The Falling Shadow: One Patient's Mental Health Care 1978-1993*, Duckworth, London.

179

Bluglass, R. (1984), *A Guide to the Mental Health Act 1983*, Churchill Livingstone, London.

Boorse, C. (1981), 'On the Distinction Between Disease and Illness', in Cohen, M., T. Nagel, and T. Scanlon (eds), *Medicine and Moral Philosophy*, Princeton University Press, Princeton.

Bott, E. (1976), 'Hospital and Society', *British Journal of Medical Psychology*, Vol. 46, pp. 97-140.

Bottoms, A. E., and R. Brownsword (1982), 'The Dangerousness Debate After the Floud Report', *British Journal of Criminology*, Vol. 22, No. 3, pp. 229-54.

Brackx, A., and C. Grimshaw (eds) (1989), *Mental Health Care in Crisis*, Pluto Press, London.

Brain, L. (1960), *Brain's Clinical Neurology*, 5th edition, OUP, Oxford.

Braine, D., and H. Lesser (eds) (1988), *Ethics, Technology and Medicine*, Avebury, Aldershot.

Brazier, M. (1987), *Medicine, Patients and the Law*, Penguin, Harmondsworth.

Breggin, P. (1972), 'The Return of Lobotomy and Psychosurgery', *Congressional Record*, Vol. 118. pp. E1603-12.

Breggin, P. (1993), *Toxic Psychiatry*, Fontana, London.

British Association for Counselling (1984), *Code of Ethics and Practice for Counsellors*, British Association for Counselling, Rugby.

British National Formulary (1994), *British National Formulary*, BMA and British Pharmacological Society, London.

Brohn, P. (1986), *Gentle Giants,* Century Publishing, London.

Brown, G. (1973), 'The Mental Hospital as an Institution', *Social Science and Medicine*, Vol. 7, pp. 407-24.

Brown, G. W., and T. Harris (1978), *The Social Origins of Depression: A Study of Psychiatric Disorder in Women*, Tavistock Publications, London.

Brown, R. (1977), 'Physical Illness and Mental Health', *Philosophy and Public Affairs*, Vol. 7, pp. 17-38.

Browning, R., (1968), *Browning: Poems and Plays*, vol. two, Dent Everyman's Library, London.

Bruce, E. M., N. Crone, G. Fitzpatrick, S. J. Frewin, A. Gillis, C. F. Lascelles, L. J. Levene, and H. Merskey (1960), 'A Comparative Trial of ECT and Tofranil', *American Journal of Psychiatry*, Vol. 117, p. 76.

Buchanan, A. (1978), 'Medical Paternalism', *Philosophy and Public Affairs*, Vol. 7, pp. 370-90.

Burns, C. R. (1976), 'The Non-naturals: A Paradox in the Western Concept of Health', *Journal of Medicine and Philosophy*, Vol. 1, pp. 202-11.

Burton, L. (1975), *The Family Life of Sick Children*, Routledge and Kegan Paul, London.

Butler, A., and C. Pritchard (1983), *Social Work and Mental Illness*, Macmillan Education, Basingstoke.

Butler, S. (1987), *Erewhon,* Penguin, Harmondsworth.

Campbell, R. (1992), *Philosophy and Suicide*, The Second Richard Finlayson Lecture edition, The Samaritans, London.

Camus, A. (1975), *The Myth of Sisyphus,* Penguin, Harmondsworth.

Caplan, A. L., H. T. Engelhardt, and J. J. McCartney (eds) (1981), *Concepts of Health and Disease: Interdisciplinary Perspectives*, Addison-Wesley, Reading, Massachusetts.

Castoriadis, C. (1991), *Philosophy, Politics, Autonomy: Essays in Political Philosophy*, OUP, New York.

Cavadino, M. (1989), *Mental Health Law in Context: Doctors' Orders?*, Aldershot, Dartmouth.

Chalmers, A. F. (1982), *What Is This Thing Called Science? An Assessment of the Nature and Status of Scientific Method*, second edition, Open University Press, Milton Keynes.

Chatterton v. Gerson and Another (1980), All ER 257 *The Times*, London, 7th February.

Chesler, P. (1972), *Women and Madness*, Avon Books, New York.

Chitty, S. (1985), *Now to My Mother*, Weidenfeld and Nicholson, London.

Chodoff, P. (1976), 'The Case for the Involuntary Hospitalisation of the Mentally Ill', *American Journal of Psychiatry*, Vol. 133, pp. 496-501.

Chodoff, P. (1984), 'Involuntary Hospitalisation of the Mentally Ill as a Moral Issue', *American Journal of Psychiatry*, Vol. 141, pp. 384-89.

Clare, A. (1980), *Psychiatry in Dissent*, Tavistock Publications, London.

Clark, A. F., and N. L. Holden (1987), 'The Persistence of Prescribing Habits: A Survey and Follow-Up of Prescribing to Chronic Hospital In-Patients', *British Journal of Psychiatry*, Vol. 150, pp. 88-91.

Clark, P., and C. Wright (eds) (1988), *Mind, Psychoanalysis and Science*, Basil Blackwell, Oxford.

Clouser, K. D., C. M. Culver, and B. Gert (1981), 'Malady: A New Treatment of Disease', *Hastings Centre Report*, Vol. 11, No. 3, pp. 29-37.

Coate, M. (1964), *Beyond All Reason,* Constable, London.

Cocozza, J., and H. Steadman (1976), 'Predictions in Psychiatry: An Example of Misplaced Confidence in Experts', *Social Problems,* Vol. 25, No. 23, pp. 265-70.

Cohen, D. (1989), *Soviet Psychiatry,* Paladin, Grafton Books, London.

Cohen, D. (1988), *Forgotten Millions: The Treatment of the Mentally Ill - A Global Perspective*, Paladin, London.

Cohen, D. (ed.), (1990), *Challenging the Therapeutic State: Critical Perspectives on Psychiatry and the Mental Health System*, The Institute of Mind and Behaviour, New York.

Cohen, S. (1972), *Folk Devils and Moral Panics*, McGibbon and Kee, London.

Coles, E. M. (1975), 'The Meaning and Measurement of Mental Health', *Bulletin of the British Psychological Society*, Vol. 28, March, pp. 111-13.

Committee of Enquiry (1976), *Report of the Committee of Enquiry, St Augustine's Hospital, Chatham, Kent*, South East Thames Regional Health Authority, London.

Conrad, J. P. (1982), 'The Quandary of Dangerousness', *British Journal of Criminology*, Vol. 22, pp. 255-67.

Conrad, J. P., and S. Dinitz (eds) (1977), *In Fear of Each Other: Studies of Dangerousness in America*, Lexington Books, Lexington.

Costello, C. G. (1976), Electroconvulsive Therapy: Is Further Investigation Necessary?, *Canadian Psychiatric Association Journal*, Vol. 21, pp. 761-7.

Coulter, J. (1973), *Approaches to Insanity: A Philosophical and Sociological Study*, Martin Robertson, London.

Covi, L., R. S. Lipman, and J. H. Pattison (1973), 'Length of Treatment with Anxiolytic Sedatives and Responses to Their Sudden Withdrawal', *Acta Psychiatrica Scandinavia*, Vol. 49, pp. 51-64.

Cresswell, J., and N. Johnson (1990), 'The One-Sided Wall', in *Plays By Women*, ed. M. Remnant, Vol. 8, Methuen, London.

Crichton, J. (ed.) (1995), *Psychiatric Patient Violence: Risk and Response*, Duckworth, London.

Cronholm, B., and J. O. Ottosson (1960), 'Experimental Studies of the Therapeutic Action of Electroconvulsive Therapy in Endogenous Depression', *Acta Psychiatrica et Neurologica Scandinavica*, Vol. 35, Suppl. 145, pp. 69-97.

Crow, T. J., J. S. Macmillan, A. L. Johnson, and E. C. Johnson (1986), 'The Northwick Park Study of First Episode Schizophrenia: A Controlled Study of Neuroleptic Treatment', *British Journal of Psychiatry*, Vol. 148, pp. 120-27.

Culver, C. M., and B. Gert (1982), *Philosophy in Medicine*, OUP, Oxford.

Dahlberg, C. (1970), 'Sexual Contact Between Patient and Therapist', *Contemporary Psychoanalysis*, Vol. 6, pp. 107-24.

Dalley, G. (1988), *Ideologies of Caring*, Macmillan, London.

Daniel, S. L. (1986), 'The Patient as Text: A Model of Clinical Hermeneutics', *Theoretical Medicine,* Vol. 7, pp. 195-210.

Davidson, D. (1982), 'Rational Animals', *Dialectica,* Vol. 36, pp. 318-27.

Davidson, D. (1989), 'Psychology as Philosophy', in *The Philosophy of Mind*, ed. J. Glover, OUP, Oxford.

Davidson, V. (1977), 'Psychiatry's Problem With No Name: Therapist-Patient Sex', *American Journal of Psychoanalysis*, Vol. 37, pp. 43-50.

Delgado, J. M. R. (1969), *Physical Control of the Mind: Toward a Psychocivilised Society*, Harper and Row, New York.

Department of Health and Welsh Office (1993), *Code of Practice: Mental Health Act 1983*, HMSO, London.

Department of Health: Mental Health Task Force (1994), *London Project*, HMSO, London.

Deveson, A. (1992), *Tell Me I'm Here*, Penguin, Harmondsworth.

Dinnage, R. (1988), *One to One: Experiences of Psychotherapy*, Viking, Penguin Books, New York.

Donne, J. (1987), *Devotions Upon Emergent Occasions*, ed. A. Raspa, OUP, New York.

Dowie, J., and A. Elstein (eds) (1988), *Professional Judgement: A Reader in Clinical Decision Making*, CUP, Cambridge.

Downie, R. S., and K. C. Calman (1987), *Healthy Respect: Ethics in Health Care*, Faber and Faber, London.

Dubos, R. (1987), *The Mirage of Health: Utopias, Progress and Biological Change*, Rutgers University Press, New Brunswick.

Duff, A. (1977), 'Psychopathy and Moral Understanding', *American Philosophical Quarterly*, Vol. 14, No. 3, pp. 189-200.

Durkheim, E. (1952), *Suicide,* Routledge Kegan Paul, London.

Dworkin, G. (1988), *The Theory and Practice of Autonomy*, CUP, Cambridge.

Dyer, A. R., and S. Bloch (1987), 'Informed Consent and the Psychiatric Patient', *Journal of Medical Ethics*, Vol. 13, pp. 12-16.

Editorial (1989), 'Clozapine', *Lancet,* Vol. 2, p. 1430.

Editorial (1993), 'Therapy that Women Could Do Without', *The Independent*, 6 April, London.

Editorial (1993), 'Clozapine: Progress in Treating Refractory Schizophrenia', *British Medical Journal*, Vol. 306, p. 1427.

Edwards, R. B. (1981), 'Mental Health as Rational Autonomy', *Journal of Medicine and Philosophy*, Vol. 6, pp. 309-22.

Edwards, S., and V. Kumar (1984), 'A Survey of Prescribing and Psychotropic Drugs in a Birmingham Psychiatric Hospital', *British Journal of Psychiatry*, Vol. 145, pp. 502-7.

Eisenberg, N., and D. Glasgow (eds) (1986), *Current Issues in Clinical Psychology*, Gower, Aldershot.

Ellenberger, H. F. (1970), *The Discovery of the Unconscious*, Allen Lane, London.

Elliott, D. W., and J. C. Wood (1974), *A Casebook of Criminal Law*, 3rd edition, London.

Ennis, B. J., and T. R. Litwak (1974), 'Psychiatry and the Presumption of Expertise: Flipping Coins in the Courtroom', *California Law Review*, Vol. 62, No. 5, pp. 693-752.

Ennis, B. J., and T. R. Litwak (1976), 'Prediction in Psychiatry: An Example of Misplaced Confidence in Experts', *Social Problems*, Vol. 25, No. 23, pp. 265-70.

Eysenck, H. J. (1986), *Decline and Fall of the Freudian Empire*, Penguin, Harmondsworth.

Eysenck, H. J. (1952), 'The Effects of Psychotherapy: An Evaluation', *Journal of Consulting Psychology*, Vol. 16, pp. 319-24.

Eysenck, H. J. (1969), *The Effects of Psychotherapy*, Science House, New York.

Fabrega, H. (1978), 'Disease Viewed as a Symbolic Category', in *Mental Health: Philosophical Perspectives*, eds T. Engelhardt and S. F. Spicker, D. Reidel, Dordrecht.

Farrell, B. A. (1981), *The Standing of Psychoanalysis*, OUP, Oxford.

Fields, L. (1987), 'Exoneration of the Mentally Ill', *Journal of Medical Ethics*, Vol. 13, pp. 201-5.

Flew, A. (1973), *Crime or Disease?*, Macmillan, London.

Floud, J. (1981), *Dangerousness and Criminal Justice*, Heinemann, London.

Floud, J. (1982), 'Dangerousness and Criminal Justice', *British Journal of Criminology*, Vol. 22, pp. 213-28.

Floud, J. (1985), 'Dangerousness in Social Perspective', in *Psychiatry, Human Rights and the Law*, eds M. Roth, and R. Bluglass, CUP, Cambridge.

Fodor, J. A. (1994), 'The Mind-Body Problem', in *The Mind-Body Problem: A Guide to the Current Debate,* eds R. Warner and T. Szubka, Blackwell, Oxford.

Ford, M. D. (1980), 'The Psychiatrist's Double Bind: The Right to Refuse Medication', *American Journal of Psychiatry*, Vol. 137, No. 3, pp. 332-9.

Freidson, E. (1970), *Profession of Medicine: A Study of the Sociology of Applied Knowledge*, Dodd, Mead and Co., New York.

Fromm, E. (1950), *Psychoanalysis and Religion*, Yale University Press, New Haven.

Fulford, K. W. M. (1989), *Moral Theory and Medical Practice*, Press Syndicate of the University of Cambridge, Cambridge.

Fulford, K. W. M., G. Gillett and J. M. Soskice (eds) (1994), *Medicine and Moral Reasoning*, CUP, Cambridge.

Furrow, B. (1980), *Malpractice in Psychotherapy*, Lexington Books, Lexington.

Gardos, G., and J. O. Cole (1980), 'Overview: Public Health Issues in Tardive Dyskinesia', *American Journal of Psychiatry*, Vol. 137, pp. 776-81.

Garfield, S. L., and A. E. Bergin (eds) (1978), *Handbook of Psychotherapy and Behaviour Change: An Empirical Analysis,* John Wiley and Sons, New York.

Gartrell, N., J. Herman, S. Olante, M. Feldstein, and R. Localio (1986), 'Psychiatrist-Patient Sexual Contact', *American Journal of Psychiatry*, Vol. 143, No. 9, pp. 1126-31.

Gaylin, W. M., J. S. Meister, and R. C. Neville (eds) (1975), *Operating on the Mind: the Psychosurgery Debate*, Basic Books, New York.

Geller, J. L. (1986), 'Rights, Wrongs and the Dilemma of Coerced Community Treatment', *American Journal of Psychiatry*, Vol. 143, No. 10, pp. 1259-64.

Gert, B. (1988), *Morality: A New Justification of the Moral Rules*, OUP, Oxford.

Gillon, R. (1986), *Philosophical Medical Ethics*, John Wiley, Chichester.

Glover, J. (ed.) (1989), *The Philosophy of Mind*, OUP, Oxford.

Goffman, E. (1987), *Asylums: Essays on the Social Situation of Mental Patients and Other Inmates*, Peregrine, London.

Goldberg, D., and P. Huxley (1992), *Common Mental Disorders: A Bio-Social Model*, Routledge, London.

Goodwin, S. (1990), *Community Care and the Future of Mental Health Service Provision*, Avebury, Aldershot.

Gordon, R. A. (1982), 'Preventive Sentencing and the Dangerous Offender', *British Journal of Criminology*, Vol. 22, pp. 285-314.

Gorman, J. (1990), *The Essential Guide to Psychiatric Drugs*, St Martin's Press, New York.

Gostin, L. (1985), 'Human Rights in Mental Health', in *Psychiatry, Human Rights and the Law*, eds M. Roth and R. Bluglass, CUP, Cambridge.

Gostin, L. (ed.) (1985), *Secure Provision: A Review of Special Services for the Mentally Ill in England and Wales*, Tavistock Publications, London.

Granville-Grossman, K. (1971), 'Convulsive Therapy', in *Recent Advances in Clinical Psychiatry*, ed. K. Granville-Grossman, J. and A. Churchill, London.

Griffiths, S. R. (1988), *Community Care: Agenda for Action - A Report to the Secretary of State for Social Services*, HMSO, London.

Gross, H. (1978), *The Psychological Society*, Random House, New York.

Grubb, A. (ed.) (1994), *Decision-Making and Problems of Competence*, John Wiley, Chichester.

Grunbaum, A. (1985), *The Foundations of Psychoanalysis: A Philosophical Critique*, University of California Press, London.

Gustafson, D. A. (ed.) (1967), *Essays in Philosophical Psychology*, Macmillan, London.

Gutheil, T., R. Shapiro, and L. St. Clair (1980), 'Legal Guardianship in Drug Refusal: An Illusory Solution', *American Journal of Psychiatry*, Vol. 137, pp. 347-51.

Habermas, J. (1972), *Knowledge and Human Interests*, Heinemann, London.

Hall, J. E., and R. T. Hare-Mustin (1983), 'Sanctions and the Diversity of Ethical Complaints Against Psychologists', *American Psychologist*, Vol. 38, pp. 714-29.

Hall, S. A. (1992), 'Should Public Health Respect Autonomy?', *Journal of Medical Ethics*, Vol. 18, pp. 197-201.

Hands, T. (ed.) (1976), *Pleasure and Repentance*, A Wheaton & Co., Exeter.

Hankinson, J. (1989), *Bluff Your way in Philosophy*, Ravette Books, Horsham.

Harris, J. (1985), *The Value of Life: An Introduction to Medical Ethics*, Routledge Kegan Paul, London.

Hart, H. L. A. (1961), *The Concept of Law*, Clarendon Press, Oxford.

Hays, P. (1964), *New Horizons in Psychiatry*, Penguin, Harmondsworth.

Healy, D. (1990), *The Suspended Revolution*, Faber and Faber, London.

Healy, D. (1993), *Images of Trauma: From Hysteria to Post-Traumatic Stress Disorder*, Faber and Faber, London.

Heelas, P., and A. Lock (eds) (1981), *Indigenous Psychologies: the Anthropology of the Self*, Academic Press, London.

Hemmenki, E. (1977), 'Polypharmacy Among Psychiatric Patients', *Acta Psychiatrica Scandinavia*, Vol. 56, pp. 347-56.

Herink, R. (1981), *The A-Z Guide to Different Therapies in Use Today*, New American Library, New York.

Hervey, N. (1986), 'Advocacy or Folly: the Alleged Lunatics' Friends Society, 1845-63', *Medical History*, Vol. 30, pp. 245-75.

Herxheimer, A. (1976), 'Ignorance: Educating Doctors to Use Drugs Well', *British Journal of Clinical Pharmacology*, Vol. 3, pp. 111-12.

Hill, D. (1985), *The Politics of Schizophrenia*, University Press of America, London.

Hinton, J. (ed.) (1982), *Dangerousness: Problems of Assessment and Prediction*, Allen and Unwin, London.

Hobson, R. F. (1985), *Forms of Feeling: The Heart of Psychotherapy*, Tavistock Publications, London.

Holly, L., and B. Webb (1992), *The Four Projects in the Advocacy Alliance: Some Commonalities and Differences*, Evaluation Development and Review Unit edition, Evaluation Workshop No. 2, The Tavistock Institute, London.

Holyroyd, J. C., and A. M. Brodsky (1977), 'Psychologists' Attitudes and Practices Regarding Erotic and Non-erotic Physical Contact With Patients', *American Psychologist*, Vol. 32, pp. 843-9.

Honderich, T. (1982), 'On Justifying Protective Punishment', *British Journal of Criminology*, Vol. 22, pp. 268-75.

House of Commons Health Committee (1993-94), *Better Off in the Community? The Care of People Who Are Seriously Mentally Ill*, vol. 1 & 2, HMSO, London.

Howe, G. (1991), *The Reality of Schizophrenia*, Faber and Faber, London.

Howell, M., and P. Ford (1980), *The Elephant Man*, Allison and Busby, London.

Human Rights and Equal Opportunities Commission (1993), *Human Rights and Mental Illness: Report of the National Enquiry into the Human Rights of People with Mental Illness*, vol. 1&2, Australian Government Publishing Service, Canberra.

Hume, D. (1978), *A Treatise of Human Nature*, ed. L. A. Selby-Brigge and P. H. Nidditch, 2nd edition, Clarendon Press, Oxford.

Humphrey, N. (1992), *A History of the Mind*, Chatto and Windus, London.

Huxley, P. J., T. Hagan, R. Henelly and J. Hunt (1990), *Effective Community Mental Health Services*, Avebury, Aldershot.

Ignatieff, M. (1990), *The Needs of Strangers*, Hogarth Press, London.

Illich, I. (1988), *Limits to Medicine*, Pelican, London.

Illich, I. (1977), *Medical Nemesis: The Expropriation of Health*, Penguin, Harmondsworth.

Ingleby, D. (ed.) (1981), *Critical Psychiatry: The Politics of Mental Health*, Penguin, Harmondsworth.

Jameson, A. (1984), *Nursing Practice: The Ethical Issues*, Prentice-Hall, Eaglewood Cliffs, New Jersey.

Jeffrey, R. (1979), 'Deviant Patients in Casualty Departments', *Sociology of Health and Illness*, Vol. 1, pp. 90-98.

Johnson, D. McI., and N. Dodds (eds) (1957), *Plea for the Silent*, Christopher Johnson, London.

Johnstone, E. C., J. F. W. Deakin, P. Lawler, C. D. Frith, M. Stevens, K. McPherson and T. J. Crow (1980), 'The Northwick Park ECT Trial', *Lancet*, Vol. ii, pp. 1317-20.

Johnstone, L. (1989), *Users and Abusers of Psychiatry*, Routledge, London.

Jones, K. (1988), *Experience in Mental Health*, Sage Publications, London.

Jones, K., and A. Poletti (1986), 'The "Italian Experience" Reconsidered', *British Journal of Psychiatry*, Vol. 148, pp. 144-50.

Joseph, Sir K. (1971), *Hospital Services for the Mentally Ill*, White Paper, HMSO, London.

Kafka, F. (1961), *Metamorphosis and Other Stories*, Penguin, Harmondsworth.

Kardener, S. H., M. Fuller and I. N. Mensch (1973), 'A Survey of Physicians' Attitudes and Practices Regarding Erotic and Non-erotic Contact with Patients', *American Journal of Psychiatry*, Vol. 130, pp. 1077-81.

Kellam, A. M. P. (1987), 'The Neuroleptic Syndrome, So-called: A Survey of the World Literature', *British Journal of Psychiatry*, Vol. 150, pp. 752-9.

Kendell, R. E. (1975), 'The Concept of Disease and Its Implications for Psychiatry', *British Journal of Psychiatry*, Vol. 127, pp. 305-15.

Kerwin, R. (1993), 'Adverse Reporting and the New Antipsychotics', *Lancet*, Vol. 342, p. 1440.

Kidel, M., and S. Rowe-Leete (eds) (1988), *The Meaning of Illness*, Routledge, London.

Kington, M. (1992), 'Vacant Places Upstairs', *The Independent*, 7 May, p. 28.

Klass, A. (1975), *There's Gold in Them Thar Pills: Enquiry into the Medical Industrial Complex*, Penguin, Harrnondsworth.

Kleinig, J. (1985), *Ethical Issues in Psychosurgery*, Allen and Unwin, London.

Klerman, G., and G. Schechter (1984), 'Ethical Aspects of Drug Treatment', in *Psychiatric Ethics*, eds S. Bloch and P. Chodoff, OUP, Oxford.

Klerman, G. L. (1972), 'Psychotropic Hedonism versus Pharmacological Calvinism', *Hastings Center Report*, Vol. 2, pp. 1-3.

Komrad, M. S. (1983), 'A Defence of Medical Paternalism: Maximising Patients' Autonomy', *Journal of Medical Ethics*, Vol. 9, No. 1, pp. 38-44.

Kovel, J. (1978), *A Complete Guide to Therapy*, Penguin, Harmondsworth.

Kramer, P. D. (1994), *Listening to Prozac: A Psychiatrist Explores Antidepressant Drugs and the Remaking of the Self*, Fourth Estate, London.

Kraupl-Taylor, F. (1976), 'The Medical Model of the Disease Concept', *British Journal of Psychiatry*, Vol. 128, pp. 588-94.

Kubie, I. S. (1971), 'Retreat from Patients', *Archives of General Psychiatry*, Vol. 24, pp. 98-106.

Kuhn, A. (1985), *The Power of the Image*, Routledge Kegan Paul, London.

Lacey, R. (1991), *The Complete Guide to Psychiatric Drugs*, Ebury Press, London.

Lader, M., and H. Petursson (1983), 'Long-term Effects of Benzodiazepines', *Neuropharmacology*, Vol. 22, pp. 527-33.

Laing, J., and D. McQuarrie (1992), *Fifty Years in the System*, Corgi Books, London.

Laing, R. D. (1967), *The Politics of Experience and The Bird of Paradise*, Penguin, Harmondsworth.

Laing, R. D. (1969), *Politics and the Family*, Penguin, Harmondsworth.

Laing, R. D. (1979), *The Divided Self*, Penguin, Harmondsworth.

Lakin, M. (1988), *Ethical Issues in the Psychotherapies*, OUP, Oxford.

Lakin, M. (1991), *Coping with Ethical Dilemmas in Psychotherapy*, Pergamon Press, Oxford.

Lamb, D. (1988), *Down the Slippery Slope: Arguing in Applied Ethics*, Croom Helm, London.

Lambert, M. J., A. E. Bergin, and J. L. Collins (1977), 'Therapist-induced Deterioration in Psychotherapy', in *The Therapist's Contributions to Effective Treatment*, eds A. M. Gurman and A. M. Rogers, Pergamon, New York.

Lambourn, J., and D. Gill (1978), 'A Controlled Comparison of Simulated and Real ECT', *British Journal of Psychiatry*, Vol. 133, pp. 514-9.

Langan, M. (1990), 'Community Care in the 1990s: The Community Care White Paper Caring for People', *Critical Social Policy*, Vol. 29, pp. 58-70.

Langs, R. (1985), *Madness and Cure*, Newconcept Press, Emerson, NJ.

Langsley, D. G. (1980), 'The Community Mental Health Center: Does it Treat Patients?', *Hospital and Community Psychiatry*, Vol. 31, pp. 815-9.

Lasch, C. (1991), *The Culture of Narcissism*, W W Norton & Co., London.

Ledermann, E. K. (1984), *Mental Health and Human Conscience: the True and the False Self*, Avebury, Amersham.

Ledermann, E. K. (1986), *Philosophy and Medicine*, Revised edition, Gower, Aldershot.

Leff, J. P., and J. K. Wing (1971), 'Trial of Maintenance Therapy in Schizophrenia', *British Medical Journal*, Vol. 5, pp. 559-606.

Lesser, H. (1983), 'Consent, Competency and ECT: A Philosopher's Comment', *Journal of Medical Ethics*, Vol. 9, pp. 144-5.

Levitt, E. E. (1977), 'Unpublished Paper on Sexual Transgressions Between Physician and Patient Presented at American Medical Association Annual Convention', *AMA Annual Convention*, June 21.

Loga, S., S. Curry, and M. Lader (1975), 'Interactions of Orphenadrine and Phenobarbitone With Chlorpromazine: Plasma Concentrations and Effects in Man', *British Journal of Clinical Pharmacology*, Vol. 2, pp. 197-208.

Lomas, P. (1981), *The Case for a Personal Psychotherapy*, OUP, Oxford.

Lorber, J. (1975), 'Good Patients and Problem Patients: Conformity and Deviance in a General Hospital', *Journal of Health and Social Behaviour*, Vol. 16, pp. 213-25.

Lowe, C. M. (1969), *Value Orientations in Counselling and Psychotherapy: The Meaning of Mental Health*, Chandler, San Francisco.

Luborsky, L., B. Singer, and B. Luborsky (1975), 'Comparative Studies of Psychotherapies: Is it True that "Everyone Has Won and All Must Have Prizes?"', *Archives of General Psychiatry*, Vol. 32, pp. 995-1008.

Macalpine, I., and R. Hunter (1974), The Pathography of the Past, *TLS*, March 15, p. 256.

Mack, J. E., and H. Hickler (1981), *Vivienne: The Life and Suicide of an Adolescent Girl*, Little, Brown and Company, Boston.

Mackie, J. L. (1977), *Ethics: Inventing Right and Wrong*, Penguin, Harmondsworth.

Macklin, R. (1982), 'Refusal of Psychiatric Treatment: Autonomy, Treatment and Paternalism', in *Psychiatry and Ethics*, ed. R. Edwards, Prometheus, New York.

Marks, I. M., J. L. T. Birley, and M. G. Gelder (1966), 'Modified Leucotomy in Severe Agoraphobia: A Controlled Series Inquiry', *British Journal of Psychiatry*, Vol. 113, pp. 53-73.

Masson, J. (1989), *Against Therapy*, Collins, London.

Mayer, J., and N. Timms (1970), *The Client Speaks*, Routledge Kegan Paul, London.

Mays, D. T., and C. M. Frank (1985), *Negative Outcomes in Psychotherapy and What to do About It*, Springer, New York.

McCall-Smith, A. (1987), 'Commentary: Exoneration of the Mentally Ill', *Journal of Medical Ethics*, Vol. 13, pp. 206-8.

Mcintyre, K., M. Farrell, and A. David (1989), 'What Do Psychiatric Inpatients Really Want?', *British Medical Journal*, Vol. 298, pp. 159-60.

Mechanic, D. (1980), Readings in Medical Sociology, Free Press, New York.

Medical Research Council (1965), 'Report by Clinical Psychiatry Committee on ECT', *British Medical Journal*, Vol. 1, pp. 881.

Mental Health Act Commission (1991-93), *Fifth Biennial Report*, HMSO, London.

Mental Health Foundation (1994), *Creating Community Care: Report of the Mental Health Foundation Inquiry into Community Care for People with Severe Mental Illness*, Mental Health Foundation, London.

Michel, K., and T. Kolakowska (1981), 'A Survey of Psychotropic Drug Prescribing in Two Psychiatric Hospitals', *British Journal of Psychiatry*, Vol. 138, pp. 217-21.

Midgley, M. (1986), *Wickedness: A Philosophical Essay*, Ark Paperbacks, London.

Midgley, M. (1991), *Can't We Make Moral Judgements?*, The Bristol Press, Bristol.

Miller, J. (1991), *Madness*, BBC2, 3 November.

Miller, J. (1991), 'The Doctor's Dilemma: Miller on Madness', *Open Mind*, Vol. 49, pp. 31.

Milton, J. (1972), *Paradise Lost, Book 1*, ed. C. A. Patrides, Macmillan, Basingstoke.

MIND (1986), *Special Report on the Major Tranquillisers*, MIND Publications, London.

Monahan, J. (1981), *The Clinical Prediction of Violent Behavior*, U S Department of Health and Human Services, Rockville.

Montandon, C., and T. Harding (1984), 'The Reliability of Dangerousness Assessments', *British Journal of Psychiatry*, Vol. 144, pp. 149-55.

Moore, M. (1975), 'Some Myths About Mental Illness', *Archives of General Psychiatry*, Vol. 32, pp. 1483-97.

Moore, M. (1980), 'Legal Conceptions of Mental Illness', in *Mental Illness: Law and Public Policy*, eds B. Brody and H. T. Engelhardt, Reidel Publishing, Boston.

Murphy, E. (1991), *After the Asylums: Community Care for People with Mental Illness*, Faber and Faber, London.

Neville, R. C. (1975), 'Zalmoxis or the Morals of ESB and Psychosurgery', in *Operating on the Mind: The Psychosurgery Conflict*, eds W. M. Gaylin, J. S. Meister and R. C. Neville, Basic Books, New York.

Newton, J. (1988), *Preventing Mental Illness*, Routledge Kegan Paul, London.

North, C. (1988), *Welcome Silence*, Simon and Schuster, London.

Office of Health Economics (1990), *Mental Health in the 1990s - From Custody to Care?*, HMSO, London.

Ottosson, J. O. (1979), 'Simulated and Real ECT', *British Journal of Psychiatry*, Vol. 134, p. 314.

Parsons, T. (1951), *The Social System*, Free Press, Glencoe, Illinois.

Parsons, T. (1958), 'Definitions of Health and Illness in the Light of American Values and Social Structures', in *Patients, Physicians and Illness*, ed. E. G. Jaco, Free Press, New York.

Parsons, T. (1978), 'Health and Disease: A Sociological and Action Perspective', in *Encyclopaedia of Bioethics*, ed. W. T. Reich, Free Press, New York.

Pellegrino, E. D., and D. C. Thomasma (1981), *A Philosophical Basis of Medical Practice*, OUP, New York.

Penfold, P. S., and G. A. Walker (1984), *Women and the Psychiatric Paradox*, Open University Press, Milton Keynes.

Perriam, W. (1991), *Fifty-Minute Hour*, Paladin, London.

Pfohl, S. (1977), 'The Psychiatric Assessment of Dangerousness: Practical Problems and Political Implications', in *In Fear of Each Other*, eds J. P. Conrad and S. Dinitz, Lexington Books, Lexington.

Pies, R. (1979), 'On Myths and Countermyths: More on Szaszian Fallacies', *Archives of General Psychiatry*, Vol. 36, pp. 139-44.

Pilkonis, P. (1984), 'A Comparative Outcome Study of Individual, Group and Conjoint Psychotherapy', *Archives of General Psychiatry*, Vol. 41, pp. 431-7.

Podvoll, E. M. (1990), *The Seduction of Madness*, Century, London.

Pope, K. S., P. Keith-Spiegel and B. G. Tabachnik (1986), 'Sexual Attractions to Clients: The Human Therapist and (Sometimes) Inhuman Training System', *American Psychologist,* Vol. 41, pp. 147-58.

Pope, K. S., L. R. Schover and H. Levenson (1980), 'Sexual Behavior Between Clinical Supervisors and Trainers: Implications for Professional Standards', *Professional Psychology*, Vol. 11, pp. 157-62.

Porter, R. (1987), *A Social History of Madness: Stories of the Insane*, Weidenfeld and Nicholson, London.

Porter, R. (1990), *Mind Forg'd Manacles: A History of Madness in England from the Restoration to the Regency*, Penguin, Harmondsworth.

Porter, R. (ed.) (1991), *The Faber Book of Madness*, Faber and Faber, London.

Presthus, R. V. (1962) 'Authority in Organisations', in *Concepts and Issues in Administrative Behaviour*, eds S. Mailick and E. H. van Ness, Prentice-Hall, Englewood Cliffs, New Jersey.

Price, T. R. P., T. B. Mackenzie, G. J. Tucker, and C. Culver (1978), 'The Dose Response Ratio in Electroconvulsive Therapy', *Archives of General Psychiatry*, Vol. 35, pp. 1131-6.

Priest, S. (1991), *Theories of the Mind*, Penguin, Harmondsworth.

Psychosurgery Review Board (1993), *Annual Report of the Psychosurgery Review Board (1993)*, Melbourne.

Rachman, S. (1971), *The Effects of Psychotherapy*, Pergamon Press, Oxford.

Radden, J. (1985), *Madness and Reason*, Allen and Unwin, London.

Ramon, S., and Giannichedda (eds) (1991), *Psychiatry in Transition: The British and Italian Experiences*, Pluto Press, London.

Rawls, J. (1989), *A Theory of Justice*, OUP, Oxford.

Redlich, F., and R. F. Moilica (1976), 'Overview: Ethical Issues in Contemporary Psychiatry', *American Journal of Psychiatry*, Vol. 133, pp. 125-36.

Reiman, E. M. (1989), 'Neuroanatomical Correlates of Anticipatory Anxiety', *Science*, Vol. 243 (4894, Pt 1), pp. 1071-4.

Reiser, S. J. (1980), 'Refusing Treatment for Mental Illness', *American Journal of Psychiatry*, Vol. 137, No. 3, pp. 329-31.

Report into the Care and Treatment of Christopher Clunis (1994), HMSO, London.

Reznek, L. (1991), *The Philosophical Defence of Psychiatry*, Routledge, London.

Rickels, K., W. G. Case, and R. W. Downing (1983), 'Long-term Diazepam Therapy and Clinical Outcome', *Journal of the American Medical Association*, Vol. 250, pp. 767-71.

Rickels, K., and E. E. Schweizer (1986), 'Low-dose Dependence in Chronic Benzodiazepine Users: A Preliminary Report on 119 Patients', *Psychopharmacology Bulletin*, Vol. 22, pp. 407-15.

Ricoeur, P. (1988), *Hermeneutics and the Social Sciences*, CUP, Cambridge.

Robertson, G. (1981), 'Informed Consent to Medical Treatment', *The Law Quarterly Review*, January, pp. 102-26.

Robitscher, J. (1980), *The Powers of Psychiatry*, Houghton Mifflin, Boston.

Rogers, A., D. Pilgrim, and R. Lacey (1993), *Experiencing Psychiatry: Users' Views of Services*, Macmillan in association with MIND Publishing, Basingstoke.

Rogers, W. S. (1991), *Explaining Health and Illness*, Harvester Wheatsheaf, London.

Ross, W. D. (1930), *The Right and the Good*, Clarendon Press, Oxford.

Roth, J. (1972), 'Some Contingencies of the Moral Evaluation and Control of Clientele: The Case of the Hospital Emergency Service', *American Journal of Sociology*, Vol. 77, pp. 839-55.

Roth, M. (1976), 'Schizophrenia and the Theories of Thomas Szasz', *British Journal of Psychiatry*, Vol. 129, pp. 317-26.

Roth, M., and R. Bluglass (eds) (1985), *Psychiatry, Human Rights and the Law*, CUP, Cambridge.

Rowe, D. (1988), *Choosing Not Losing: The Experience of Depression*, Fontana Paperbacks, London.

Royal College of Psychiatrists (1977), 'Memorandum on the Use of Electroconvulsive Therapy', *British Journal of Psychiatry*, Vol. 131, pp. 261-72.

Rubenstein, L. S. (1986), 'Treatment of the Mentally Ill: Legal Advocacy Enters the Second Generation', *American Journal of Psychiatry*, Vol. 143, pp. 1264-9.

Rutter, P. (1990), *Sex in the Forbidden Zone: When Men in Power - Therapists, Doctors, Clergy, Teachers and Others - Betray Women's Trust*, Unwin Paperbacks, London.

Ryle, A. (1982), *Psychotherapy: A Cognitive Integration of Theory and Practice*, Academic Press, London.

Sacks, O. (1982), *Awakenings*, Picador, London.

Sacks, O. (1986), *The Man Who Mistook His Wife for a Hat*, Picador, London.

Sainz, A. (1959), 'Clarification of the Action of Successful Treatments in the Depressions', *Diseases of the Nervous System*, Vol. 20, pp. 53-7.

Salzman, C. (1977), 'ECT and Ethical Psychiatry', *American Journal of Psychiatry*, Vol. 134, No. 9, pp. 1006-9.

Sargant, W., and E. Slater (1972), *Introduction to Physical Treatments in Psychiatry*, fifth edition, Livingstone, Edinburgh.

Scheff, T. (1966), *Being Mentally Ill*, Aldine, Chicago.

Schrag, P. (1980), *Mind Control*, Marion Boyars, London.

Schreiber, F. R. (1974), *Sybil*, Penguin, Harmondsworth.

Scott, W. A. (1958), 'Research Definitions of Mental Health and Mental Illness', *Psychological Bulletin*, Vol. 55, pp. 29-45.

Scull, A. (1976), 'The Decarceration of the Mentally Ill: A Critical View', *Politics and Society*, Vol. 6, pp. 173-211.

Scull, A. (1984), *Decarceration: Community Treatment and the Deviant*, second edition, Polity Press, Cambridge.

Scull, A. (1991), 'Deinstitutionalisation: Cycles of Despair', *Journal of Mind and Behavior*, Vol. 11, Nos. 3&4, pp. 301-12.

Searle, J. (1984), *Minds, Brains and Science: the 1984 Reith Lectures*, Penguin, Harmondsworth.

Sedgwick, P. (1982), *Psychopolitics*, 2nd edition, Pluto Press, London.

Shakespeare, W. (1967), *Macbeth*, New Penguin Shakespeare edition, Penguin, Harmondsworth.

Shakespeare, W. (1980), *Hamlet*, New Penguin Shakespeare edition, Penguin, Harmondsworth.

Shakespeare, W. (1981), *As You Like It*, New Penguin Shakespeare edition, Penguin, Harmondsworth.

Shapiro, D. A., and D. Shapiro (1982), 'Meta-analysis of Comparative Therapy Outcome Studies: A Replication and Refinement', *Psychological Bulletin*, Vol. 92, pp. 581-604.

Sheppard, C., L. Collins, D. Florentino, J. Fracchia, and S. Merliss (1969), 'Polypharmacy in Psychiatric Treatment: Incidence in a State Hospital', *Current Therapeutic Research*, Vol. 11, pp. 765-74.

Sherlock, R. (1983), 'Consent, Competency and ECT: Some Critical Suggestions', *Journal of Medical Ethics*, Vol. 9, pp. 141-3.

Shields, P. (1985), 'The Consumer's View of Psychiatry', *Hospital and Health Services Review*, May, pp. 117-9.

Showalter, E. (1987), *The Female Malady: Women, Madness and English Culture, 1830-1980*, Virago, London.

Sider, R. C. (1984), 'The Ethics of Therapeutic Modality Choice', *American Journal of Psychiatry*, Vol. 141, No. 3, pp. 390-94.

Siegler, M., and H. Osmond (1966), 'Models of Madness', *British Journal of Psychiatry*, Vol. 112, pp. 1193-1203.

Siegler, M., and H. Osmond (1974), 'The Sick Role Revisited', *Hastings Centre Studies*, Vol. 1, No. 3, pp. 41-58.

Simons (1993), *Citizen Advocacy: The Inside View*, Norah Fry Research Centre, Bristol.

Sims, A. C. P. (1986), *Symptoms in the Mind*, Balliere Tindall, London.

Sims, A. C. P. (1988), 'The Psychiatrist as Priest', *J. Roy. Soc. Health*, Vol. 5, pp. 160-63.

Sims, A. C. P. (1992), 'Symptoms and Beliefs', *J. Roy. Soc. Health*, Vol. 112, No. 1, pp. 42-6.

Sloane, R. B., A. H. Cristol, N. J. Yorkston, and K. Whipple (1975), 'Short-term Analytically Oriented Psychotherapy vs. Behavior Therapy', *American Journal of Psychiatry*, Vol. 132, pp. 373-7.

Smail, D. (1987), *Taking Care: An Alternative to Therapy*, J. M. Dent & Sons, London.

Smith, F. B. (1982), *Florence Nightingale: Reputation and Power*, Croom Helm, London.

Smith, J. C., and B. N. Hogan (1973), *Criminal Law*, 3rd edition, London.

Smith, M. L., G. V. Glass and T. I. Miller (1980), *The Benefits of Psychotherapy*, Johns Hopkins University Press, Baltimore.

Smith, P. S., and O. R. Jones (1988), *The Philosophy of Mind*, CUP, Cambridge.

Sontag, S. (1988), *Illness as Metaphor*, Penguin, Harmondsworth.

Sontag, S. (1990), *AIDS and Its Metaphors*, Penguin, Harmondsworth.

Spring, J. (1987), *Cry Hard and Swim: The Story of an Incest Survivor*, Virago, London.

Steere, J. (1984), *Ethics in Clinical Psychology*, OUP, Cape Town.

Steering Committee of the Confidential Inquiry into Homicides and Suicides by Mentally Ill People (1994), *A Preliminary Report on Homicide*, Confidential Enquiry Steering Committee, London.

Stone, A. A. (1982), 'Psychiatric Abuse and Legal Reform: Two Ways to Make a Bad Situation Worse', *International Journal of Law and Psychiatry*, Vol. 5, pp. 9-28.

Stone, A. A. (1984), *Law, Psychiatry and Morality*, American Psychiatric Association Press, Washington, DC.

Storr, A. (1970), *Human Aggression*, Pelican, Harmondsworth.

Storr, A. (1987), *The Art of Psychotherapy*, Secker and Warburg, London.

Styron, W. (1991), *Darkness Visible: A Memoir of Madness*, Jonathan Cape, London.

Sutherland, J. D. (1968), 'The Consultant Psychotherapist in the National Health Service: His Role and Training', *British Journal of Psychiatry*, Vol. 114, pp. 509-15.

Sutherland, S. (1987), *Breakdown*, Weidenfeld and Nicholson, London.

Symonds, B. (1991), 'Sociological Issues in the Conceptualization of Mental Illness', *Journal of Advanced Nursing*, Vol. 16, pp. 1470-77.

Szasz, T. (1970), *The Manufacture of Madness: A Comparative Study of the Inquisition and the Mental Health Movement*, Harper and Row, New York.

Szasz, T. (1971), 'The Ethics of Suicide', *The Antioch Review*, Vol. 31, pp. 7-17.

Szasz, T. (1972), *The Myth of Mental Illness*, Paladin, London.

Szasz, T. (1983), *Ideology and Insanity*, Marion Boyars, London.

Szasz, T. (1989), *Law, Liberty and Psychiatry*, Syracuse University Press, Syracuse.

Tarasoff vs the Regents of the University of California (ed.) (1974), *118 California Reporter*, 129, 529, P 2d 553.

Taussig, M. (1980), 'Reification and the Consciousness of the Patient', *Social Science and Medicine*, Vol. 14b, pp. 3-13.

Thompson, A. (1990), *Guide to Ethical Practice in Psychotherapy*, John Wiley, Chichester.

Thorogood, M., P. Cowen, J. Mann, M. Murphy, and M. Versey (1992), 'Fatal Myocardial Infarction and Use of Psychotropic Medication', *Lancet*, Vol. 340, p. 1067.

Tomlinson, D. (1991), *Utopia, Community Care and the Retreat from the Asylums*, Open University Press, Milton Keynes.

Toombs, S. K. (1993), *The Meaning of Illness: A Phenomenological Account of the Different Perspectives of Physician and Patient*, vol. 42, Philosophy and Medicine, Kluwer Academic Publishers, Dordrecht.

Torrey, E. F. (1989), *Nowhere to Go: The Tragic Odyssey of the Homeless Mentally Ill*, Harper and Row, New York.

Townsend, P., and N. Davidson (eds) (1988), 'The Black Report', in *Inequalities in Health*, Penguin, Harmondsworth.

Tschudin, V. (1986), *Ethics in Nursing: The Caring Relationship*, Heinemann, London.

Tyrer, P. (1987), 'Benefits and Risks of Benzodiazepines: The Benzodiazepines in Current Practice', *Royal Society of Medicine International Congress and Symposium Series*, Vol. 114, pp. 7-11.

US National Commission for the Protection of Human Subjects of Biomedical and Behavioral Research (1977), *Report and Recommendations: Psychosurgery*, US Department of Health, Education and Welfare, Bethesda.

Valenstein, E. S. (1977), 'The Practice of Psychosurgery', in *US National Commission for the Protection of Human Subjects of Biomedical and Behavioural Research*, vol. (OS) 77-0002, US DHEW, Bethesda.

Valenstein, E. S. (ed.) (1980), *The Psychosurgery Debate: Scientific, Legal and Ethical Perspectives*, Freeman, San Francisco.

Vardy, P. (1992), *The Puzzle of Evil*, Fount Paperbacks, London.

Veatch, R. M. (1974), 'Drugs and Competing Drug Ethics', *Hastings Center Studies*, Vol. 2, No. 1, pp. 68-80.

Vice, J. (1989), 'The Morality of Mental Illness: Thomas Szasz's Critique of Psychiatry', *Journal of Humanistic Psychology*, Vol. 29, pp. 385-93.

Virchow, R. (1971), *Cellular Pathology as Based Upon Physiological and Pathological Histology*, trans. F. Chance, Dover, New York.

Walker, N. (1982), 'Unscientific, Unwise, Unprofitable or Unjust?', *British Journal of Criminology*, Vol. 22, pp. 276-83.

Wallace, M. (1987), *The Forgotten Illness*, Times Newspapers and SANE, London.

Warner, R. (1985), *Recovery from Schizophrenia: The Political Economy of Psychiatry*, Routledge Kegan Paul, London.

Warner, R., and T. Szubka (1994), *The Mind-Body Problem*, Blackwell, Oxford.

Waterhouse, R. (1993), 'Mother Gets £352,777 After Attack By Her Son', *The Independent*, 27 January, p. 9.

Watt, J. A. G. (1979), 'Simulated and Real ECT', *British Journal of Psychiatry*, Vol. 134, pp. 314.

Wellings, K. (1983), *Sickness and Sin: the Case of Genital Herpes*, Paper presented to the British Sociological Association Medical Sociology Group Annual Conference 1983.

White, A. (1982), *Beyond the Glass*, Fontana Paperbacks, Glasgow.

Whitehead, M. (1988), 'The Health Divide', in *Inequalities in Health*, Penguin, Harmondsworth.

Williams, J. (1990), *The Law of Mental Health*, Fourmat Publishing, London.

Wilson, H. S. (1982), *Deinstitutionalised Residential Care for the Mentally Disordered: The Soteria House Approach*, Grune and Stratton, New York.

Wilson, I. C., J. T. Vernon and T. Guin (1963), 'A Controlled Study of Treatments of Depression', *Journal of Neuropsychiatry*, Vol. 4, pp. 331-7.

Wilson, O. M. (1976), '"The Normal" as a Culture-related Concept: Historical Considerations', *Mental Health Society*, Vol. 3, pp. 57-71.

Wing, K. (1988), 'Abandoning What?', *British Journal of Clinical Psychology*, Vol. 27, pp. 325-8.

Winokur, A., K. Rickels, and D. J. Greenblatt (1980), 'Withdrawal from Long-term, Low Dosage Administration of Diazepam: A Double-blind, Placebo Controlled Case Study', *Archives of General Psychiatry*, Vol. 37, pp. 101-5.

Wittgenstein, L. (1972), *Blue and Brown Books*, OUP, Oxford.

Woodman, T. (1987), 'First Person Account: A Pessimist's Progress', *Schizophrenia Bulletin*, Vol. 13, No. 2, p. 330.

Wootton, B. (1959), *Social Science and Social Pathology*, Allen and Unwin, London.

Wulff, H. W., S. A. Pedersen and R. Rosenberg (1990), *Philosophy of Medicine: An Introduction*, second edition, Blackwell Scientific Publications, Oxford.

Index

198